WOODLANDS OF BRITAIN

A NATURALIST'S GUIDE

WOODLANDS OF BRITAIN

A NATURALIST'S GUIDE

RON FREETHY

PRC

To my father
and my grateful thanks to Carole Pugh for
her line drawings

This edition published 1991 by The
Promotional Reprint Company Limited for
Bookmart Limited, Leicester, U.K.

First published in 1986 by
BELL HYMAN LIMITED

ISBN 1 85648 008 9

Printed and bound in Hong Kong

Contents

Woodland history

HUGE areas of Britain have been clothed in trees since megalithic times although the species have always varied with climate and occasionally as a result of man's intervention. These ancient woodlands gave early human tribes places to hunt for food and hide from their enemies. The timber has been used variously for firewood and industrial fuel; for ship and house building and for furniture making. Large areas have been cleared for agriculture, mining and metal smelting sites.

Despite such rough treatment our woodlands remain one of Britain's most enduring and endearing features. Winding paths lead through mighty trees, their leaves and branches dripping with dew or rainwater, or their bark glowing in each shaft of penetrating sunlight. Huge red and tiny roe deer roam free whilst red squirrels, tits and the occasional flock of crossbills swarm acrobatically in the branches. Bees hum, moths hover and butterflies flutter among the boughs of ash and oak whilst graceful birches grow tall in the many clearings. In the darker recesses trees starved of light grow gnarled and twisted, many of the dead and dying providing holes for fungi, along with the hordes of insects which feed upon them. These in turn provide food for the birds, especially the woodpeckers. To the woodland stroller there is the delight of coming across great stretches of wild bluebells and primroses or discovering the rare ghost orchid or seeing a woodcock. The pleasures are endless.

Oliver Rackham, an undisputed authority on British woodland history, invented the term 'wildwood' to describe the original woodlands of Britain, made up of 60 species of trees now listed as native to Britain. Approximately 10,500 years ago, Britain was still gripped by ice north of a line from the Severn to the Wash. But as the last glacier – the Weichselian – began to melt, sea levels rose dramatically. The land bridge between Britain and the continent was submerged, producing an island and the wildwood then began to advance very rapidly. However, the spread of both animals and plants was made almost impossible by the surrounding seas, explaining why a greater variety occur on the continent than in Britain. There was also a bridge between Britain and Ireland which had been inundated earlier and accounts for the fact that Ireland has even fewer species of animals and plants.

The subsequent development of the wildwood over the next 10,500 years has conveniently been divided by scientists into five periods.

The earliest of these is the Pre-Boreal during which the ice slowly began to melt and only the toughest of trees were able to push northwards. The earliest of the pioneers was almost certainly juniper (*Juniperus communis*). Perhaps more of a shrub than a tree, juniper is one of only three conifers native to Britain, the other two being yew (*Taxus baccata*) and Scots pine (*Pinus sylvestris*). Large areas must

OPPOSITE: **Beech woodlands are only native to south eastern England. Elsewhere beech was almost always planted.**

have initially been clothed with juniper, but as the climate improved taller trees established themselves and shaded out the pioneer. Its decline must also have been accelerated by the human demands on its useful timber, and juniper is now only common in exposed areas, especially on limestone.

Juniper can easily be identified by its sharply pointed blue-green, needle-like leaves which occur in groups of three and the timber also retains both the resinous scent and the bluish tint so evident in the leaves. The tree seldom approaches 15.2m (50ft) in height and is never more than 0.9m (3ft) in girth. The resinous and fragrant aroma is even more attractive if the timber or the leaves are burned and this scent, combined with a hot, bright flame often made juniper a popular tree on the household fire. It was also burned to produce high quality charcoal (sold under the name of savin) which was used in the manufacture of gunpowder when reliable explosive qualities were required. Drinking bowls and dirk handles were fashioned from this versatile wood, its hard texture similarly making it popular in Sweden for the production of the bows of narrow bowsaws which were used to clear forests. During the writing of this book I made a crude saw of juniper wood and following a high wind collected a number of fallen branches. My primitive saw easily cut through oak, ash, elm and Scots pine as well as a number of introduced trees including spruce and larch. Hornbeam (*Carpinus betulus*), however, proved quite beyond its powers.

Writing in the seventeenth century John Evelyn noted that the blue, dusty looking juniper berries were used as a spice and as a medicine since they were reputed to be a powerful tonic. The wood, leaves and berries were burned in the bedrooms of the sick with 'invigorating effects'. Until well into the present century the country-folk in Sweden converted the berries into a preserve, which was usually eaten at breakfast.

The old vernacular names used in various parts of the world prove just how well our ancestors knew their plants. In Germany, juniper was known as wacholder which meant supple or spring wood. In Ireland it was called iubhar beine meaning Yew of the Hills – an ideal description considering its favoured habitat. In Norse, juniper was known as en and some workers suggest that the Cumbrian river Ehen gets its name from the trees growing along the side of Ennerdale in the Lake District, an early settlement of the invading Norsemen. In France, where its berries were used to flavour gin, the tree was called genevrier. The berries were often used both as a spice and as a powerful tonic.

When the Pre-Boreal period was coming to an end and the Boreal period began some 9,500 years ago, birch (*Betula pubescens*) had joined juniper and soon afterwards came the tall and stately Scots pine. This would soon have cast a shade too dense to allow juniper to flourish except on the exposed edges of the now extensive woodlands.

A visit to one of the few remaining native pine woods quickly dispels the dour reputation of such areas. The Black Wood of Rannoch is seldom as sombre as its name implies with splendid views through the trees revealing loch Rannoch gouged out by moving glaciers and stately birches growing in its open glades. A native pine wood is nothing like the regimented rows of a modern profit-motivated forest of alien species. Nature organized her plantations without any need to worry about maximum yield, profit margins or, most importantly, time.

The Boreal period continued until 7,500 years ago and at its beginning the species described above were dominant although other species gradually began to assert themselves. Hazel (*Corylus avellana*) was beginning to occupy a considerable area of woodland beneath the dominant trees – the understorey – and elm (*Ulmus procera*) and the oaks were also becoming increasingly common together with several species of willow (*Salix spp*), aspen (*Populus tremula*) and rowan (*Sorbus aucuparia*). The spread was never even across Britain since the more southerly areas were comparatively rich in oak and northern Britain was still dominated, even at the end of the period, by birch and Scots pine, with only some juniper remaining.

The Atlantic period lasted from 7,500 to 5,000 years ago and was, on average, 2.5°C warmer than today's climate. Trees and other vegetation thrived in these conditions, and the high rainfall also helped many species to spread. New species appearing in Britain included alder (*Alnus glutinosa*), small leaved lime (*Tilia cordata*) and holly (*Ilex aquifolium*). Both native species of oak found the warm, moist conditions much to their liking, and expanded their range thus shading out pioneer species such as birch and pine. Apart from areas of high altitude, cliffs and the flood plains of rivers, most of Britain was covered in trees during the Atlantic period until 5,000 years ago when the tree cover began to decline due in part – but only in part – to climatic changes.

The tree which suffered most during the subsequent Sub-Boreal period would seem to have been the elm. The change to colder, drier conditions doubtless had its

Pollen grain analysis

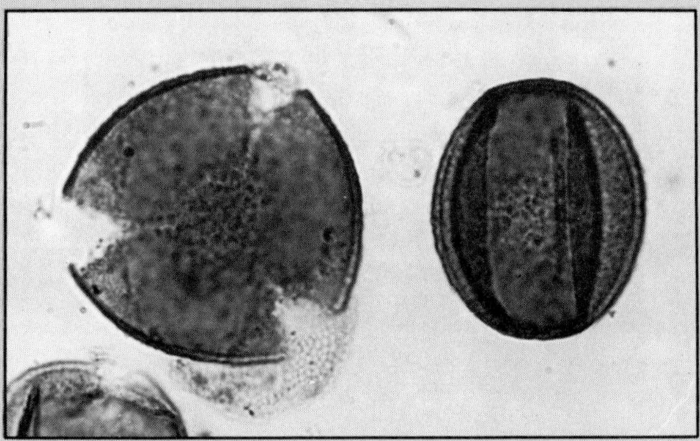

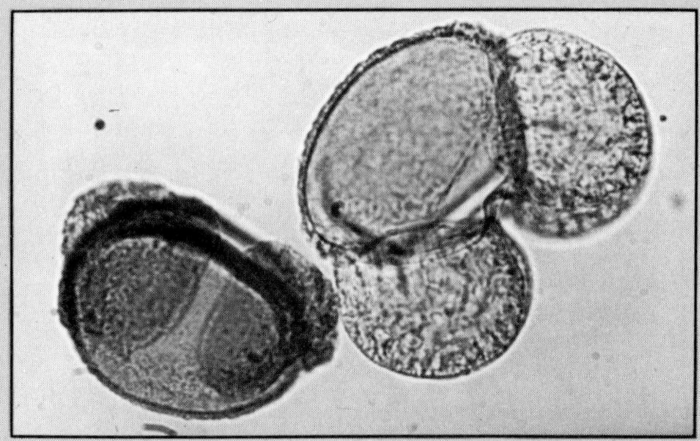

IT has proved possible to trace the vegetational history of Britain by an analysis of pollen grains which became trapped in acid soils, mud and especially peat. Although the interior of the grains soon disintegrates the walls are almost indestructible. Furthermore, each species of tree has grains of a unique shape and pattern making them as identifiable as human finger prints. Once the presence of a particular species has been identified by means of its pollen grains, all that is required is to calculate the age of the deposit in which they are found. This is now done by the sophisticated technique of radio carbon dating and depends upon the modern scientists' ability to compare the weight of an atom of one element with that of another.

The basic scale is the weight of the lightest element, hydrogen – said to have an atomic weight of one. On this scale, carbon has an atomic weight of 12, but a few atoms are heavier and weigh 14. These heavier atoms, called isotopes, occur in a very definite proportion in atmospheric carbon dioxide. As soon as the carbon 14 (C^{14}), which is harmlessly radioactive, is absorbed by a green plant and converted into sugar by photosynthesis, it begins to decay at a slow but predictable rate. After thousands of years all the C^{14} reverts to C^{12} – the normal weight for the atom. Thus by measuring the relative proportion of C^{14} and C^{12} in the peat deposits containing the embedded pollen grains, it is possible to date the sample and work out the dominant trees of the period.

Great care, however, must be taken when interpreting pollen grain data. It was once confidently assumed on the basis of exhaustive pollen analysis that the wildwood was almost totally dominated by the oaks and there was very little small leaved lime in evidence. It is now realized that oak is wind pollinated producing great volumes of pollen grains light enough to be easily carried on the slightest of breezes. Lime on the other hand, is insect pollinated and the grains are larger and heavier. This must mean that lime pollen will be under-represented in the peat. Once these factors are known, and allowed for, a really accurate early history of British woodlands can be formulated.

The magnified grains illustrated are of oak (left) and Scots pine (right).

effect, but human activities also began to have a noticeable effect for the first time.

During this period, known to historians as Neolithic, man became less of a wandering hunter-gatherer and learned to create clearings and cultivate crops. Although many woodland areas were disturbed, there were no wholesale clearances and the creation of fields and their subsequent abandonment helped pioneer species such as birch to return temporarily to areas previously lost to oak, lime and elm. These changes can be proved by reference to peat dated by the radio-carbon technique since such peat contains pollen grains of trees and cereal grasses together with some contemporary artefacts.

Human tree felling activities accelerated the leaching process, too, especially in areas of high rainfall. It was almost certainly a combination of man and weather which led to the formation of heaths and bogs. The fact that elm was the main tree to suffer could have been due to some ancient equivalent of the catastrophic Dutch elm disease. But it is more likely that it was the demand for young elm leaves collected by early European societies for use as winter fodder now that the domestication of wild cattle, pigs, goats and sheep had become more common.

The Sub-Atlantic period extends from 2,700 years ago to the present day, and it is during this time that substantial areas of woodland have been cleared. As the wildwood was cleared for growing crops or for grazing, trees such as lime and Scots pine almost disappeared from England. Limes prefer to grow in deep, mineral-rich soil much in demand by the new agriculturalists and were soon cut down, the timber being used for building and probably for firewood. It was even easier to eliminate Scots pine because it could be cleared by burning its richly resinous trunk and highly flammable leaves. This species will not grow again from its roots (suckering) or from severed trunks (pollarding) so areas cleared of Scots pine did not regenerate. Even when farmsteads were abandoned, frequently because the soil had become impoverished after a few years' growth of the same crop on unfertilized ground, Scots pine did not grow again. Land, however, was freely available and the farmer simply moved on to pastures new which he hacked from the wildwood.

The Black Wood of Rannoch.

The Celts began to arrive in Britain around 2,500 years ago and their knowledge of iron enabled them to make ploughs and other tools with which they could bring more land under cultivation since trees could be felled more efficiently. It must not be assumed that the Iron Age Celts, who built the hill forts, were always at war. The society seems to have been remarkably stable and there were several kingdoms important enough to mint their own coins. Their settlements were always situated on high land since the wildwood of the valleys was often swampy and jungle-like. Much of Britain's woodland was still wild and free and the climate still favoured the growth of oak, alder, birch and eventually beech (*Fagus sylvatica*) which seems to be truly native only in the more southerly areas of Britain.

Until the Roman invasion, the history of the woodlands can only be based upon some scientific facts and a lot of intelligent guesswork on the part of several generations of woodland historians. However, from then on, an increasing insistence upon keeping written legal records enables the demise of Britain's woodland to be plotted with much more confidence.

The four centuries of occupation of Britain by Imperial Rome affected the woodlands in several very important ways. Large quantities of timber were required to build towns and also to provide fuel for the sophisticated heating systems typical of Roman society. The Celts were far from friendly away from the main settlements and many stretches of woodland were laid waste to deny the revolutionaries a hiding place. The Romans were also very skilled in putting their colonies to work and the fertile earth of Britain was soon providing a surplus of grain for export.

Many new fields were created by tree felling, especially in the south and east of the country. Romans were not only agriculturalists, but were also among the first to systematically organize industry. Iron smelting was soon in full swing in several forests including the Weald, Dean and, to a lesser extent, in the north west of England. In Derbyshire, lead smelting was, for the time, a huge industry because this metal was used extensively in Roman plumbing. The smelting of these and other metals including Cornish tin, required a constant supply of timber – a demand which continued even after the seventeenth century when wood shortages led to the use of coal as a substitute. Even the Romans, however, must have eventually felt the lack of accessible suitable timber and some attempt at woodland management seems to have evolved at this time. Archaeologists have found that deposits of Roman charcoal show it to have been prepared from branches of similar size which suggests that they were aware of the techniques of coppiced woodland.

Obviously life did not grind to a halt when a series of domestic crises, which were to ruin their Empire, drew the Roman legions home. But the organized society in Britain so typical of the Imperialists' rule crumbled. Agriculture, both arable and what little pastoral there was, declined and there was some regeneration of woodland. Trees such as birch pioneered the recovery which was then predictably replaced by oak, ash (*Fraxinus excelsior*) and in the south by beech. Two types of British woodland can be recognized from this time onwards. One is primary woodland consisting of original wildwood, while the other is secondary woodland – that which has returned to areas once cleared of their tree cover.

With the gradual infiltration of the Saxons into Britain came an agricultural revolution. They reclaimed many Roman fields and also made inroads into primary woodlands mainly in southern areas. The Saxons' demand for timber was

Red deer roam in the pine and birch forests of Scotland.

Large bindweed twists and binds around other plants. Its flexible stems were once used as string.

huge as all their buildings were constructed of wood and their timber framed houses and cruck-built barns which were supported by huge beams. The forest of Arden was almost certainly devastated during the Saxon period to provide timber for smelting. The Saxons did not worry about attacking the wildwoods, unlike the Scandinavians who were to follow and, more especially, the Celts, whose religions were based upon natural objects. Many Celtic traditions still live on in the assemblies of some modern day witches, whose beliefs are buried deep in the wildwoods.

To the Saxons, the woods were valuable commodities and written laws and deeds were required to preserve them or at least to ensure that only the owner had a right to cut them down. For the first time, parts of the wildwood did not belong to Everyman. The practice of coppicing was popular in Saxon times and the more substantial pieces of timber were obtained from large trees called standards which were deliberately not coppiced. It also seems highly likely that the Saxons obtained some standard timber from the vast areas of wildwood which still remained.

One of the earliest types of land deed was the Perambulation which described in detail a walk around the land in question pointing out the obvious features of the area. This is almost certainly the origin of the beating of the bounds which is still ceremoniously carried out in some English villages.

The Vikings and Danes later laid even rougher hands on the northern areas of Britain, clearing primary woodland mainly for use in their magnificently proportioned long ships and also for building and firewood. Their woodland clearings were called thwaites and are still marked as such on the Ordnance Survey maps of today. Bassenthwaite, Thornthwaite and Greythwaite in Lakeland and the village of Thwaite in the Dales are an indication of a Scandinavian assault on Britain's wildwood. The origins of Saxon clearings can also be seen in some place names. A ley (as in Bromley) or a hay (as in Roundhay) were clearings made by one farmer and if several families operated close together the settlement was called a ham (as in Birmingham or Nottingham).

The Domesday survey was completed in 1086 and shows just how much of the wildwood was being managed for profit. The only substantial area left blank and therefore unclaimed appears to have been in the Forest of Dean. It was much easier for the crown to lay claim to this area since it lay so close to the King. It may well have remained in royal hands and relatively intact until 1241 when Henry III sold 71 mature oaks to be used in the construction of a Dominican Friary at Gloucester, which was completed in 1265.

In Wales the Celts had not been subdued and their culture was less likely to destroy the wildwood. Similarly in Scotland, the presence of peat for burning and easily quarried stone outcrops for building served to preserve the native woods for longer than was the case in England.

Norman rule was anything but benevolent and their forest laws, although based upon Saxon traditions, were vigorously enforced by a number of well defined officials each well aware of his part in ruling the woods. It is hard for us to imagine just how restrictive the old forest laws could be. Take a walk through your local wood and nobody is likely to challenge you. Smell the fragrant blossoms and the damp fungus-rich earth. But things were very different in a Norman wood – each man from peasant to king knew what could be gathered, how many animals could be legally grazed, what type of dog could be kept and to whom each species of game belonged. All land belonged to the King and William originally placed a chief forester in charge of all the English woodlands.

By the middle of the thirteenth century it became apparent that this post was beyond one man and two forest justices were appointed. One had responsibility for lands south of the river Trent and the other over the more rebellious north. Each forest – and some were less densely populated with trees than others – had its own master forester to rule over it. This official was also called the warden or the steward and to help him preserve the forest for the sovereign he had a lieutenant and a varying number of verderers who were almost always knights. Such officials acted like magistrates and tried those who broke the forest laws.

The patrol work was done by salaried foresters who were responsible for the preservation of trees (termed vert) and venison, then a term used for all species of deer and wild boar, which were valued as animals to be hunted and eaten.

Last in the chain of command was the woodward, who was charged with the task of cutting timber as directed by those above him. The name woodward may have had its origin in the Anglo-Saxon woodland where he was the official appointed by a community to see that no one abused the privileges within the wildwood. The agister was an official who was likely to come in contact with the peasants more often than most of the others since he had control over the grazing of the animals in the forest. The regarder was there in the capacity of woodland accountant working rather like an auditor. The Eyre court occasionally visited each forest and ensured that justice was seen to be done. It would appear then that the peasants hardly dare venture into the forest but this was not the case since they had their own rights and were fully aware of them.

Estovers, evesfold, pannage, firebote, turbary and free warren were all the right of Everyman. Estovers gave the right to remove fallen timber from the wood for the repair of hedges and houses. Dead twigs could also be removed from living trees providing they could be reached either 'by hook or by crook' – a term which survives in our vocabulary today. Evesfold and pannage had a similar meaning, the former giving everyone the right to allow his quota of pigs to feed on fallen beech nuts. Since beech is far more common in the south of England than in the north, pannage would have been much more relevant in those areas allowing the pigs to feed in the woods on both fallen beech nuts and acorns from oaks.

From the ancient Cheshire town of Frodsham, there are clear signs to Delamere forest, at one time one of the most impressive of Britain's wildwoods. It is now but a remnant mainly because of the demands of the salt industry for timber. This was operating around Droitwich long before the arrival of the Romans and has not diminished in any way since. Cheshire stands on what was once a huge, shallow sea which evaporated in a long hot period before the ice ages, and the brine was buried under a mass of silt. In Anglo-Saxon times over 300 salt houses were busy evaporating the brine to produce salt – the demands for timber to stoke their boilers must have been immense.

Ireland's native woodlands do not echo to the nocturnal hootings of the tawny owl or the laughing trills of the green woodpecker. It was not St Patrick who banished snakes from the Emerald Isle, but an impenetrable barrier of water preventing them from extending their range.

Tawny owls do not breed in Ireland but delightful youngsters like this one are a feature of most deciduous woods in the rest of the British Isles.

Firebote was also a fiercely defended right enabling the often hard-pressed peasants to cut firewood to cook their food and keep themselves warm in winter. Turbary was the right to gather bracken, turf and, in some areas, peat. Game was also subject to strict rules. No one save the king or those designated by him could kill venison but other edible animals and birds were all fair game and this right was known as free warren. A minor official known as the warrener ensured that all kept to the law. Although some periods appear to have been more lenient than others, the penalties for breaking the law were often extreme, for the offender was made to pay with his body.

A trip backwards in time into a medieval woodland would reveal the retreating wildwoods as the focus of industry just as much as a retreat for outlaws. Fuel for the salt industry, mining of ore, smelting and the production of charcoal would all add their own sounds, sights and smells. Bark was stripped for tanning hides, potash produced to make glass and soap, trees were carefully selected for buildings and for ships. Furniture was produced in woodland clearings, as were wooden clogs. The woollen industry expanded rapidly from the middle ages onwards and there is nothing more efficient than sheep in preventing the development of secondary woodland once the wildwood has been cleared. The real death knell for peasants' rights in the woodland, however, was the passing of the Enclosure Acts. The effect of these acts is still being felt today.

In modern times with easy and efficient transport systems, raw materials can be taken to permanent industrial bases. Thus the mining areas and the extraction plants to remove the metals from the ore are usually separated. However, things were different in the early days of metal exploitation. Most of the ore deposits were discovered as outcrops underneath the wildwood so the trees often had to be cleared before mining began. Thus the fuel for smelting was readily available and the trades of miner, smelter and smith tended to be itinerant.

Miners of the Forest of Dean were in great demand during the Middle Ages when towns and castles came under siege. These old time sappers burrowed under the fortifications and set charges. For this service the men of Dean earned special privileges which made them immune from many of the forest laws, although these rights were only verbally agreed and apparently never had the backing of any legal document.

Iron smelting required charcoal, and itinerant charcoal burners had their own life style. Many folk worked in the old woodlands but few actually lived on the job as the charcoal burners were obliged to since the production of this once vital commodity needed careful watching. At times the job must have been tough since it was more of an autumn and winter activity, although there is no doubt that increasing demands would require some burns during the sappy months of spring and summer.

The demand for charcoal continued for centuries and the craft tended to be practiced by closely knit family groups with Ashburner being a common name. Great inroads were made into timber stocks despite some effort to coppice and thus conserve stocks.

The Weald and the Lake District had good iron deposits in places and also had two other attractions for the iron masters in wood and water which meant that even very rural areas were often industrialized for a short time. The iron masters only operated small furnaces which were dismantled and moved to another tree rich area when timber supplies were used up. The charcoal burners could begin their destructive work once again and it was only the discovery of coke for smelting that brought some reprieve to the wildwoods.

Potash pits can still be found in old woodlands by those with the patience to find them in the tangle of bramble and other herbage. Here is an example of one which burned wood and bracken. A brick or stone lined kiln was constructed, usually against a sloping bank. This allowed it to be loaded from the top. A current of air entered at the base and timber and bracken was literally burned to an ash which was in great demand when the soap and glass industries expanded from their woodland base.

Bark, especially that of oak, has always been in great demand by tanners since it contains high levels of tannin. At one time oak was coppiced to supply the industry, but what little traditional tanning remains now obtains its supply from felled trees.

During the production of leather, the hide must go through a process called leaching. The hides are placed in a series of vats containing increasingly strong solutions of tanning liquor made by adding powdered bark to water. Each tannery had a mill to grind bark into this fine powder which would be added in measured amounts to the leaching vats. The hide was then dried and curried during which it was greased and made pliable enough to be used for boot uppers, saddles, belts and, in the days before the use of synthetic fibres, items of clothing.

Messrs Barker and Tanner were important fellows in the days of woodland based industry, as was Mr Ashburner who produced the potash needed for the production of soap and glass. The name potash derives from the ash of the wood from which it was obtained and the pots in which the ash was dissolved and then strengthened by evaporation.

Soap is produced when caustic potash (potassium hydroxide), which is an alkali, neutralizes the stearic acid contained in animal fat. Potash can also be mixed with sand (an oxide of silicon) to produce glass. As the medieval manors and towering cathedrals took shape and the population became more hygiene conscious, the demands for potash were high – until the increasingly skilful chemists came up with cheaper alternatives.

Ship and house building were two more enormous users of timber. The old Celtic bards called Britain 'clas Merddin' meaning a green place defended by sea and the ancient Britons had to build many stout oak boats with anchors lowered on iron chains to protect themselves from Julius Caesar's invading forces. King

A charcoal burn

THESE two pictures show a charcoal burn at Pitshead and a charcoal burner's hut in which they lived during the burning season. The huts always resembled a Red Indian tent and were made from sloping branches tied at the top and lined with sods and leaves.

As a boy in the Lake District during the 1940s I was once taken to see a 'burn' being staged in order to record the dying craft on film. The whole idea of the manufacture of charcoal is to make sure that the patiently seasoned wood burns almost in the absence of air apart from a small volume which is essential to allow slow combustion. This removes all the volatile elements as well as the water contained in the wood.

First the burner, whose weather beaten face I can remember to this day, arranged a number of split logs to produce what he called the chimney and around this he stacked his timbers all facing inwards and sloping towards the top. Once this large dome was complete he covered it with turf before adding more logs and completing the structure with a coat of leaves and earth. The chimney was plugged with a bung of timber, called a motty peg. When the charcoal burner was sure that his pitshead was airtight he removed the motty peg and dropped a burning piece of charcoal into the centre. The burn was thus begun from the middle and billows of white smoke had taken on a blue haze.

At this point we all had to go home and return at intervals since the burn takes up to ten days during which time the charcoal men get little rest because they have to ensure that the burn does not go too quickly or unevenly. A careless workman in the old days would have ended up with one mighty bonfire and no charcoal and therefore no wages. Eventually, even the blue haze around the pitshead faded away and the finished charcoal was raked out, allowed to cool and packed into sacks.

Alfred later expanded this Celtic navy. His ships had 60 oars each and were also made of oak together with other suitable timber which must have been diligently searched for in the woodlands and skilfully felled.

Although William of Normandy was successful in his invasion of England he was far too intelligent not to appreciate his luck. His own fleet of 900 had greatly outnumbered the Anglo-Saxon ships, but these had proved superior in quality. The new king was therefore very quick to give special privileges to the cinque ports to keep the naval elements loyal. Successive monarchs strengthened the navy but Henry VIII was particularly conscious of Britain's need to rule the waves. He established dockyards at Portsmouth, Dartford and Woolwich and passed laws to conserve vital supplies of oak. His foresight proved invaluable when Elizabeth I's admirals, aided by a mighty storm, devastated the Spanish Armada. William III also realized the value of a strong navy and signed a statute enclosing 2,000 acres of the New Forest in which oaks were nurtured. These mighty trees provided timber for the Trafalgar fleet and this act is still in force today. Conservation is not a twentieth-century invention.

The focal point of ship building developed at Buckler's Yard close to the New Forest, at the mouth of the deep water estuary of the Beaulieu river. As early as the sixteenth century, wooden ships were sliding into the river but the real prosperity came in the late eighteenth century when mighty ships such as the *Agamemnon* were built and in 1800, the 1,917 ton *Spenser* was launched carrying over 600 crew.

Ship-building and the proliferation of large, half timbered manor houses took a heavy toll of the wildwood as bands of skilled tree fellers scoured the land for suitably shaped timber. This took care of short term requirements, and in the long term, attempts were made to grow oak with gnarled branches suitable for making joints and beams.

Before a tree was felled a cushion of brushwood was made for it to fall on, to prevent the twisted crown being damaged and to protect the valuable joints. Once felled, the sawyers burrowed under the trunk and a pair worked together with one, usually the boss, working above ground, while the other worked in the dusty pit below. Thus the two could work a two-handed saw and produce straight planks. Although oak was always in demand both for ships and houses, other trees also had their uses. Elms (*Ulmus sp*) are very durable under damp conditions and were used for keels whilst the tough heavy timber of box (*Buxus sempervirens*) was useful in the construction of wheels, pulley blocks and pins. British industry was obviously based on native trees but the value of introduced larch (*Larix decidua*) was soon realized. Larch doesn't splinter and was therefore thought to be 'shot proof' and also the high concentration of resin in the wood meant that iron bolts did not rust.

Improved stone quarrying techniques for building and the development of iron-based, steam-powered shipping gave the woodlands some respite, but modern housing and furniture still need large amounts of wood.

With the notable exception of bodging, the furniture maker carried out his craft indoors. Traditionally, the bodger fashioned chair legs from beechwood and he was an itinerant worker setting up his temporary workshed in a suitable glade. Because of the quantity and quality of the beech trees around High Wycombe chair making became well established there and the occasional bodger still works in the traditional manner although no full time craftsmen remain. The old method of chair manufacture involved six distinct processes. The benchman carefully draws out and saws the chair, the bottomer adzes the seat (an adze is a cutting tool with an arched blade at right angles to the handle) and the bender literally bends the timber to form the back. The framer smooths all the parts and assembles them before passing the chair on to the finisher and polisher. All these men worked indoors whilst the bodger made the chair legs in the woodland. Early bodgers made temporary work shops by cutting saplings and producing a frame from them. This frame was then walled with shavings and the roof roughly thatched. In modern times, however, pre-fabricated huts can be moved about, saving valuable time.

Like the bodger, the clog block cutter was also confined to the woodlands. Together with the clogger, these two craftsmen would make the clogs that were in common use even before the cobbled streets of the northern mill towns echoed to the beat of workers' feet – the British clog and also the French sabot and Dutch klompen probably date back to the early Middle Ages.

Block cutters worked in teams buying their wood when still standing trees, which they felled in spring and early summer. Two men would use a cross-cut saw to produce billets of four sizes which were used as soles for the different sizes of clog. The clogger then used his stock knife which was a 75cm (30in) steel blade slightly bent in the middle. One end was sharpened into a blade ending with a hooked projection which fitted into a ring hammered into a bench. This acted as a

Bodging

WATCHING a bodger at work is a fascinating experience. A practiced eye selects a suitable beech tree which is then felled and sawn into billets which are cleft into a suitable size for rounding off into a chair leg. This is done by turning the still green wood on the pole lathe – one of the oldest established machines, taking its name from the long flexible pole which drove it.

The ash driving pole had its thicker end secured to a support outside the hut, and the flexible end was positioned over the top of the lathe. A cord was fixed to the flexible end, wound twice around the timber to be turned and secured to a pedal which the operator pressed with his foot. When the foot was pressed on the treddle the future leg was turned and when the foot was removed, the pole sprang back to its original position.

I remember watching spellbound as the bodger pedalled away. Chippings flew around and lodged in his beard while his pole bent and arched like a fly fisherman's rod with a prime salmon leaping at its end. In those days each bodger produced chair legs and stretchers to his own traditional pattern and his work could easily be recognized. Completed pieces were stacked outside the hut and allowed to season before being transported to the factory. Unfortunately we have now long passed the stage of being self-sufficient in timber in Britain and a great deal is imported from abroad where some wildwood remains or trees are grown on a larger scale.

pivot whilst the opposite end of the knife had a handle by which the clogger could pull the blade over the sole on which he was working. Some clog-sole cutters worked at home but many were itinerant woodlanders living in crude huts like the charcoal burners and it must have been a common sight in the old days to see stacks of clog soles piled up like beehives to allow them to season.

Although these industries diminished many of Britain's woodlands, it eventually became in the workers' interest to ensure that some replanting was done or at least a sensible system of pollarding and coppicing was adopted. However, there were another two industries – it may not be too strong to say revolutions that worked directly and unashamedly against woodland conservation. These were the woollen trade and increased agricultural demand and efficiency. This meant that there was an increasing animal population which needed feeding and housing and which no longer required shelter or food from the woods. Fields replaced woods, too, as man's demand for food led to the formation of the enclosure system and

A photograph of the now extremely rare ghost orchid which can only be found in Britain in the deep, damp confines of oak and beech woodlands – particularly in Buckinghamshire, Hereford, Shropshire and Oxfordshire. If it is to survive, it is vital to preserve its habitat. This has at least been realized by such bodies as the Tree Council, the Woodland Trust and the Royal Society for the Protection of Birds.

The ghost orchid seldom sets fertile seeds, but usually reproduces from underground rhizomes, a slow process with sometimes several years between one flowering and the next. A flowering shoot arises from a subterranean bud – the lack of green leaves and the pale flower earns this rare plant its name of ghost orchid, or sometimes the coral root orchid.

The plant's food comes from the intimate connection between its roots, called mycorrhiza, and those of its host tree. The arrangement is not parasitic since both partners benefit, the tree apparently deriving some vital chemical from the orchid. It seems that its flowering from the end of May until September can be stimulated by a wet spring and if successful pollination does occur, it is carried out by bumble bees attracted to the copious supplies of nectar produced by the orchid and by its rather pleasant scent.

consequently the erosion of the associated commoners' rights in woodlands.

No one spoke more clearly for Everyman than John Clare in the nineteenth century who pointed out in verse that:

> Inclosure came and every path was stopt:
> Each tyrant fix'd his sign where paths were found:
> To hint a trespass now who cross'd the ground.

The children of the woodlanders moved to the towns and worked in industry for pay which was used to buy food. No-one needed to preserve the woods any more and their fate was sealed. John Evelyn, the seventeenth century diarist, remarked that a country would be far better off without gold providing it had timber. Britain forgot this for most of the nineteenth century which was a time mainly of peace and prosperity. Iron ships, powered by the steam from coal boilers, crossed the oceans and Britain imported what she wanted from the Empire. Then came war and the island used what little timber it had – which was precious little. Politicians knew in 1916 that some action was needed since Britain's woodlands were in danger of total extinction.

The government set up a committee in 1917 with Sir Richard Acland in the chair to examine what could be done. The result was the formation of the Forestry Commission which began operations in 1919 with the brief to plant 200,000 acres of trees within ten years and to raise this total to 1,770,000 acres by the end of this century. Naturally enough, upland areas of little or no use to agriculture were chosen and quick growing foreign conifers were preferred to the more slowly maturing native hardwoods. This should not detract from the efforts made and by 1939, 230 new forests had been earmarked and 360,000 of the Commission's 655,000 acres of land had been planted.

The Second World War came before these trees were mature enough to harvest, however, and another 373,000 acres of native woodlands were cleared to provide essential services. It has also been estimated that a further 150,000 acres of woodlands were seriously damaged. This underlined the objectives of the Commission and its 1919 targets were raised to 5,000,000 acres and the government encouraged private landowners to join in by the provision of grants and tax incentives.

The Forestry Commission at the present time has more than 2,000,000 acres of trees to which must be added around 1,500,000 acres of private woodland. Another 200,000 acres are regarded as approved but not permanent meaning that woodland has been planted on land not owned by the Commission. Once the trees have been felled, the area reverts to the landowner who may then use it for another purpose.

Perhaps for the first time in our history we are planting more trees than we are using. But many naturalists are still not happy. The majority of them feel that not enough native hardwoods are being planted and also that only 8 per cent of Britain's land area is under a canopy of trees. This is the smallest figure of any country in Europe with the exception of Ireland. We are still chipping away at our ancient woodlands and since 1947 the remaining area of native forest has been halved. This clearly cannot be allowed to continue, but the folly has, at last, been realized.

There is no richer habitat than the old wildwood which supports almost 250 species of flowering plant and fern. It should be stressed that cutting down a few trees can be beneficial: it allows light to reach the woodland floor which stimulates the growth of dormant seeds and a subsequent spurt of flower growth which is often prevented by dense shade. A wood managed for standard and coppiced wood can thus be ecologically rich and it is alarming when a whole wood is cut down without any replanting and the bare land is then used for building or transportation networks. Native birds such as the woodcock (*Scolopax rusticola*) are declining because of loss of habitat, while many flowers such as the primrose (*Primula vulgaris*), herb Paris (*Paris quadrifolia*) and the ghost orchid (*Epipogium aphyllum*) are also adversely affected.

Having said this, however, there at last seems to be an increasing concern for the future of our woodland and many species are in less danger today than they were ten years ago. The Forestry Commission is now opening up many forests providing nature trails, information centres, organized walks and lectures on wildlife. A few forests, such as Grizedale in the Lake District, also have well organized natural history displays and there is even a theatre in the forest. The Tree Council favours the case, pioneered in Switzerland over a century ago, that woodlands should be managed on behalf of the community with the dual object of generating a profit and the provision of a public amenity, and both the Woodland Trust and the RSPB have purchased woods in order to leave a reservoir in which wildlife can thrive. There is no doubt that as more people wander and enjoy the woodlands the greater area we shall need – man's need for communion with trees is the key to the survival of woodland plants and animals.

A clogger at work. Unlike the French and Dutch who made their footwear entirely of wood, British craftsmen had soon added the embellishment of a more comfortable leather upper secured to the sole block usually made of alder, although some preferred sycamore or even birch.

The woodland year

MIGHTY trees have a magic all of their own, and whatever the season, the play of light on the branches and foliage will never be the same from one minute to the next. Dripping with spring rain, sweltering in the summer's heat, bent almost double by the awesome storms of the autumn or hanging heavy with winter's snow, every tree retains its majesty. Each season will bring a fresh challenge to the naturalist trying to unravel the secrets of the lives of woodland, plants, and the animals which depend upon them, and a true picture will only appear after many visits spread over the whole year.

Because we find the battle against the cold, dark weeks of **winter** a struggle, there exists in our minds a special bond between us and wildlife in winter. We still have a primitive urge to stoke up the fire to provide heat for our bodily comfort, and light so that the evil forces of darkness can be kept at bay. It is a good time to feed the neighbourhood robin, to celebrate the new year with decorations of greenery, to promise the return of spring and to think about how tough the delicate looking flowers must be to survive under the carpet of frozen snow. It is worth driving miles to see a birchwood etched out in frost and mirrored in the waters of a tranquil lake.

Winter is a good time to begin a study of wildlife since the flowers are few, making learning their names easier and many trees are bare of leaves and therefore not obstructing the view. The hungry birds and other animals are so intent upon searching for food that they are often much less wary than they are at other seasons. Despite this, the skilled naturalist can often walk through a woodland and see no living creature, yet he knows what is there by the signs they leave behind.

Birds and mammals leave recognizable tracks either in snow or in the soft mud after rain. Identification takes time and patience but can be helped along by a little organization – whenever I go out into the countryside I always take a ruler and a notebook in addition to my camera.

Start by learning to eliminate the prints of domestic animals such as dogs, cats, sheep and horses. For instance, some animals leave a two toed print made by their hooves. These include deer, sheep and cows and are called unguligrade. Always measure the print and reference to books will then enable the correct species to be identified. A friend of mine always carries a ten pence coin and places this next to the print so giving him a size reference on his photographs. Others find that the presence of the coin detracts from the subject and prefer to record the dimensions.

Other mammals walk on tip toe and four, sometimes five, digits can clearly be seen – often the claws also show. This is true of many rodents, rabbits and hares as well as the carnivores which hunt them.

OPPOSITE: **The speckled wood butterfly. The life history of this species is unique in the sense that the speckled wood can hibernate either as a pupa or as a larva. In a good year the butterfly can be seen on the wing from April to October. At one time it was known as the wood argus and while many other butterflies are searching for hot sun to warm their wings this species seems quite content to flit about in the shade. It loves the narrow winding paths running through woodlands and seldom ventures into the full blaze of the sun unless disturbed. Even on a dull day it keeps its lonely vigil, patrolling its beat, and may even be seen on the wing as the soft summer rain bathes the dripping foliage. Both sides of the wings are prettily marked with shades of brown and buff and have white centred eyespots from which it has been given its name of Argus. Although it is still widely spread throughout Britain it does not seem quite as common as it once was in the north of England.**

The story told in the snow can often be exciting as I discovered early one Boxing day morning. My dog and I were first in the woodland just after dawn, and the path lay under a couple of inches of snow. As soon as I noticed the tracks of a rabbit I called my Labrador to heel and began to follow the trail. From a burrow the tracks led through a patch of hawthorn scrub, under a stile and passed close to a wall. Suddenly the tracks deepened telling me that the rabbit had sensed danger and had accelerated. Some little distance on, the rabbit's tracks were joined by those of a stoat which had approached out of some bushes and at an angle to its intended prey. A small area of blood was soon discovered and then the path taken by the stoat as it dragged its victim's body into the cover of a holly bush was easily followed. Insisting that the excited dog sit still, I peered beyond the holly to a pile of stones which had fallen from an old wall. There was the stoat enjoying its meal. It raised itself on its hind legs, glared myopically at me, spat like a cat, and continued with its breakfast. I left it in peace, feeling rather pleased with myself and cursing the fact that snow was beginning to fall again and obliterate the tracks.

It is not so easy to follow tracks when there is no snow on the ground, but many streams which run through woods have areas by the shallows which are worn smooth by animals coming down to drink. The prints of an amazing number of animals including voles, deer, hedgehogs, badgers, foxes and even squirrels turn up at my local water hole along with birds such as the moorhen, which spends much of its time in woodland, and the heron which comes in search of frogs and fish.

Searching for nests in winter may seem a fruitless exercise, but most naturalists these days prefer not to approach birds during the breeding season when disturbance may cause desertion of the eggs or young. In any event, the nests are easier to see when the concealing leaves have fallen from the trees. The details of construction can be examined at leisure and there will be one or two surprises.

One of the easiest to find is the domed nest of the wren (*Troglodytes troglodytes*). They are always covered on the outside with leaves or fronds of bracken and as they dry out the rusty red colours stand out against the tree or tangles of bramble. Look inside and you will find that only about one nest in eight has feathers inside it. This

Some prints are very distinct and a reference collection can easily be made using plaster of paris and a frame made out of cardboard. The cardboard is bent around the print and the circle completed by fastening with a paper clip. A small bowl is then used to mix the plaster with water from a stream and poured into the mould which is left for half an hour to set. This time should never be wasted and can be used to look carefully for other tracks and signs – it is surprising how much more you can see when confined to a small area. When the plaster has set it is removed and gently wrapped in tissue and taken home. The print must first be cleaned and then painted to bring out each tiny detail. I have heard it said that this method is time consuming and requires a great deal of organizing. This is true, but this is also what being a naturalist means. Those who wish to know which creatures are active in a particular woodland must make an effort to get to know them.

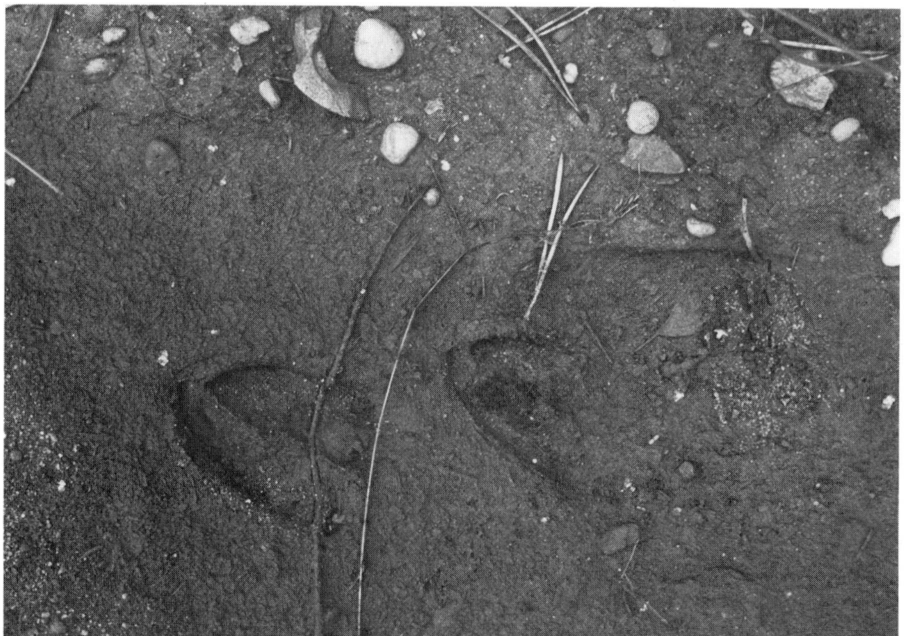

Here are fallow deer tracks in soft soil – notice that there are only two toes.

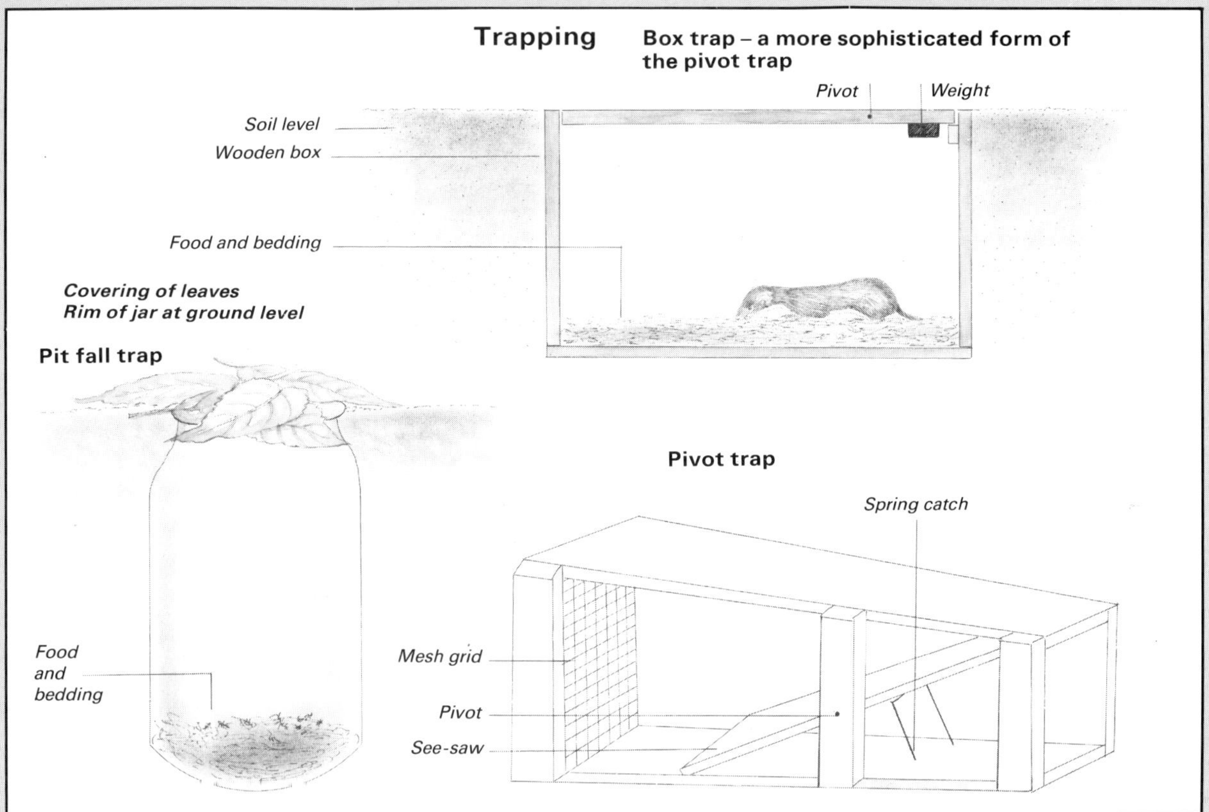

GREAT fun may be had and no harm is caused to wildlife by setting up a series of baited traps to catch invertebrates and small mammals. A pit-fall trap, for example, can be made from a jam jar which should be filled with hay to keep the captive animal warm and plenty of suitable food to persuade it to enter the trap. The jar is buried in soil so that the neck is at ground level and it is covered by a strip of bark supported by stones to lift it just clear of the entrance, leaving room for the animal to enter. A bait of oatmeal will attract vegetarians such as the bank vole (illustrated) and short tailed field vole while minced meat or cat food will bring both common and pigmy shrews in search of food. Surprisingly few British mammals hibernate, and with the exceptions of the dormice, bats and the hedgehogs, all our species are actively searching for food. Larger animals, such as stoats and weasels can be caught by means of a see-saw trap simply made from a stout wooden box. The top is pivoted and provided with a return weight as a counterbalance. The device is baited and buried to ground level in the same way as the pit fall trap. All traps should be looked at regularly to avoid the animals dying of cold or shortage of food. The bedding is absolutely essential to avoid the creatures becoming cold and they should be released carefully both for their own sake and for the sake of the fingers of those who release them.

Commercial traps can be obtained, the best on the market being the Longworth, originally designed by the Animal Ecology research group at Oxford. They are now produced by the Longworth Instruments Co Ltd at Abingdon in Berkshire. The trap is made from aluminium and is in two parts which fit together easily. The fact that it is made of metal means that it can become cold if left overnight so on really cold nights I do not set my traps at all and always provide a great deal of bedding. One half of the trap is the nest section and the other is a tunnel leading into it. The tunnel door is closed firmly behind it as soon as the mammal steps on a treddle at the entrance to the nest box. Providing the trap is carefully concealed it will catch voles, long tailed field mice and shrews very efficiently and they can be released without harm. On one occasion I had to abandon trapping one particular area because as fast as I released it a short tailed vole headed straight back into the trap for a meal and a sleep!

Snow on hawthorn branches during the winter of 1981–82.

is because the male wren, once he has established his territory, sets about the task of building a number of nests and then takes his new mate on a tour of inspection. Finally she selects one which is then lined with feathers whilst the others are discarded. They come in useful during the cold nights of winter when they are used as roosts. In the evil winter of 1962–63, for instance, I found the pathetic corpses of 13 wrens which had died of cold despite being huddled together in an old nest in an effort to conserve heat.

The examination of old nests often reveals infertile eggs which have failed to hatch. I collect these and keep them in my garden shed until the spring. There is no point in trying to blow an addled egg and all I do is wait until my local ant's nest has become active in spring. I then make a hole in each of my eggs and place them near the nest – within a day or two the ants have cleaned out the eggs and they are ready for labelling and sending to my local natural history museum.

Old nests have one final surprise in store. In the hollow, where the eggs are laid – the cup – there are often supplies of hawthorn berries, hazel nuts, rose hips and other fruits. These cannot have been blown in by accident but have been deliberately carried there by the long tailed field mouse (*Apodemus sylvaticus*).

The dreys of the red and grey squirrels, neither of which hibernates, are often confused with birds' nests. Their breeding season can begin as early as February and caches of food are hidden throughout the wood both on the ground, in hollow trees and in nests, including their own dreys, of which one squirrel may have several. The grey squirrel (*Sciurus carolinensis*), introduced from North America in the late nineteenth century, seems to prefer parks and deciduous woodlands and the native red squirrel (*Sciurus vulgaris*), now much more restricted in distribution, favours coniferous woods. However, the two can occur together and the winter naturalist in search of nests must learn to distinguish between them.

Both build their dreys (also sometimes called jugs) in two layers. The outer layer consists of interwoven branches and then there is an inner lining of grasses and leaves which makes the interior snug, dry and warm. The grey squirrel chooses deciduous branches and twigs, especially those with leaves still attached, thereby giving the drey an untidy appearance. In contrast, the drey of the red is much neater, being composed of an interwoven mass of thin, usually coniferous twigs. I once found a red squirrel's drey in a Lakeland wood which was in the fork of a larch tree blown down by a winter gale. I was able to pull the drey to pieces and discovered in the lining lots of feathers, including those of a song thrush and a jay which was easy to understand, but also several feathers from a mallard (*Anas platyrhynchos*). These ubiquitous ducks are found with surprising frequency in woodlands. Any drey is between 24cm and 35cm (9in to 14in) in diameter and its spherical shape has no obvious entrance – squirrels 'close the door' when they enter and leave – so distinguishing it from any bird's nest.

By far the best way to master the identification of trees is to make a collection of winter twigs. The autumn gales, falls of heavy winter snow on the branches as well as the activities of birds and mammals break off twigs which fall onto the relatively bare ground and can be collected. Dead leaves are also abundant and can be gathered but this is best done in late summer and autumn.

Towards the end of winter, buds begin to swell with sap and prepare to burst. Buds are really the undeveloped shoots usually containing frail young leaves, whilst others protect the flower parts. During the developmental period they are subject to many dangers including hungry animals, hard frost and loss of essential water during periods of strong, cold dehydrating winds. Thus the close packing of the bud prevents the radiation of heat and transpiration of moisture, whilst special structures have developed to give additional protection. These include hairs and furry coverings, rough scales and even sticky resins and gums to prevent both water vapour from evaporating and too much water entering during wet weather. This sticky material is often so distasteful that many animals ignore it completely. This is particularly obvious in the horse chestnut (*Aesculus hippocastanum*), the resin being produced by glands situated on the bud scales. As the scales grow and shift position, the sticky substance gets smeared all over the huge reddish brown bud, which can be up to 2.5cm (1in) long and almost as broad.

The ash (*Fraxinus excelsior*) can easily be identified by the unique black colour of its buds. A close look will show that its shape resembles the hoof of a deer and if the twig is held up to the light it will be found to be a very dark olive green in colour rather than blue. This dark colour contrasts beautifully with the grey branch on which it grows.

The bud of the beech (*Fagus sylvatica*) is about 2cm ($\frac{3}{4}$in) long and is slim and sharply pointed. At one time these buds were gathered, dried in ovens and used as tooth picks. Their graceful shape enhances the delicate branches on which they grow and when light shines through them, the whole area is flooded with a brownish glow. The buds are arranged spirally and almost alternately on the twig. Beech twigs are very similar to those of hornbeam but the latter are rather smaller, blunter and are not so shiny. They also tend to bend inwards towards the twig whilst those of beech usually point outwards. Oak (*Quercus sp*) twigs bristle with bright brown buds and there are usually five or six clustered around a central bud, usually the largest of the group. The twig has something of a rugged appearance due to the prominent leaf scars which stand out from the twig.

Elms also have unique buds which are very tiny, seldom exceeding 3mm ($\frac{1}{8}$in) in length, and they are almost as broad. They are reddish brown in colour – a feature which is beautifully apparent when the tree is lit by the low light of a winter's

Buds are always consistent in their shape and colour – especially the terminal bud, although the lateral buds below it are also arranged in a specific manner along the stem. Late winter twigs can be kept in fresh water where they will develop and the magic of the unfolding process can be watched in the comfort of your own home.

The green buds of the sycamore (above) are ovoid and about 1.2cm ($\frac{1}{2}$in) long. The lateral buds are arranged in pairs. Most lateral buds do not develop unless the terminal bud is damaged in which case one or perhaps both of a pair of laterals takes over. The age of any twig can be calculated by counting the conspicuous scars left by the scales of the terminal bud each year.

dawn. A collection of twigs made during a winter's walk through a wood can be identified at home – I like to do it in front of a crackling fire made from pieces of dead wood collected on the same journey together with the smell of smouldering holly or beech, a good book and a glass of wine made from elderberries or sloes gathered from the same wood in autumn.

Buds on twigs of oak (top), elm (middle) and ash (bottom).

The weather changes during the equinoxes of **spring** and autumn are seldom smooth and March often roars in like a lion, the wild old winter king having a terrifying last fling. The lengthening days slowly cause a rise in temperature and the combination of light and heat triggers some birds to begin their breeding rituals.

Many woodcocks leave our woods for more northerly regions although some remain to breed in Britain, a favoured nest site being at the foot of a tree. Other species which grace our woodlands in winter are the brambling (*Fringilla montifringella*), fieldfare (*Turdus pilaris*) and the red wing (*Turdus iliacus*) all of which have very occasionally bred in Britain but usually return to Iceland and Scandinavia. To replace them our April woods begin to echo with the songs of the warblers, two of the commonest being the willow warbler (*Phylloscopus trochilus*) and the chiff-chaff (*Phylloscopus collybita*). The two species are very difficult to separate by their physical appearance but the onomatopoeic call of the chiff-chaff soon indicates its presence.

The cuckoo also enjoys woodlands, especially those with open rides and suitable song posts for the vociferous male. As soon as the cuckoo (*Cuculus canorus*) arrives towards the end of April the myths regarding its migration, song and breeding are given yet another airing. Bird song builds up to the crescendo of the May dawn chorus and the relative merits of the nightingale (*Luscinia megarhynchos*) and the blackbird (*Turdus merula*) as nature's best choristers are put to the test.

Birds are divided into 28 orders, and the birds which can be truly said to sing are only found in the last and most advanced order, the perching birds or passerines. Song may be defined as a connected string of vocalizations concerned with procuring and maintaining a territory. It has evolved by the linking together of a number of calls such as alarm calls or flight calls. The song of the chaffinch still contains its *wheet* alarm call so familiar to those who wander through our woodlands and startle the bird. There is little doubt that song is still evolving and the most highly developed of the passerines are often superb vocalists and as such are often referred to as oscines or song-birds.

If one conducted a survey amongst non-ornithologists and asked for the name of Britain's most accomplished avian songster, the nightingale would be the easy victor. You would also be told that, as its name implies, it only sings at night. I will accept that the song is fluid and accomplished, but I would point out that the species is often highly vocal during the hours of daylight. My vote, however, would not go to the nightingale but to the blackbird, which can also sing beautifully during the shortening nights of springtime.

The male nightingales arrive in England a couple of weeks before the females and as the species is very shy it may take some time to warm up and develop a full blooded song. I must confess to being rather puzzled as to why a collection of nightingales should be called a watch when they are so difficult to see! Perhaps a choir of nightingales might be considered a more appropriate appelation. Their song was certainly well known to Pliny, the Roman natural historian. He has this to say about the nightingale:

> 'The song is to be heard without intermission, for fifteen days and nights continuously when the foliage is thickening, as it bursts from the bud; a bird which deserves our

The anatomy of bird song

Cross section of a bird's syrinx.

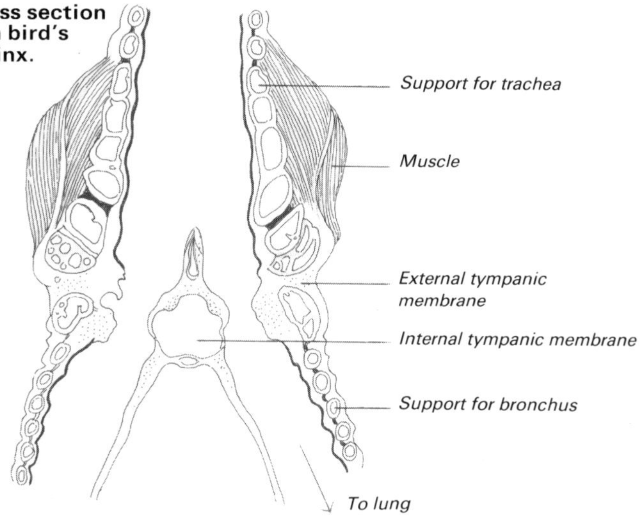

A nightingale singing.

IT is a great deal easier to explain how birds are able to sing than it is to account for why they do so. At one time it was only those of a more artistic temperament who made any attempt to interpret the intricacies of avian acoustics. Beethoven included the songs of the nightingale (played on the flute) and the quail (performed on the oboe) in his Pastoral Symphony. These are quite obvious when one listens carefully, and there is no problem at all in recognizing the cuckoo call faithfully copied by the clarinet. But how are these often quite wonderful sounds produced by our birds? To understand what happens, we must forget all about our own vocal apparatus. We have a larynx (the Adam's apple) and by forcing air through the vocal chords within this apparatus we produce a sound of varying quality which we shape into language using tongue and teeth. Birds however, do not have a larynx but a much more complex structure called the syrinx situated very close to the lungs.

In addition to its lungs a bird has a series of air sacs which allow it to hold a much larger volume of air than is the case with a mammal. Doubtless this evolved in response to the extra demands made upon the respiratory system by a flying animal, but it also enables birds to sustain long streams of liquid notes without having to pause for breath.

The syrinx itself consists of muscles, membranes, and a substantial resonating chamber. Experiments have shown that the activity of the syrinx is controlled to some extent by nerves linked to the brain, but also by the reproductive hormones. In the case of many birds, the delivery rate of the notes is so rapid that the human ear is not able to detect a tune. In the wren, for example, it has been estimated that ten separate notes can be produced every second. If this sound is tape recorded and slowed down the song becomes much more understandable to the human ear and since the middle 1950s man's electronic ingenuity has enabled sonograms to be constructed.

Firstly, the sound of the singing bird is recorded, every attempt being made to cut out all background noises. This tape is then played into an instrument known as a sound spectograph, which produces a visual tracing representing the component pulses of the bird's song. Gradually the technique has become more sophisticated and can not only be used to distinguish one species from another, but can also show that birds, like human beings, have regional accents. We do indeed have cockney sparrers, Lancastrian blackbirds and Scots thrushes. The sonograph has made a recent and very significant step. On the telephone you can tell which of your friends you are speaking to so why should a bird not be able to distinguish the sound of its own mate? Indeed this is almost certainly the case, since the sonographs do show individual variations and we now have a much fuller understanding of bird language than would ever have been thought possible a few years ago.

admiration in no slight degree. First of all what a powerful voice in so small a body! Its note how long and how well sustained. And then, too, it is the only bird the notes of which are modulated in accordance with strict rules of musical science.'

This last sentence is not strictly true but it does show that even the ancients, without the benefit of modern notation and technology, could detect music in the song of birds.

The nightingale is a summer visitor in Britain and is usually present from mid-April to mid-September although the British Trust for Ornithology do have records as early as March and as late as December. The earliest arrival date listed is of a bird present near Farley in Wiltshire on 10 March 1961 and the latest record is 20 December 1958 at Long Melford in Suffolk. There seem to be no records for January or February.

Although *The Atlas of Breeding Birds of Britain and Ireland* offers a figure of some 10,000 breeding pairs, these are almost all concentrated in the south eastern corner of Britain and no breeding records occur further north than Yorkshire. The species does not breed at all in Scotland or in Ireland. It is, however, mentioned that the numbers have drastically declined due to the loss of suitable habitat. There seems to be a rule, with but a few exceptions, that dull looking birds which spend much of their life skulking about in the undergrowth should have loud and very penetrating songs. This actually makes a great deal of sense for how else will the sexes be able to find each other? The chosen environment provides both nesting site and food so the bird need not venture far out of the blackthorn thickets to which they become so attached.

The yellow flag iris adds a lovely flash of colour to damp woodlands and its roots were once a source of starch used in food and the laundry.

Some blackbirds, unlike the nightingale, are with us all through the year and because of this it is not always realized that it is also a migratory species. Evidence obtained from ringing birds shows that some individuals are indeed home birds but many, especially young birds, may wander considerable distances. Because the blackbird is such a common species and the male is so easily recognized, their habits and idiosyncrasies tend to be well catalogued, but none the less interesting for that. A browse through the back numbers of magazines such as *The Field* reveals many fascinating observations. In March 1916 Mr F W Berry wrote from a vicarage at Wenden near Saffron Walden:

'The night of March 10, 1916 was extremely mild with a full clear moon. At 10pm I was surprised to hear a number of blackbirds in full song. After a time the singing ceased, but on going out again at midnight it had recommenced and in various directions I could hear a dozen or more birds in full chorus.'

This habit of singing at night is well documented. In recent years the sprouting of street lights around the perimeters of our parks and along roads and suburban gardens has resulted in an artificial daylight so that night singing has become habitual. It would also seem safe to assume that birds breeding in trees which are artificially illuminated tend to breed even earlier than those birds abiding in the dark depths of the countryside.

A further journey through the yellowing pages of the back numbers of *The Field* brings the rich reward of an altruistic tale concerning the blackbird. Mr B Baise of Wellbrook House, Mayfield, Sussex wrote on 28 May 1921:

'Whilst busy digging a few days ago, with an old retriever lying close by, my attention was attracted to the behaviour of a hen blackbird towards the dog. The dog was looking bored and somewhat perplexed and disturbed, for he got up and lay down again further away. The blackbird then paid its attentions towards me, carried on the same performance by running towards me instead of towards the dog, stopping close by, opening its bill and uttering a plaintive cry; then running away some distance, always in the same direction. I thought perhaps it wanted a worm, so I threw it one or two, but these it utterly ignored. I then came to the conclusion that there must be some good reason for its strange behaviour, so sticking my spade in the ground I followed the bird. As soon as it saw me doing so its excitement seemed to grow. When I reached the orchard it flew into an apple tree, and called as loudly as it could. On looking up I saw another blackbird (a male) partially hanging and very much spent. As the helpless victim was out of my reach I went to get a short ladder, and so find out the trouble. Whilst I was gone the hen bird remained with its mate never ceasing its plaintive cry. On reaching the helpless bird I found that one leg was tightly wedged in a ragged end of a small splintered bough. With little difficulty I released the sufferer and, on examining the limb found it unbroken. When I let him go he flew away somewhat weakly accompanied by his clever little mate. This episode which goes far to prove the intelligence of wild birds, I am not likely to forget, nor the wonderful way that blackbird *made* me understand it wanted my services.'

So much for a wonderfully emotional oddity, but what about the normal behaviour of the species? Breeding behaviour can begin as early as January providing the weather is sufficiently mild, but the cycle reaches its peak during the spring period. Two and sometimes three broods are raised which means that there may be young, not yet at the flying stage, as late as September. Thus for *Turdus merula* the breeding season is a protracted one.

The nest itself is interesting. I used to think that the song thrush was more industrious than the blackbird, taking the trouble to line its nest with mud or smoothed cow pat. If a disused blackbird's nest is dissected, or if one has the good fortune to witness the actual construction, it can be seen that the blackbird first lines with mud and then adds a further lining of dried grasses. Into this cradle four

As might be expected, the ever popular daffodil has a good number of vernacular names including goose-flop, but most are much more complimentary. I particularly like Whit Sunday, bell-flowers, daffy-dilly and golden trumpets. As with many of our wild flowers the daffodil has been associated with the cuckoo, being called the cuckoo rose in Devon.

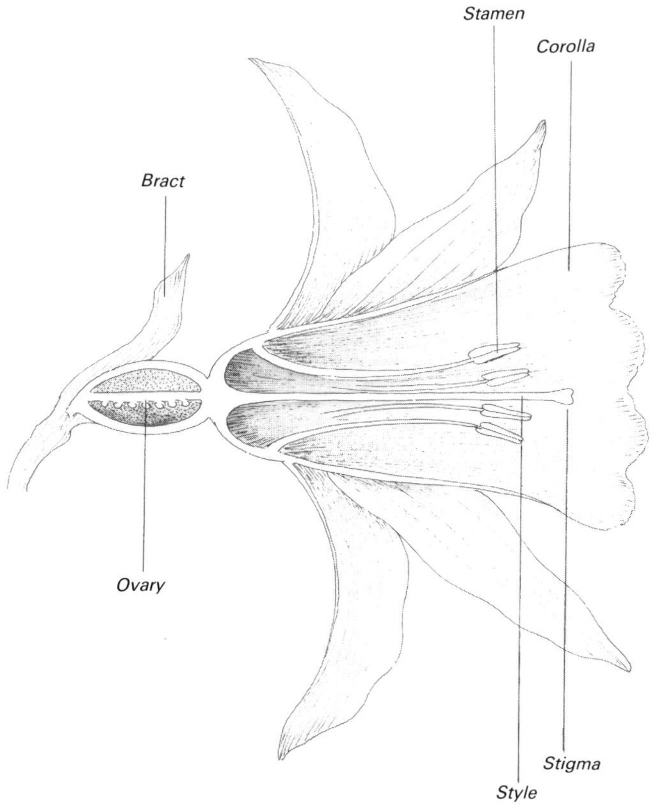

or five blue-green eggs, freckled with varying amounts of brown, are laid. The hen is said to incubate alone and although I am well aware that it is stated in many books not to happen, I have two personal observations of a male blackbird sitting on a clutch of eggs. In neither case, however, did the male spend long on the nest, and he may not have had any serious intent of infringing the feminine territory. The cock plays his full part in the feeding of the young, though, which have a diet consisting mainly of earthworms, but often includes wireworms and other invertebrates.

When the young are tiny they swallow the droppings, but later on the parent birds assiduously remove the droppings leaving them at a safe distance from the nest. Many young birds, including blackbirds, release their excreta in a gelatinous sac, a sort of pre-packaging developed by the natural world. The nestlings grow with great speed and after about a fortnight the young are ready to fly. The parents very soon leave them to fend for themselves, and get on with the business of raising another brood, usually but not always, using a different nest.

As far as feeding is concerned the blackbird, as with all thrushes, is very versatile. After a summer spent feasting upon invertebrates it turns its attention to seeds and fruits.

Spring flowers – especially those in a woodland – are involved in a desperate race against time. They must produce their flowers and their leaves and must get on with the vital task of producing food before the larger, dominant plants cast their dark shade, cutting off the essential sunlight.

Flowering plants are divided into two groups termed monocotyledons (monocots) and dicotyledons (dicots). Monocots have only one leaf within the seed whereas the much more numerous dicots have two. Monocots have their flower parts in multiples of three whilst dicots have theirs in twos, fives or in multiples of these numbers.

The daffodil is sadly much rarer in the wild than it used to be because of the people who have snatched the blooms and hacked the bulbs out of the ground over the years. It flowers in March and April and has a crinkled corolla which is about 5cm (2in) long which is about the same length as the perianthal structures. Both the drooping head as well as the corolla protect the delicate stamens from rain. The equally sensitive bud is protected by a thin sheath called the bract, which after the flower has bloomed becomes dry and papery.

Snowdrops – the most well-known of Britain's spring flowers.

A lot of folk insist that the Fair Maid of February, as the snowdrop (*Galanthus nivalis*) is often called, is not a true native of Britain. This may be, but it is so much at home in churchyards, old orchards and small woodlands that we must surely admit it to our list of wild plants. In their *Flora of the British Isles* Clapham, Tutin and Warburg note that the species is probably native. An old English rhyme records that:

> 'The Snowdrop in purest white arrae
> First rears her head on Candlemass day.'

This is on 2 February but in mild winters the first blooms may have risen from their bulbs as early as mid January. There seems ample proof to suggest that the monks of the late Middle Ages brought back many holy snowdrops from their journeys to Rome, and Gerard noted that:

> 'These plants doe grow wilde in Italy and the places adjacent, notwithstanding our London gardens have taken possession of them these manie years past.'

Thus we are left with the compromise that the snowdrop may have been a rather uncommon native plant in some areas of our wildwoods, but frequent introductions have made it much more common. We should all be grateful to the monks because if any flower deserves to be worshipped it must be the Fair Maid of February bringing us a promise of the spring to come.

Mammals such as the fox (*Vulpes vulpes*) and, more especially, the badger (*Meles meles*) give birth to their young early in the year and by the time the sweet smelling primroses and bluebells (*Endymion non-scriptus*) are gracing the woodlands it is time to go looking for cubs. There is nothing skilful about these watches but the basic rules of woodcraft *must* be obeyed. The bright anoraks and waterproofs which can be seen for miles and crackle at the slightest movement are utterly useless. A visit to an army surplus store in search of combat jackets, which were obviously designed for camouflage, is essential and it must also be remembered that spring nights can be just as cold as some in winter. Plenty of sweaters should be worn underneath and do not neglect the legs. A pair of pyjama trousers or long thermal underwear may not be glamorous, but they are certainly functional.

The den of the fox or the sett of the badger should be approached quietly about an hour before sunset. Take care that you select a spot with the wind blowing from the entrance towards you. I remember one memorable watch which began with a heavy shower of sleet just as I settled myself down in the fork of an ash tree overlooking a badger sett. This had been shown me by a friend, but I had never watched it before. Expecting a badger to emerge I was astounded when a dog fox came out and after spending some time scenting the air, he set off down wind and disappeared into the gathering gloom. It often happens that fox and badger share a particularly secluded, and therefore safe, home. Neither appears to mind the presence of the other despite their differing habits. An hour later, just as I had resigned myself to a silent night and begun to think about my cramped position and the falling temperature, a boar badger emerged and began to have a good scratch. The sky had cleared and a pale moon and the stars shone bright in the frosty air. He grunted into the funnel of the sett and was soon joined by his mate who was followed first by one and then another cub blinking at the unaccustomed light. Judging from the information my friend had given me the young badgers were on their first visit to the surface. One tried to suckle, but the sow was far too wary to relax to this extent and soon bullied them to return underground. This was the first of many sightings during the spring and summer and just goes to prove that careful preparation and a knowledge of the animal's behaviour leads to successful watches.

Many naturalists prefer to walk in the woods on the hot days of summer and the fruitful days of autumn, but there is so much to see both in winter and spring, and neither must we neglect the night. Some creatures, however, are at their most active when the temperatures begin to rise. As spring gives way to summer and the bluebells fade, the drainage ditches, streams and old ponds warm up and the bees buzz. Spring has gone for another year and it is high summer.

As the sun beats down from the clear blue sky in the **summer**, the leaves of the trees gather heat and light but deny this to the woodland floor. Insects still live in the leaf litter but there is much more going on in the open spaces and rides of the woods and also at the woodland's edge. It is in these areas and on the canopies of the trees themselves that the greatest activity occurs. Much of this is lost to naturalists unless they make full use of their binoculars or are prepared to sit in a hide. Some of the Forestry Commission woodlands have deer observation towers which can provide splendid views of the tree tops and I have found that good use can be made of photographers' hides supported on stilts. If you possess none of these

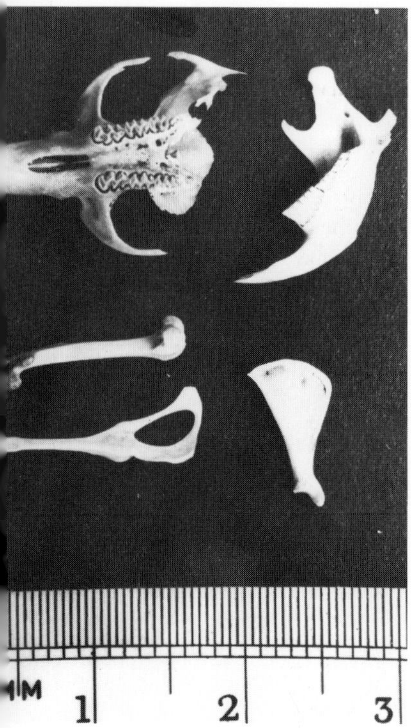

The tawny owl is a regular member of most woodlands and usually has a favourite roost under which the pellets are dropped and can be collected. Separating and identifying the material within the pellet is one of the most exciting parts of a field naturalist's craft. Small mammals can be identified by the shape of bones and markings on the teeth, and birds from their claws and feathers. Very occasionally a bird ring may be found to give an even more fascinating history of the woodland's web of life. Although tawny owls do sometimes partly dismember their prey before swallowing it there is usually enough evidence to work out its diet.

advantages then choose a woodland growing on a slope, and look down from the highest bank onto the canopy. You will be rewarded by good views of insects, especially butterflies, whilst the bird world has its insect specialists which are always on the hunt.

The holly and the ivy are usually associated with winter but they are linked in summer by the fascinating life history of the holly blue butterfly (*Celastrina argiolus*). This species overwinters as a pupa and then goes through two generations. The caterpillars of the first feed on the buds and berries of holly (*Ilex aquifolium*) whilst the second generation feed upon ivy (*Hedera helix*). Occasionally this second brood will also feed on alder buckthorn (*Rhamnus frangula*). Holly blues have the upper surface of their lilac blue wings bordered with black, a feature that is much more obvious in the males. Adults are on the wing from late April through into June and the second brood are active during August and September. Holly blues are more common in the south of England but are also found in a few sheltered woods in Scotland in which the essential food plants grow. Another butterfly which is seen in the high canopy is the silver washed fritillary (*Argynnis paphia*). This depends entirely on the oak for its survival and adults are not seen on the wing until July when the female lays her eggs in the gnarled bark of old oaks. In around a fortnight the caterpillars hatch first, eat their own egg shells and then go straight into hibernation. This period lasts from August until late March, when the hungry caterpillars descend the trunk and go off in search of the leaves of violets on which they feed.

Butterflies are also common along the rides and woodland edges and these habitats are now more important than they have ever been before. Valuable habitat such as hedges, field boundaries and roadside verges are being landscaped, treated with herbicides or removed altogether and butterfly populations have declined in consequence. In our woodland clearings peacocks (*Inachis io*) and small tortoishells (*Aglais urticae*) can find fresh nettles on which to lay their eggs whilst August sees the peak population of the speckled wood (*Pararge aegeria*). Those on the wing in August come from the second brood, the caterpillars feeding mainly upon the common couch grass (*Elymus repens*) or cock's-foot (*Dactylis glomerata*).

As a rule, the best places to observe butterflies are in woodland clearings early in the morning. Being cold blooded they cannot control their body temperature themselves and must obtain some body heat from the sun. Early in the morning they are very sluggish and hold out their wings which function like solar panels before flying away. Whilst they are warming up, their wing patterns can be studied and photographs taken. The well informed naturalist will also soon learn the areas where other cold blooded animals such as reptiles come to bask in the sun.

I remember as a boy being lucky enough to be caught trespassing by our local policeman who may well have saved my life. A single track railway line ran down from a granite quarry through a fine old lakeland wood. In the summer, common lizards and slow worms came out of the wood to lie on the railway sleepers and soak up the sun. He gave me a telling off, but was a naturalist himself and pointed out an old stone wall in the dip of a damp wood on which adders regularly basked. The adder (*Vipera berus*) can be distinguished from the larger grass snake (*Natrix natrix*) by dark markings on the head of the poisonous species. One of these marks on the adder resembles an inverted 'V' which is also the first letter of its alternative name of viper. Like the common lizard, vipers give birth to live young but the female takes more care of them and they are sometimes seen on a sunlit bank soaking up the sun. Once recognized the adder should be looked at from a distance and if left alone it will not be at all aggressive. It is not able to raise its head and strike in the manner of several species of poisonous tropical snakes.

The early summer sees many birds, especially the migrants, completing the breeding season and once this has ended they enter the period of moult which is usually during August. The skilful bird watcher can identify some of these woodland birds by their feeding methods and others by the evidence they leave behind them. The flycatchers, for example, have an easily recognized way of catching flies. They wait on a perch and then fly out quickly to capture one or several flies only to return to the same perch to repeat the process. There are two species in the British woodlands. The spotted flycatcher (*Muscicapa striata*) is marginally larger than the pied flycatcher (*Ficedula hypoleuca*) which is around 12.5cm (5in) long. Male spotted flycatchers are clearly black and white whilst the female is brown and white. Around 20,000 pairs of the pied flycatcher breed in the damp oakwoods of Britain whilst the population of spotted flycatchers is probably ten times this figure. The species is widely distributed but found at its highest densities in deciduous woodland. Both sexes are alike with streaked breast and grey brown back.

The tree-creeper (*Certhia familiaris*) is also easily recognized because it moves its way spirally up a tree trunk and when it reaches the top it flies down to the base of the next and begins the whole process again. It has strong claws to help it climb and its tail feathers are specially stiffened so that the bird can lean backwards and take a rest using them as a support.

Some species leave behind evidence of their presence which the experienced naturalist can read. The song thrush (*Turdus philomelos*) loves snails but can find the shells difficult to break. Not many birds have learned to use a tool, but the song thrush knows where the local outcrops of rock and loose stones are to be found. It carries its snails to its 'anvil' which soon becomes littered with broken shells. The sparrowhawk (*Accipiter nisus*), likewise, has a regular plucking post – often an old tree stump in a secluded part of the wood, and the area around it looks as if some thoughtless person has just cut open a feather mattress. It is only when you look closer that you find strips of bone and flesh. The carnage is greatest at the time when the female is confined to the nest with the young and the male has to keep her supplied with plucked birds which the hen dismembers for her young. Owls are much tidier feeders but still leave plenty of evidence for those with the time to look and the eyes to see. Owls usually swallow their prey whole but cannot afford to allow the sharp bones and feather quills to pass into the main gut. These potentially dangerous structures are therefore separated in the crop prior to entering the delicate areas of the rest of the digestive tract and regurgitated as a pellet.

The common or vivaparous lizard is widely distributed throughout Britain and Ireland. Lizards vary in size from 10–15cm (4–6in), including the tail and although it is possible to separate the sexes in the field it is not easy. The belly of the male tends to be reddish while that of his mate is yellow. After breeding, the female's gestation period seems to depend upon temperature and so young tend to be born earlier in the south of England than in the north and births are earlier in hot summers than in cold. It may well be that a pregnant female deliberately sits in the sun exposing her abdomen to the heat in order to accelerate development. The number of young varies from two to fifteen, each being born in a transparent bag which soon ruptures. Neither parent takes much interest in their young which can catch their own food, mainly live insects, within an hour of being born.

The slow-worm is neither slow nor a worm. Other folk called it a blind worm and yet it can see perfectly well. It is, in fact, a legless lizard and may be distinguished from snakes by the fact that it has eyelids enabling it to blink – an activity completely beyond the snakes which are also reptiles. It is often said that snakes have no eyelids at all which is not true but they are transparent and permanently closed over the eyeball to form a useful protective layer as they creep through low and often sharp vegetation.

The green woodpecker (*Picus viridis*) and the jay (*Garrulus glandarius*) both have an unusual habit which has been called 'anting'. These species appear to enjoy dancing up and down on the nest of the wood ant (*Formica rufa*). Some writers have suggested that the birds close their eyes in ecstasy. It seems, however, that the exercise serves two purposes. Firstly wood ants are an important part of the diet, but just as important may be the fact that when ants are in danger they inject a stream of formic acid which serves to deter the majority of predators. The acid is also strong enough to kill the feather lice which infect the birds explaining why it is essential that they keep their eyes closed. The ceremony is fascinating and I well remember watching a green woodpecker performing in Hardcastle Crags woodland at dawn on a wet morning in late June, and how much the dance reminded me of old witchcraft ceremonies. Midsummer's day – St John's Day – was a day when witches were said to be active and country-folk went diligently in search of magical plants with the power to keep Old Nick at bay.

The St John's wort family are well represented in the summer woodland and include the fascinating shrub tutsan (*Hypericum androsaemum*). The yellow flowers are approximately 2cm ($\frac{3}{4}$in) across whilst the leaves can be as long as 7.5cm (3in). At one time country-folk used them as book marks and called them bible-leaves. They were often gathered on midsummer's eve and replaced by fresh leaves every year to renew the protection of the Good Book from the Devil.

The name tutsan derives from the French toute-saine meaning all-heal, since the plant had an unrivalled reputation as a healer of wounds. It differs from the rest of the family, which produce dry seeds, by forming juicy berries. At first these are red but during the autumn they turn black. When squeezed a red juice is produced and accounts for the scientific name of androsaemum which means the blood of a man. Our ancestors believed that God placed a sign on each plant to let us know what He intended it to be used for. The Doctrine of Signatures obviously suggested that tutsan should be used in the treatment of wounds. There was an old superstition in the New Forest which suggested that tutsan grew where a battle had been fought and the plant was sucking the blood of the slaughtered Danish soldiers out of the soil.

There are several other species of St John's wort, but the one most likely to be found in the woods on St John's eve (29 June) is *Hypericum perforatum*. It was believed that God placed a sign on each plant to tell His people the function of that plant. Hence, those which looked like a body organ were used to cure ills in that organ, while those with red sap were used for blood disorders or staunching the blood from a wound. These plants became known as signature plants. All the species of St John's wort are signature plants because the leaves bear red spots thought to represent the blood of John the Baptist martyred on 29 June. Anything so holy was bound to keep the Devil at bay as well as curing wounds, thus its old name of Devil's flight.

The old herbalists were also convinced that self heal (*Prunella vulgaris*), which grows in clearings, had the power to cure wounds its signature being its ability to bloom again with surprising speed after being cut. Yarrow (*Achillea millefolium*) was supposed to cure melancholy and its close relative sneezewort (*Achillea ptarmica*) – was used to treat heavy colds. Both are named after Achilles who was reputed to be the first to realize the healing powers of both plants.

The precise demarcation of the seasons is merely for human convenience and summer merges imperceptibly into **autumn**. As the days shorten, migrant birds prepare to leave, fruits and seeds ripen, fungi grow beneath the trees stripped of their leaves by the seasonal gales, and nature battens down her hatches in preparation for another winter. There are, however, the autumnal colours to delight us and the sun's rays are often warm and cheery.

The casual woodland naturalist strolls happily about, perfectly aware of the rudiments of fruit and seed dispersal. But how many, I wonder, can distinguish between a fruit and a seed? A fruit is really a seed container and differs from the seeds within it both in external appearance and internal structure. The fruit is usually carried upon a stalk (technically known as the pedicel) which once bore the blossom. Seeds do not have pedicels but they do have a small scar called the hilum where the seed was attached to the fruit. A fruit obviously does not have such a structure but almost always carries the withered remains of one or more styles. These are the female part of the flower connecting the stigma, on which the pollen is deposited, to the ovary in which the ovules are fertilized. Look at a crab-apple and you will find the remains of the styles at one end and the stalk at the other. If a fruit is cut in half you will find seeds within. If you cut a seed in half all you find is the embryo plant. Since fruits and seeds of plants can be stored over winter to provide essential food they have been valuable, and indeed are still so, in the evolution of the human species.

The greengrocer's distinction between a vegetable and a fruit is not always clear but to a botanist a fruit is any structure containing seeds and therefore cucumbers, marrows, tomatoes, peas and beans are technically fruits and not vegetables. However, the scientific classification of fruits is rather more technical. In a strawberry or a rose hip, for example, the pips are actually fruits in their own right since they have seeds within them and the colourful fleshy part is the receptacle. In the apple and the pear the receptacle has become fused to the outside of the ovary wall and has then swollen up to produce a succulent meal which, like the strawberry and rosehip, are therefore not true fruits and are sensibly called false fruits.

It obviously makes no sense for seeds to fall to the ground below their parents since a seedling is bound to be shaded out in competition with its larger relative, and the youngster's roots would also be unsuccessful in its search for water. The fruits and seeds of plants are therefore dispersed by one of four methods, wind, animals, water or by their own explosive mechanism.

Fruits and seeds dispersed by wind either develop growths which are referred to as wings so that they spin through air even in quite light breezes, the most familiar example being those of the sycamore (*Acer pseudoplatanus*) which children accurately call helicopters. Both ash and limes (*Tilia sp*) have winged seeds and lime has a long thin bract under which the fruits are suspended. An equally ingenious arrangement is found in campions and poppies and called a censer mechanism. The flower stalk is long and at the end the ovary swells up and becomes dry and hollow with its top perforated like a pepper pot. The wind then shakes the flower and the seeds are scattered away from the parent plant. The chances are that the distance travelled by seeds dispersed in this way will be less than either parachute or winged fruits, but it is quite efficient nevertheless.

Seeds are dispersed by animals either by being sticky or edible. Goosegrass (*Galium aparine*) and burdock, for instance, both have hooked fruits which catch on the fur or feathers of passing creatures and fall off or are preened off some distance from the parent plant. Edible fruits like blackberry, elderberry or mistletoe are swallowed and after passage through the gut are defecated at a considerable distance from the parent. Recent research has shown that some seeds, blackberry (*Rubus fruticosus*) and mistletoe (*Viscum album*) for example, germinate more efficiently after they have been exposed to animal digestive fluids. Thus both plant and animal benefit from this arrangement and primitive human societies must be an integral part of this arrangement because they ate so many plants whilst wander-

Old man's beard or clematis. This species, together with dandelion (*Taraxacum officinalis*), rosebay willow herb (*Chamgenerion angustifolium*) and the thistles have small seeds with a tuft of feathers acting just like parachutes.

ing over large areas of the country. The bright colours of many fruits such as holly and rowan (*Sorbus aucuparia*) are obviously adaptations evolved to enable animals to spot them more easily. A minor variation on this theme occurs in mistletoe which has seeds that stick to a bird's bill and when the bird accurately named mistle thrush, wipes its bill on a branch it allows the parasitic plant to find another host.

Few fruits and seeds are dispersed by water and of those found in woodland only alder (*Alnus glutinosa*) has seeds which may fall into the woodland stream and so be carried away from the parent. The majority of alder seeds, however, are dispersed by birds such as the siskin (*Carduelis spinus*) and the long tailed tit (*Aegithalos caudatus*), which greedily feed on them during the autumn and winter.

All the dispersal methods described so far depend upon an outside agency moving the seeds but some plants, especially those of the pea family (the leguminosae), are able to provide their own dispersive force. I was forcibly reminded of this on a hot day in late September as I lay watching a pair of woodpigeons (*Columba palumbus*), which often breed late in the year, feeding a pair of young. I was concealed in a thicket of gorse (*Ulex europaeus*). There was no wind and so I could clearly detect faint clicking noises and I first felt a sharp pain in my eye and then another on my ear. I then realized that the gorse pods (called legumes) were twisting in the heat and then bursting. The force of the explosion was firing the seeds in all directions. I forgot about the pigeons for a while and concentrated on watching the exploding gorse, the shower of seeds ensuring that this sloping bank of the wood would continue to be clothed in gorse for many years to come. The cover it provides for nests is so enjoyed by the summer breeding birds, especially the whinchat (*Saxicola rubetra*) and the yellowhammer (*Emberiza citrinella*), that their offspring are protected by a formidable barrier of thorns.

A collection of wild fruits and an examination of them can be a further guide to animal life. The nuts of the hazel are one of the best clues for the nature detective. A wood mouse (*Apodemus sylvaticus*) holds the nut in its front paws and turns it almost as if it was in a lathe. It then chisels away with its sharp rodent teeth to produce a neat oval hole with bevelled edges. The squirrels are much less patient and rip the shell almost in half whilst the dormouse (*Muscardinus avellanarius*) seems unable to decide where to attack the nut leaving teeth marks all over the surface.

The fly agaric is one of Britain's most lovely fungi. It is poisonous, but in the past it was brought into the house to kill flies.

Evidence of the presence of the nuthatch (*Sitta europaea*) takes the form of a nut jammed neatly into a crevice on the bark of a tree near a convenient perch. The bird then earns its old country name of nut-hatchet by hammering away at the natural line of cleavage until the hazel nut falls naturally into two halves. The great tit (*Parus major*) has, rather surprisingly, a bill powerful enough to hammer a nut all over its surface until it finally gets at the rich kernel within.

When deciduous leaves shed their leaves in the autumn the fall is anything but haphazard. Cells at the base of the leaf stalk become separated from each other thus creating a definite area of weakness. It is here that the leaf eventually breaks away, the dividing layer being called the absciss layer. Either during the time that the cells are separating in the absciss layer or just afterwards, a band of cork forms in the area healing what would otherwise be an open wound. Before the cork finally seals off the leaf, however, there is an exchange of materials between the leaf and the branch that carries it. Any remaining food in the leaves is passed backwards into the branch via the veins. This is stored in the branch just below the buds which will grow the following year by drawing on these reserves. There is also a movement in the reverse direction as the plant passes waste materials into the deciduous leaves and it is this two way traffic and the break down of the chlorophyll

A female wood mouse. This species is a wonderful climber and spends much of the winter wandering about the upper branches of trees above the snow and water of the woodland floor. I once disturbed a wood mouse fast asleep in an old blackbird's nest in a hawthorn tree on the edge of a Dorset woodland. I watched in amazement as it climbed the thorny branches, jumped across into the next tree and then disappeared amid a cloud of disturbed dead and wrinkled leaves.

in the leaves which results in the magnificent tints which make our autumn woodlands so attractive.

At the same time as the cork layer forms over the leaf scar, the lenticels in the bark through which the tree breathes are sealed by a similar protective layer. This is an equivalent reaction to that of a hibernating animal such as the hedgehog (*Erinaceus europeaus*) which ensures that respiration is reduced during winter, thus conserving vital food reserves. In spring, the thin cork layer plugging the lenticels crumbles and they are again fully functional.

As herbaceous perennials prepare for winter, the upper herbage dies off. But before this, food is passed downwards into underground perennating, or food storing, organs which can be roots, rhizomes, bulbs or corms. Annual plants die completely and over-wintering is only possible in the form of seeds. Biennials follow the same pattern as perennials after their first year of life, but during their second year all the plant dies and over-wintering is also in the form of seeds.

Reproduction by seeds is an advantage because the offspring may be the product of two parents – providing, of course, that cross pollination has taken place. In addition to this the further the seeds are dispersed the better chance they have of avoiding competition both with other seedlings and, more importantly with their parents. A third important factor is that new areas can be colonized. Vegetative reproduction, or propagation to give it the correct term, may occur in plants when one of its vegetational parts splits and no sexual process is involved. In some cases this method has advantages since it does not depend upon wind or insects and cutting out the flowering stage allows quick reproduction. The disadvantages are that having only one parent means no mixing of genes, severe competition between parent and several offspring and new areas cannot be colonized. From the point of view of providing the future offspring with food, however, vegetative propagation is an ideal method since all the plant has to do is to store large volumes of food in the organ which is about to reproduce. The plant makes more food than it uses and it stores the surplus for the next growing season, a process called perennation. This food supply can also be used to initiate the growth of new plants and the function of perennation and vegetative propagation can often be combined within one organ.

Some plants have large pointed tap roots and in the carrot family (the umbelliferae) these become swollen with food. Other plants do not have one large tap root but a spreading fibrous system which is so typical of grasses whilst in the lesser celandine (*Ranunculus ficaria*) the food is stored in a number of tuberous roots.

In a few plants, the uncommon member of the cabbage family, kohl rabi, for example, the food is stored in an upright stem above the ground, but most storage stems are subterranean. Those which grow parallel to the surface – either above or below – are called rhizomes. The whole structure is swollen with food in such plants as Solomon's seal (*Polygonatum multiflorum*) found in dry woodlands and the yellow flag iris (*Iris pseudacorus*) which is a typical plant of swampy woods. In other cases the underground stems are short and swollen. They are called corms and fine examples can be seen in the bulbous buttercup (*Ranunculus bulbosus*) and the crocus (*Crocus nudiflorus*). If only the end of the stems are swollen as in the potato, the structure is known as a stem tuber.

In some plants, the leaf stalks (called petioles) swell up and this is the portion we eat when we enjoy rhubarb and celery whilst in other plants, the wood sorrel (*Oxalis acetosella*) for example, both the leaf bases and a rhizome hold food reserves. The most typical situation, however, is for the swollen leaf bases to store food or perhaps the scale leaves may perform this function. This arrangement is called a bulb which can be seen in the bluebell and in the daffodil (*Narcissus pseudonarcissus*).

All these structures are perennating organs which enable the plant to survive the winter below ground but rhizomes, corms, tubers and bulbs all have tiny buds on their surfaces or within the tissues. Should growth occur during the following spring from two or more of these buds, then vegetative propagation has also been accomplished.

Each season has its own smells, sounds and sights. Autumn brings the evocative aroma of rotting leaves, the sound of song as birds complete their moult and are full of excess energy rather than amorous vigour. Many woods echo to the sound of roaring red deer (*Cervus elaphus*) as the stags compete to gather a harem of hinds around them.

On the way home to a tiny cottage with its crackling fire and old fashioned range with a wise woodlander one day, we collected several fungi to eat with our breakfast and I have made full use of autumn fungi ever since. It always surprises me that so many people refuse to eat fungi since so very few species are poisonous. It does pay to be very careful, but even the fly agaric (*Amanita muscaria*) with its characteristic red cap spotted with white is not actually lethal. The death cap (*Amanita phalloides*) has a greenish cap between 7.5cm and 10cm (3 to 4in) in diameter and is a killer. Many fungi, however, are not only edible but also very tasty and both the field mushroom (*Agaricus campestris*) and, more especially, the horse mushroom (*Agaricus arvensis*) may be found in the open glades of woodlands as well as around the edges. The Jew's ear fungus (*Hirneola auricula-judae*) grows particularly well on elder and can grow up to 10cm (4 in) across and is far from appetizing to look at. In dry weather the fungus becomes hard and shrivelled, and in wet weather it becames limp and gelatinous. If collected after rain it can be eaten raw or boiled in milk and added to soup or stocks.

Much more commonly found in woods is the lawyer's wig (*Coprinus comatus*) also known as the shaggy ink cap. It seems to grow well on disturbed land and I often find it in my local wood soon after the owner has burned branches when he has felled some trees. It can grow up to 25cm (10in) and the white, slightly upturned scales easily account for its alternative name of lawyer's wig. As the fungus ripens and the black spores shed, the body liquifies and turns to a black sloppy mass. This is called auto-digestion and as a boy I used to scrape this into a jam jar to use as ink – I also gathered bird feathers to use as quills. There is no doubt that this use was well appreciated by those country-folk who were lucky enough to be able to write. Ink cap in this state should never be eaten but if gathered when young they make a very pleasant meal. I like them best when the wig-like tops are peeled, sliced and fried in butter.

Native trees & shrubs

TREES are defined as woody perennial plants which increase in size year by year but I well remember two questions asked me by an intelligent ten year old. 'What', she asked, 'is the difference between a tree and shrub?' and she followed this with the disarmingly simple 'and what is wood?' There is, in fact no botanical distinction between a tree and a shrub although it is generally accepted that a tree has one stem or trunk from ground level which does not exceed 6m (almost 20ft) in height whilst a shrub is said to branch from ground level and ranges from 0.5m to 0.6m (19in to 20in) in height. Clearly this is not a scientific definition since hawthorn (*Crataegus monogyna*) and many other species including gorse (*Ulex europaeus*) and blackthorn (*Prunus spinosa*) can fall into both categories according to the conditions in which they are growing and also whether or not they are cut by hedgers. The term woody perennial is, therefore, best used to cover all eventualities.

The second question is far easier to answer, although to understand the term we need to know how trees grow. Trees increase in length by the division of cells at the tip of the stem and in thickness by the production of wood. A deciduous tree trunk can easily be seen to contain larger numbers of thick walled tubes called xylem vessels, and it is these which make up the wood. They not only strengthen the trunk and the branches but also carry water and salts in solution from the spreading root system to the leaves and other organs. Outside the xylem vessels is an area containing another set of tubes called the phloem or bast. This tissue serves to carry the sugar produced by the leaves around the rest of the tree. Between these two layers is a thin strip of cells called the cambium which divide to produce new xylem and phloem. Obviously the growth of deciduous trees varies according to season and this will be reflected in the relative amounts of xylem produced. In the spring, growth is very rapid, large volumes of water are demanded and the tree thus produces many big xylem vessels which make up what is known as the spring wood. In the summer and autumn, growth slows down and fewer and much narrower xylem vessels are formed. In the winter, with the leaves gone from the trees, growth stops altogether and the whole year's growth is therefore recorded on the trunk of the tree as an annual ring. This enables the trunk to be examined and the age of the tree can be calculated. It is possible to get an estimate of the age of a living tree by extracting a core from the trunk, counting the rings, pushing back the core rather like a cork into a bottle and then sealing the wound with a protection of harmless wax.

In mature trees not all the annual rings contain functional xylem vessels which form the water carrying tissue of the plant. In trees this is called sapwood and is towards the outside of the trunk. The central area of the trunk is made up of dead

OPPOSITE: **Birch trees often seem to have their branches infested with birds' nests but these tangled masses called witches brooms are deformaties caused by buds being attacked by either insects or fungus such as the fly agaric. This fungus is actually attached to the trees' roots and both partners benefit from the association – symbiosis. The fungus derives sugars from the tree and the fly agaric assists the tree by speeding up the absorption of nutrients from the soil. All these fungal attacks do much to weaken and eventually kill the tree and dead, decaying specimens are typical features of any birch wood. They are full of insects and potential nesting holes making the areas popular with woodpeckers, especially the great spotted.**

The leaves and fruits of the oak.

vessels called a heartwood and is usually much darker than the sapwood since it is impregnated with waste materials from the tree including tannins and resins, both of which help to preserve the wood.

A field lecture, this time to a group of adults, prompted two more questions – 'What is grain?' and 'how does bark differ from wood?' Grain is caused by medullary rays which are rows of thin walled cells running through the xylem vessels and across which vital food supplies are carried. It is a combination of annual rings and the medullary rays which give timber its attractive graining.

Bark is a corky substance formed outside the phloem and developed from a second band of dividing cells which are called the bark cambium. This is the sappy, green tissue situated just under the bark. The function of bark is to provide the tree with a barrier against rain and frost which would rot the wood and it conversely prevents loss by evaporation of the vital water supplies contained in the xylem on its way from the roots to the leaves. The bark also prevents the entry of bacteria and fungi thus acting in a very similar way to our own skin. The bark cannot, however, be completely impermeable since the living cells within the tree have to breathe – it therefore has a series of pores called lenticels. These are small enough to prevent water molecules from evaporating or entering, but large enough to allow oxygen to enter and carbon dioxide to leave the trunk. The texture and patterning of the bark and the positioning of the lenticels is often a good way to identify trees and many naturalists learn these different patterns by taking photographs or by making bark rubbings. These are made by placing a piece of good quality plain paper against the bark and rubbing a wax crayon over the surface. This, plus a collection of twigs, leaves and fruit in the appropriate seasons, will soon make tree identification easy.

Some of Britain's native trees are able, when conditions are ideal, to completely dominate a woodland. This occurs because they are so tall consequently shading out those plants beneath them. The root systems are also so efficient that they take most of the available water. Such species include oak, beech, birch, ash, alder, elm and the conifers Scots pine and yew.

Britain's magnificent **oak** woodlands with their rich understorey of shrubs and herbs, scented with thousands of blossoms and hundreds of singing birds are still one of the joys of Britain. Badgers (*Meles meles*) push through the undergrowth, butterflies and other insects swarm in the trees all adding their contribution to one of the richest communities of living organisms anywhere on earth.

Section through a tree trunk.

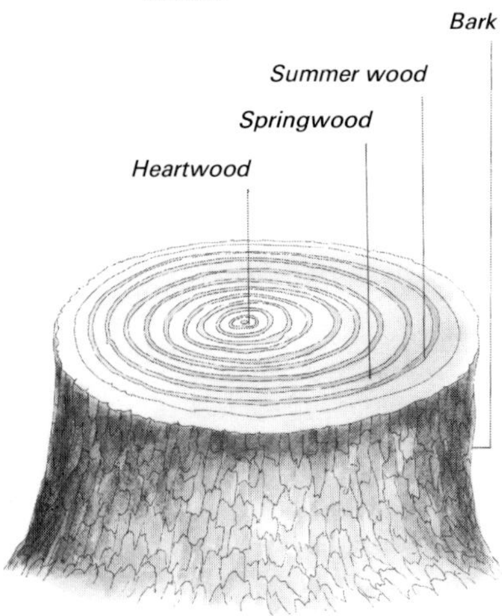

Although there are over 450 species of oak in the world Britain only has two that are native. The common or pedunculate oak (*Quercus robur* also known as *Q. pedunculata*) can grow as high as 30m (nearly 100ft) and prefers deep, heavy soils and even grows well on clay. It is typical of south eastern Britain and can be recognized by its hairless twigs, deeply lobed leaves carried on short stalks and indentations called auricles at the bases. The acorns are carried on long stalks.

The durmast or sessile oak (*Quercus petrae* or *Q. sessiliflora*), in contrast, is found mainly in the more exposed north westerly hills and can thrive on shallower, more acidic soils. The leaves are larger, less deeply lobed, taper into the base and have long stalks. The sessile acorns lack stalks altogether and the twigs are hairy.

Important as these differences are, it should be stressed that the two species are often found growing together. Hybrids between the two commonly occur and the uses to which they are put are similar, as is the wildlife supported by them.

The Saxon name for oak was ac from which the name oak derives and the old village of Acton, now swallowed up in London's sprawl, was once a clearing in an oak forest. The Celts knew it as derw from which the word Druid originated relating to that forest based religion.

Oaks are by no means exceptional in height but their strength is in their stout gnarled trunks and more especially in the deep tap roots. The latter send out huge horizontal branches which take such a firm grip on the ground that the oak is seldom disturbed by the fiercest of storms which often leave a trail of fallen birches and beeches behind them. It is said that Smeaton looked long and hard at the shape of an oak trunk as he set about designing his lighthouse on the Eddystone rock.

Just after the leaves have opened, usually in May, the oak flowers appear and are of two types. The slender male catkins are greenish-yellow and occur in pendant-like clusters on single stalks at intervals along the shoot. The female flowers appear a little later and thus avoid cross-pollination. They are carried on long stalks either singly or in groups in the leaf axils or at the end of shoots and the red stigmas stand out clearly from the round, pale brown flowers. The acorns are never produced in any quantity until the tree is over 60 years old and are then usually ripe and beginning to fall off the tree by October. This fall was eagerly awaited not only by the wildlife but also by the woodlander with his herd of pigs. The timber was and is widely used for doors, furniture, coffins, boats, gates and a host of other artefacts, but it does have the major disadvantage of its mutually corrosive effect when in contact with metals.

Because the natural vegetation over much of Europe is dominated by oak and because its leaves and fruit are so nutritious, it is not surprising that more species of animal live amongst its gnarled branches than in any other species of tree. The insects dominate the scene and are often present in such numbers that they strip off all the leaves. The tree seems to be able to withstand these attacks, however, providing they do not occur in successive years. Three moth larvae which are particularly destructive defoliators are those of the winter moth (*Operophtera brumata*), the mottled umber (*Erannis defoliaria*) and the oak tortrix (*Tortrix viridana*) which is also known as the green oak roller. The latter is often so numerous that it falls in clouds whenever an oak bough is shaken but is usually kept in check by hordes of small birds, especially the titmice which not only sustain themselves but also feed their young on the succulent moth larvae.

The great spotted woodpecker, with its stiff tail feathers and special arrangement of the toes is perfectly designed for climbing trees in search of food or a nest site.

Ancient **beechwoods** occur in the Chilterns, the Thames and Wye valleys, in the Cardiff area and encircling the Weald. When beechwoods occur outside these areas they tend to have been planted – the oak held such a dominant position in the wildwood that it is doubtful that the beech could gain a significant root hold.

Beech produces many dark green leaves which overlap to such an extent that little light reaches the woodland floor and the flora in this area is impoverished. The roots also grow close to the surface of the soil and this, together with the thick carpet of dead leaves which decay very slowly, means that only plants which have evolved a strategy to handle this difficult environment will survive.

Saprophytic and mycorrhizal orchids are just such plants. A saprophyte lives on the dead, decaying material and does not therefore need light to make its own food by photosynthesis. The birds-nest orchid (*Neottia nidus-avis*) is a good example of this mode of nutrition whilst the white helleborine (*Cephalanthera damasonium*) is mycorrhizal, its roots forming a partnership with an underground fungus, another example of symbiosis. Each partner – the tree and the fungus, provide a vital element for the other but the precise mechanism of mycorrhizal partnerships is not fully understood.

The bark of the beech tree not only attracts modern lovers to carve their names upon it, but it was once used as the covers for books and as writing tablets. This use is reflected in the vernacular for names for beech in several countries; in Germany it is buche, in Swedish bak and in Saxon it was bece, all of which could have been the origin of the word book. The generic name Fagus derives from phago which is

Not least among the characteristics of the oak are these marble galls which are abnormal growths on stems, leaves and even on the roots. They are formed by the oak to protect itself from the attentions of the larvae of gall wasps.

Greek for edible and refers to the seeds which were once eaten by man but are now left to birds and mammals.

Beech leaves are covered with a protective down during the early stages, which withers away as the shiny dark green foliage matures – basically oval in shape except for the pointed end. In autumn the leaves turn a magnificent red or golden brown prior to their fall in the sweeping gales. Young trees and those which are regularly clipped – beech is a popular hedging tree – tend to retain the dead leaves until the following spring when they are pushed off by the new leaves.

Flowers of both sexes are carried on the same tree but many do not breed until they are 80 years old. The male flowers are carried on swinging stems, each flower having from eight to 16 stamens. The stalks carrying the female flowers are much stiffer, however, which is an ideal arrangement for catching the pollen carried on the wind. The scales which surround the flowers swell to form the husk which closes over one or two brown nuts.

As a rule, beech in Britain does not set fertile seeds but if a mild spring prevents damage to the buds by frost and this is followed by a hot summer a large and fertile crop is produced. These are much to the liking of pheasant (*Phasianus colchicus*), wood pigeon, jay and even the rook (*Corvus frugilegus*), whose original habitat was in woodland clearings rather than its more modern choice of man-created hedgerows.

Birch, in contrast to beech, tends to grow quickly and can reach a height of 10m (33ft) in less than 20 years. It tends to be fully mature before it is 60 years old and seldom lives longer than a single century – a very short life span for a deciduous tree. It requires so much light that its seedlings cannot grow beneath the parents, while young oaks and ashes seem able to cope easily.

There are around 40 species of birch, only three occurring naturally in Britain. These are the dwarf birch (*Betula nana*), one of the first colonizers and is a tough little Alpine shrub now confined to northern Scotland, silver birch (*Betula pendula*) and downy birch (*Betula pubescens*). The latter two, especially the downy birch, are very resistant to frost and are therefore important pioneer species and can be readily distinguished. The silver birch has pale bark from which it gets its vernacular name and its branches always droop at the tips from which its scientific name pendula derives. Silver birch twigs are covered in pale coloured bumps. These are lacking in the downy birch which, as its scientific name pubescens implies, are hairy. The leaves also differ in shape – those of the silver birch have toothed margins and are much more pointed. Care should be taken in identification as the two have been known to hybridize.

Foresters have used birch as nursery trees for many years copying nature's own method of using the birch as a pioneering species. To see birches at their best, walk by a Scottish loch where the graceful trees hang over the water. Gnarled and twisted trees warped by the wind are draped in lichens which indicate the purity of the air.

Many trees are dead and being eaten away by spectacular growths of fungi particularly birch polypore (*Polyporus betulinus*) which grows on the trunk and the colourful honey fungus (*Armillaria mellea*) which attacks the roots of birches growing in the damper areas.

It was Coleridge who called the birch *The Lady of the Woods* but the Anglo-Saxon word beorht meaning bright and shining is just as descriptive. Apart from its old use in dealing with unruly school children and other offenders, the birch has served several other functions including the manufacture of sweeping brushes. The white timber which is faintly tinged with red is surprisingly hard, produces excellent charcoal and burns with a hot bright flame. The ashes from the fires were not wasted either since they are particularly rich in potash making efficient fertilizer and they were also used in the manufacture of soap.

The bark is very resistant to damp and birch stakes therefore make good posts for fencing. It is not surprising how many uses the old Highlanders and the northern Europeans had for birch when it is realized that the birch was the only common hardwood tree able to cope with the extreme climate of these lands. It was used for furniture, especially chairs, for making casks and the wheelwright also found it useful. In Scandinavia the tree grows taller and straighter than in Britain and birch is grown in vast plantations to be used to produce plywood.

Our name birch derives from the Old English word birk, and names such as Birkdale, Whitebirk and Birkenhead denote areas where the tree flourished. Birch belongs to the family betulacea which also includes the alder and other catkin-bearing trees such as the hornbeam and the hazel.

It seems that **ash** is more tolerant of lime than other species such as oak and beech since their shallow roots are able to grow down into the narrow cracks in limestone. The native ashwoods of Britain are centred in two main districts – the chalk downlands of the south east of England and the limestone areas of the north and west. There are few more beautiful sights than an ashwood; its open canopy allowing light to reach the field layer so that an interesting but limited community of flowers can develop. These include the rare baneberry (*Actaea spicata*), lady's slipper orchid (*Cypripedium calceolus*) and the delightfully scented lily of the valley (*Convallaria majalis*). The number of species associated with ash is not great probably because its roots are shallow and remove most of the water and nutrients.

ABOVE: **The most striking feature of the beech is its trunk, with its grey smooth bark looking like the columns of a huge arboreal temple.**

LEFT: **Slimy beech tuft – a parasitic fungus often to be found living on a beech trunk.**

Boles

Alder

Birch

Elder

Hawthorn

Holly

TREES can not only be identified by leaves, buds and fruit, but with a little practice the trunk and bark also enable them to be distinguished. Alder, for example, has long and sometimes quite deep lines rather like scratches running parallel down the trunk.

The bark of birch is pale, often marked with darker blotches. Running across the trunk are small grooves and the bark itself is easily peeled. This is well known to birds, particularly tree creepers which build their nests and find food between the peeling bark and trunk.

The bole of hawthorn is fluted and looks as if several small boles have been welded together to produce the main tree. Although elder bark is soft and uneven and looks brittle the structure is very tough indeed. Holly trunks are a delightful shade of brownish grey, spotted and blotched with darker colours. Despite these rough looking areas, rubbing the hand down the trunk reveals that it is surprisingly smooth. The patterns of boles can be shown by making bark rubbings using wax crayons. Another method which is just as effective is to press trips of plasticine hard into the bole of the tree. One particularly bright ten year old once had the idea of trying to match the colour of the plasticine with that of the natural bark to bring more than a touch of realism to her hobby.

It may also be that many herbs are also unable to grow in areas which are too rich in lime. This may account for the old belief that the 'drip' from an ash tree is fatal to most other plants.

The ash belongs to the oleaceae which is the olive family. Pollen analysis has indicated that after the ice age the ash was a late arrival which soon established itself in the forests. Some botanists believe that the spread of ash was helped by a catastrophic decline in elms approximately 5,000 years ago. Ash is late coming into leaf, but the purple clusters of hermaphrodite flowers growing from the black buds are produced long before the leaves, usually during May. The pollen is carried from male anthers to female stigmas by the wind. Once the ovules have been fertilized the fruit, known as a key, begins to develop. Each key is a flat wing-like structure which can be carried for miles during the fierce autumn gales.

Few trees retain their leaves for so short a period as the ash, but few are so attractive. The mid-stem of the leaf bears five or six pairs of leaflets arranged along it and the symmetry is completed by a single terminal leaflet. The overall length of the leaf may reach 30cm (1ft).

Even in tall specimens, the girth of the ash is seldom very great which accounts for its graceful appearance. Its strength lies in its suppleness, a factor well known to our woodland ancestors who used it both for bows and spears, for ladders, plough stocks, pulley blocks and tool handles. Coach makers loved it to make chassis with and, until 1932, motor manufacturers all used ash too. Wheelwrights and coopers demanded young, supple staves from this tree, and its smooth texture is still important in the manufacture of oars and snooker cues. Cabinet makers also find the elegant veining of the timber much in demand. Such a valuable tree was obviously coppiced and in some areas it still is providing wood for walking sticks and the handles of garden tools.

Sadly, whilst most of our ash trees appear perfectly healthy, some are threatened by ash dieback disease which can lead to serious disfigurement and occasionally death. Viruses, insects, atmospheric pollution and drought have all been suggested as possible factors but the cause has not yet been positively identified although the Department of Forestry at Oxford University are currently researching the problem.

Mention of the **alder** conjures up the music of deep running water, the plop of a trout rising to the fly and the gentle lowing of cattle cropping the rich riverside pasture. Alder at one time dominated many woods in the low lying marshy areas of Britain before man set about draining the land. Small fragments of these alder swamp forests – which were called carrs – remain, especially in East Anglia. The Broads are typically fringed by damp alder woodlands, the dripping foliage overlooking a rich carpet of mosses and ferns.

Under good conditions alder can grow to a height of 20m (almost 65ft) and the growth over the first ten years is strikingly rapid which makes it a good colonizer of recently flooded land. The soil in these areas has had most of its nutrients leached from it but the alder has proved well able to handle this situation. Its roots are covered with lumps called nodules and when these are cut open and examined under a microscope they are found to contain bacteria. These are able to absorb nitrogen directly from the atmosphere and convert it into nitrates to share with the tree. The alder provides the bacteria with the vital sugars which it needs, as well as a protected habitat, and the two exist together in a mutually beneficial partnership which biologists refer to as a symbiosis.

The leaves of the alder are heart shaped and the prominent veins branch off at acute angles from each side of the midrib to the saw-edged margin of the leaf. The leaves are often attacked by a mite called *Eriophyes laevis* causing the leaves to

The yellow male catkins of the birch tree emerge early in the spring and are already releasing pollen into the wind by April. Initially the female flowers are green and erect but when pollinated they hang down and turn dark brown before releasing large numbers of small winged seeds to be dispersed by the wind. Birds such as the siskin (*Carduelis spinus*), redpoll and the long tailed tit show surprising agility in their efforts to reach these seeds.

produce a protective growth called galls seen on the leaves as tiny yellowish bumps. The dark green epidermis of the leaf is very sticky and thus accounts for the scientific name glutinosa.

The name alder derives from two Celtic words: al meaning near and Ian meaning the border of a river. The trunk grows very straight and when young has purple bark but old trees have a rough black bark. In ideal conditions alder can live for 200 years.

Otters (*Lutra lutra*) are not usually associated with woodlands, but they find wet alder woods ideal areas in which to rest during the day. Otters build both holts, which are permanent rests, and hovers which are much less permanent hiding places from which they sally forth on their nocturnal wanderings. The gnarled, twisted and often exposed roots of alder are ideal for both these purposes.

Alder woods were once coppiced for their timber, but its use these days is somewhat limited. In parts of northern Europe it is used to produce ply-wood and coppiced alder also provides poles which are used to strengthen river banks. The timber, when freshly cut, is white but when exposed to the air a red dye is generated from the damaged tissues. This once prevented some superstitious folk from cutting it – they thought that it bled because the fairies living inside it had been slaughtered and feared the reaction of the 'little people'.

The wood is soft which carvers and furniture makers may have found to be an advantage. It is, as you would expect, very durable under water and was used for foundations of buildings, bridges and piers – it is said that Venice is supported on alder timber. It made good charcoal and many gunpowder works were built in alder woods with the additional advantage of a swift river running through them, used to drive the machinery. Alder wood was also used to make clogs and was in demand for the manufacture of herring barrels prior to the days when fishing vessels were equipped with efficient deep freeze systems.

Young ash trees.

There are many species of **elm** found in Britain, the two most common being the Scots or Wych elm (*Ulmus glabra*) and the small leaved, English or common elm (*Ulmus procera*). The latter has been much in the news in recent years because of the disastrous effect upon it of Dutch elm disease.

The disease seems to have first affected British trees in 1927 caused by the fungus *Ceratocystis ulmi* – after ten years of causing damage, however, our elms began to recover. In the 1960s, a new and much more serious epidemic began, probably imported in logs shipped from Canada. By the middle 1970s the new fungus had destroyed the majority of Britain's native elms and was particularly damaging to *Ulmus procera*. This species seldom forms woods in its own right, but is important in hedgerows and is present in some numbers in many woodlands in which other species dominate. The loss of elms has reduced the nesting sites available to birds such as the rook (*Corvus frugilegus*), kestrel (*Falco tinnunculus*) and the increasingly uncommon hobby (*Falco subbuteo*) – the loss of elms may well have caused an even more dramatic increase in the population of this delightful little raptor.

The spores of the fungus are carried from tree to tree by elm bark beetles *Scolytus multistriatus* and *Scolytus scolytus*. Both these species appear to be more common in the south of England accounting for the fact that this region has been more affected by the disease. Because the fungus blocks the vessels carrying water from the roots to the leaves one can see why the wetter northern areas have suffered less from a disease which kills mainly by dehydrating the tree. Work by Dr J Fairhurst at the University of Salford has suggested the presence of a third elm bark beetle *Scolytus laevis* identified from both County Durham and Merseyside.

The branches and twigs of the English elm are twisted and contorted, somewhat reminiscent of oak, but the brown buds are single and not carried in a terminal group so typical of the Quercus genus. The leaves are also different, those of elm being somewhat pear shaped, pointed at the end and beautifully veined.

The flowers, appearing before the leaves, occur in inconspicuous little bunches that emerge, often as early as February, from purple red scaly buds protecting them from the wintry cold. Despite the numerous flowers, elms do not usually produce fertile seeds and reproduce mainly by suckers, also growing well from cuttings. This may eventually enable elm to recover from the attacks of *Ceratocystis ulmi*.

Elm timber is brownish in colour and is so hard and fine grained that it is still in continual demand for tool handles, boat building, doors and, of course, coffins. At one time water pipes were made from elm trunks which were hollowed out and then linked together.

The wych elm can be distinguished from the common elm by the larger size and more handsome appearance of its leaves. The outer edge of the leaves are less crinkled than those of *Ulmus procera* and the flowers are larger. It is just as well that the seeds are usually more fertile as the wych elm does not reproduce from suckers although it grows well from cuttings.

The dark impenetrable confines of the **pine** woods of the Scottish Highlands once offered refuge to outlaws and wild beasts alike. Little remains today because the woods were cleared first to deny the Highlanders refuge after the 1745 rebellion and then to provide absent landowners with profit from timber.

Although conservationists are now at pains to protect the pine forests many factors are working against them, not least the British climate. Over the last few centuries the weather has been becoming warmer and wetter. As a result the forest floor is developing a spongy mass of sphagnum moss and the new trees are growing on top of a spongy cushion. I recently watched a group of naturalists demonstrat-

Alder cones. The catkins on alder become obvious as early as February and long before the leaves are in evidence. Both male and female catkins are carried on the same tree. The dull red male catkins consist of a column of stamens and in spring they quickly double their length and when ripe can reach 5cm (2in) and are covered in yellow pollen carried on the wind to the female. The female catkins seldom exceed 1cm ($\frac{1}{3}$in) and when unpollinated they are purple brown. After pollination they turn green and enlarge to form a cone inside which the seeds develop. In winter the cones harden, turn black and open to allow the winged seeds to escape. These can be dispersed by wind, water (since they float) and birds feeding upon them.

Ash is late coming into leaf, but the purple clusters of hermaphrodite flowers growing from the black buds are produced long before the leaves, usually during May. The pollen is carried from male anthers to female stigmas by the wind. Once the ovules have been fertilized the fruit, known as a key, begins to develop. Each key is a flat wing-like structure which can be carried for miles during the fierce autumn gales.

ing this phenomenon by jumping up and down and watching the young pines wobble on the surface of what amounts to a raised bog. The trees are ripped out of their spongy sockets by winds which would easily be resisted by pines growing on drier areas.

A further problem is that pine seeds, which are often spread by crossbills (*Loxia curvirostra*) as well as by wind, need to be pushed deep into the leaf litter if they are to germinate successfully. There are now no elk, reindeer or bear to do this job and these fine old woodlands are suffering in consequence.

Among the species of mammal still dependent upon these forests are the wild cat (*Felis sylvestris*), red squirrel and pine marten (*Martes martes*). Birds such as the crested tit (*Parus cristatus*) and the capercaillie (*Tetrao urogallus*) are also typical animals to be found in the pine woods. The beautiful caterpillars of the pine hawk moth (*Hyloicus pinastri*) are often found feeding on the paired evergreen leaves.

Otters are sometimes found in damp woodlands and find plenty of cover beneath the gnarled roots of trees.

The Scots pine flowers during May and June and the male and female blooms may easily be distinguished. The male catkins can be up to 2.5cm (1in) long and occur in whorls at the end of branches. The yellow pollen on the stamens is so prolific that it often gives the whole tree a sulphureous appearance. The female flowers are inconspicuous and cones often appear in pairs, although occasionally up to six can occur together. They vary greatly in colour from green to purple with the occasional red specimen. The cones usually take 18 months to ripen when they become dark brown and the scales open to release the winged nut, like seeds, into the area. On a windy autumn day I sat near the crashing falls of the Linn of Dee watching pine seeds skim through the air. Many were falling on stony ground and even more onto boggy cushions of sphagnum.

The vast acres of Scots pine forest are no more, but there are still areas where the sunlight reflects from the deep red trunks and from which trees can be harvested. Scots pine timber is usually called deal and it has been used for pit props, paper pulp, telephone poles, window frames and joists.

There are few woods dominated by the yew alone and they include the limestone area around Arnside and, more particularly, Kingley Vale near Chichester. Because it lives to a great age the yew holds a special affection in our folklore despite its sombre reputation. It is the only British tree that has kept its Celtic name – iw.

The dark, evergreen, oblong leaves which seem harmless when fresh, are fatal to cattle when dry. They are produced with the twigs in two opposite and crowded rows, each is rather less than 2.5cm (1in) long and the shiny surface is concave on the underside, with a conspicuous mid vein and ending in a sharp point. The male and female flowers are usually produced on separate trees which is why some yews – the males – never produce fruit.

Other types of flower grow on the underside of the twigs and the tiny male flowers arrive as membranous buds clustered on the twigs. The anthers are loaded with pollen during March and April and the slightest tap on the branch or the most gentle of breezes is sufficient to send clouds of the yellow dust into the air to be carried to the female flowers.

Yew branches were certainly used in the manufacture of bows for archers, but its modern usage is to provide the cabinet maker with delightfully grained timber. Although it grows very slowly, yew can easily be propagated, especially in sheltered and shady positions in heavy soils accounting for its appearance in the middle of woods dominated by oak or beech where its seeds are obviously sown by birds.

The black buds and huge leaves of the ash make the tree easily identified.

Having a less dominant, but equally important role, in the woodland are the understorey species providing food and shelter for the animals. The often dense thickets of these species, especially hawthorn, rose and blackthorn, provides the best cover for wildlife throughout the year. This is the case particularly in winter when the understorey is the warmest area in the woodland.

Hawthorn is also called white thorn, maybush and quick, the name deriving from hage or hedge although it is also to be found as an understorey species in woodland. There are two species in Britain – the midland hawthorn (*Crataegus laevigata*), much more of a woodland tree found in the oak woodlands of the midlands and south eastern England, and the other is common hawthorn. The white, occasionally pink, flowers of the common hawthorn have only one style which develops into a single seed within the scarlet haws. This accounts for the specific name monogyna, whilst Crataegus derives from the Greek word kratas meaning strength. Midland hawthorn has blossom of an even darker red and two or even three seeds are contained within each haw.

Although it is regarded mainly as a hedge tree, hawthorn can reach 16m (50ft) when growing unrestrained in a woodland habitat and there are some magnificent specimens growing in the New Forest in Hampshire. The tree grows very rapidly, reaching a height of 4m (13ft) during its first four years after which it slows down.

To the naturalist, hawthorn is a joy. What other blossom has such a beautiful scent and is surrounded by so many fascinating insects? Birds love its protective thorns and song thrushes (*Turdus philomelos*), blackbirds, magpies (*Pica pica*) and long tailed tits all find ideal nest sites. In winter hordes of birds, including the winter visiting redwings (*Turdus iliacus*) and fieldfare (*Turdus pilaris*), feed greedily on the nutritious haws.

Although it is not renowned as a timber tree the yellowish wood of hawthorn has been used to fashion tool handles and mallets, it generates a great deal of heat as a fuel and the thorny branches were used to kindle fires.

Elder (*Sambucus nigra*) grows well in damp conditions and grows so rapidly that it quickly becomes an important member of the understorey, although it seldom reaches a height of 6m (20ft). The generic name Sambucus derives from the Greek

sambuke meaning a flute and, indeed, wind instruments were made by hollowing out the soft central pith from the branches. The specific name nigra relates to the dark colour of the foliage.

As a rule, elder leaves are not popular with vertebrate animals, including sheep and deer, and this helps the species to dominate other more tasty trees. The larvae of the swallow-tailed moth (*Ourapteryx sambucaria*), however, appear to thrive upon them.

The **crab apple** (*Malus sylvestris*) is Britain's only native apple tree and may be found in hedgerows. Its original habitat was in the open areas of oak woods throughout Britain although it is quite rare in central and northern Scotland. The origin of crab is not clear but probably derives from the Norse word skrabba.

Described as a large shrub or a small tree, the crab is often thorny, and grows to a height of between 2m and 10m (6ft and 32ft). The trunk is irregularly ridged and the grey bark peels off in thin flakes. Although young shoots and leaves may be protected by a thin layer of down they soon become smooth and shiny.

The delicate pink and white blossom is a delight during late May and early June and contains rich supplies of nectar much sought after by insects, especially bees which pollinate the species. The ripe fruit is yellow-green, blushed with red and although sour they can be sweetened with honey and made into delicious crab apple jelly and brewed to produce a powerful wine.

Holly, with the exception of ivy, is Britain's most widespread evergreen, although its advance appears to have been relatively recent. It grows well in the shade of both oak and beech and is a regular member of the understorey, protected from herbivores by its prickles. It is amazing how energy conscious nature can be, however, for there are far fewer prickles on the leaves of the higher branches which are out of reach of the animals.

Holly seldom grows taller than 12m (39ft) although occasional specimens have been known to reach 20m (63ft). It grows slowly and proves very hardy in wet and windy western areas even when battered by salt spray. Despite this, holly does not thrive in areas of consistently low temperatures more typical of eastern Britain.

The flowers open in mid-May and, much like yews, the sexes are usually found on separate trees which is why some male trees never bear berries, while others are heavy with them. They are capable of producing fertile gametes from the age of around 12.

If you dare risk pushing your nose into the prickles you will find the flowers to be sweetly scented and full of nectar: an irresistible lure to the flies and bees which pollinate them. Honey bees (*Apis mellifera*) are particularly fond of holly.

The berries are mature in autumn and their consumption by birds has been the subject of debates among naturalists for many years. In some years the berries are sought out by all the fruit eating birds whilst in other years they are ignored and allowed to hang on the trees. Perhaps this depends upon the availability of more favoured foods. I once watched a group of wood pigeons performing heroic feats of acrobatics in order to pull off holly berries during a snow-storm in early December. They seemed to drop more than they swallowed and waiting beneath were a flock of crafty starlings (*Sturnus vulgaris*) with, I am convinced, very satisfied expressions.

Like hawthorn and rowan, holly is another plant bearing red berries and is consequently surrounded by a haze of superstition. It was planted around houses to prevent them being struck by lightning or invaded by evil spirits. It must have been a wrench for the superstitious woodlander to cut down, even if both bole and foliage did burn hot and bright. The wood is very white but heavy and since it takes a stain it was used to make handles for metal teapots – an ideal and much cheaper

Crossbills breed in coniferous areas and also sometimes arrive in British woodlands in large numbers when the supply of cones in Scandinavia runs out.

OPPOSITE: **The bole of the common yew tree. It never becomes a tall tree and seldom grows above 16m (52ft) but it can achieve an enormous girth and yews with a circumference in excess of 10m (33ft) have been recorded.**

alternative to ebony, which is also a good insulator. Both the joiner and carpenter find holly ideal for the production of attractive furniture since it will take a glorious high polish and its thorns made it an ideal fencing plant.

It may seem strange to classify **ivy** (*Hedera helix*), an evergreen climbing plant, as a tree but there seems little else to call it since it often has a main stem measuring 25cm (10in) in diameter. The tough roots used to be dug up to make very effective strops for sharpening knives. The wood from the main trunk is soft and porous enough to be thinly sliced and was used for filtering liquids. I often cut ivy stems from fallen trees and use the wood to filter my home made wines.

Isaac Walton wrote in *The Compleat Angler* that the resin oozing out of damaged ivy stems was sure to attract fish. I still don't know if he is right, but I was once fishing in a carp pond surrounded by old oaks festooned with ivy. Neither I nor my companions had taken anything all day so I gathered some wild raspberries and coated them with ivy resin. Unbelievably my next five casts produced three beautiful fish.

It should be stressed that ivy is not parasitic because the roots do not penetrate any living tissue, although many naturalists would still disagree with this more recent view. Its weight, however, especially when increased by a fall of snow, can cause damage to branches.

The distinctive leaves are often in-rolled due to the presence of an aphid (greenfly) called *Aphis hederae*. The shape of the glossy, shiny, green leaves varies – either three or five lobes are usually present, the three lobed variety being young leaves. Ivy flowers appear among the higher stems bearing the five lobed leaves. The yellow-green flowers are carried on long stalks and their unpleasant smell often offends the human nose but is attractive to insects.

The old scientific name for **alder buckthorn**, which is a shrub that seldom grows taller than 2m (6½ft), was Rhamnus deriving from the Greek for a thorn bush and frangula meaning easily broken. It is not thorny nor is it related to the alder, but its twigs are brittle and, when broken, sharp. It also grows in alder carrs where it was and still occasionally is, used to produce a high quality charcoal for slow burning and reliable fuses.

The leaves are small and oval, with delicate veining which may account for it being originally placed in the alder family. Alder buckthorn leaves are pointed and not depressed at their extremities. Bees are attracted to the purple and white anthered flowers and deep purple berries are produced during early autumn. Berry-bearing alder was yet another old name for the shrub – the unripe berries being used to produce a yellow dye and as a powerful purgative recommended by the apothecaries. Each berry contains two large seeds and is distinguished from buckthorn (*Rhamnus carthatica*) whose berries contain four seeds.

Whitebeam (*Sorbus aria*) was once found in the woodland understorey but is now also a frequent member of the hedgerow flora. It is native throughout Britain and is seen at its best on chalk and limestone. A full grown specimen can reach 12m (39ft) and may be recognized by its stout trunk and pyramidal form. The leaves are large, oval and toothed but they do vary a great deal in form and more especially size – from 5cm to 15cm (2in to 6in). The upper surface is a rich green while the undersurface is covered with soft white down which flashes in the sun whenever the leaf is turned by the breeze. This accounts for the name whitebeam, the latter half being the old Saxon word for a tree. I have watched the leaves flash like a semaphore from the limestone cliffs around Arnside where a wood fringed by whitebeam hangs over the beach.

The white flowers also have a covering of white down and grow in flat clusters at the end of short leafy stems. The globular fruits are around 1.25cm (½in) in diame-

OPPOSITE: **Scots pine – some remnants of the once huge Great Wood of Caledon still remain at Glen Affric, the Black Wood at Rannoch, at Beinn Eighe on the west coast and at Rothiemurchus under the shadow of the mighty Cairngorms. Pines grow naturally here, together with a sprinkling of birch although most of the three million acres have gone, along with lynx, elk, brown bear, wild boar and the ranging wolf.**

Contrary to popular belief, ivy is not a parasite, but its weight can often be harmful to trees.

ter and red when ripe – they are very popular with birds. The white wood has a delicate grain much used in turnery. Because it is so hard the timber was ideal for making cog wheels and was also burned to produce charcoal needed for high quality gunpowder.

The **wild service tree** (*Sorbus torminalis*) is a woodland shrub native to south and central England, the species is well adapted to living in clay soils, but can also be found on limestone and in open woodland. It is seldom higher than 10m (33ft) although it can occasionally be twice this size. It grows very slowly and can live for many years and the bark is grey and smooth. The maple-like leaves are variable but usually oval or heart shaped and broken into six to ten angularly toothed lobes. They can be as long as 10cm (4in) and as broad as 7.5cm (3in). The older leaves are smooth on both sides but when young the undersides are almost as white and furry as those of the whitebeam. The white flowers also appear in May and June and each 1.25cm ($\frac{1}{2}$in) bloom is grouped with others into broad flat clusters enveloped in white down when young.

The fruit has ripened by early November. Each is approximately 0.8cm ($\frac{1}{3}$in) in diameter, pear shaped or nearly spherical and of a greeny-brown colour dotted with brown corky spots marking the entry to the lenticels.

The botanist and herbalist John Gerard (1545–1612) gave the **wayfaring tree** (*Viburnum lantana*) its English name because 'it was ever on the road'. In Britain this shrub is certainly a native, but rare in the wild state. It was planted along hedges because its twigs were used in the production of bird lime – a very important substance for those whose only protein was the small birds they caught – and like the whitebeam, it is a member of the apple family.

The wayfaring tree's true niche is probably as an understorey shrub, especially in those woodlands growing on the chalk and limestone of south east England. The thick, soft, wrinkly, hairy leaves have prominent veins especially on the undersurface. They open in April and May and are followed a month later by dense creamy white bundles of flowers. They used to be boiled in water to make a cure for sore throats and a hair rinse. The ovate berry is greenish yellow at first, then turns red and by early September is shiny black. Although the shrub seldom grows more than 6m (19ft), its rich red autumnal leaves makes it a most attractive member of the woodland flora.

The clusters of small red apples which hang from the autumn boughs of the **rowan** were thought to be a certain antidote against witchcraft – perhaps this is why rowan trees are often found growing in the grounds of old houses, close to barns and along old trade roots. Its natural home, however, is as an understorey tree in the wildwoods dominated by oak and ash – especially those growing gnarled and twisted in upland areas. The fact that *Sorbus aucuparia* is often found even higher on hillsides than the dominant species accounts for its alternative name of mountain ash – to class it as an ash, however, is inaccurate despite the similarity of the leaves.

Each compound leaf is made up of opposite pairs of leaflets arranged along a stout stem and ending in a prominent terminal leaflet. Rowan leaves are, however, much smaller than ash leaves, and they are serrated at the edges whereas the leaves of the common ash are smooth at the edges.

The elegant little tree seldom grows taller than 30m (just under 100ft) and although its initial growth is fast it seldom lives longer than 100 years. There is no doubt that it would not be noticed were it not for the lovely creamy blossom which appears during June and the red berries so typical of early autumn.

The **field maple** (*Acer campestris*) is a European species usually found as a shrub, occasionally reaching heights of 20m (63ft) when it can then be confused

The flowers of holly are rich in nectar which bees are quick to take advantage of.

with the sycamore. The flowers of the field maple occur in late March before the leaves burst and are arranged in erect clusters, whereas the flowers of the sycamore hang under the leaves and appear during May or June at the same time as the leaves. There are also easily recognizable differences in the fruits since although each species has a central seed flanked by two wings, the sycamore's curve inwards and those of the field maple are horizontal.

Field maple is found in many hedgrows throughout Britain, its magnificent gold and red autumnal leaves being a joy to see. Many have been planted, but truly native trees with their palmate leaves are found in the understorey growing on the calcareous soils of England and Wales. Although the tree never grows tall enough to be an important timber tree, the wood takes a magnificent polish, especially that found in the roots, and was popular with wood turners for centuries. The woodlanders of old valued it for fuel since it burns with a hot bright flame.

Although the **guelder rose** (*Viburnum opulus*) derives its name from its cultivated variety, the snowball tree which came from the Guelderland in Holland it is, in fact, a natural inhabitant of Britain. The tree grows well in damp areas on woodland edges and rarely exceeds 4m (13ft) in height. In a warm but damp spring its blossoms can be a spectacular sight.

There are clear veins running from the apex of the stem through the lobes into which each leaf is divided. From each main vein, smaller veins continue outwards to the indented margin. The leaves, when illuminated by the autumn sunshine, show all shades from pink to bright crimson. The white blossom appears in June and July and to the inexperienced eye never seems to be ripe.

The elliptically shaped berries are shiny and bright red, very juicy but sickeningly bitter to taste. Despite this a spirit has been distilled from the berries – although I enjoy 'living off the land' I would not dream of using guelder rose.

The **wild cherry** (*Prunus avium*), often called the mazard or gean, has a shiny red bark attractively marked by horizontal lenticels and can grow to a height of 30m (almost 100ft), although on average it is usually between 6m and 12m (20ft to 40ft). It can live for up to 200 years and always seems so stately and beautifully proportioned, its lovely blossom often adding a dash of colour to a clearing in a beechwood.

BELOW: **Crab apples – although the fruit is produced each year every so often a bumper crop occurs and the woodlander can gather them from beneath the tree by the sack load. When I am collecting crabs and thinking of drinking the wine made from them by a crackling winter fire, I feel closer to our woodland based ancestors than at any other time.**

Like most of the plum family the blossom appears before the leaves, which are oval, sharply serrated and end in a prominent point. They are covered, particularly on the lower surface, with a light down.

The timber is tough and very close grained, it can be worked up into a fine polish and can be soaked in limewater to darken the texture until resembling mahogany – it is often used as a substitute for this wood in the production of musical instruments.

Bird cherry (*Prunus padus*) is a small tree often overlooked by naturalists, but to me it is very special. One late June I lay half awake in my camping van looking through a window at the thin mist rising off a Scottish loch. Suddenly a shaft of sunlight lit up the glade in which I was parked and the sound of bees humming among the leaves of bird cherry blended with the sound of a soaring lark.

The leaves always come before the lovely white blossom which is at its best in July. Bird cherry, as its name indicates, is loved by birds which do not seem to mind the bitter taste of the berries. They are usually black and occasionally red. The species grows very rapidly and can reach a height of 4m (13ft) in five years but seldom reaches more than 15m (48ft) at maturity and is often much smaller.

The trunk is purple spotted with white but it is the egg shaped leaves, so popular with insects, which give the bird cherry its real beauty. The margins are delicately indented, and there is a prominent veining system running from a thick mid-rib to the leaf edge. The wood is hard and its yellow colour and attractive graining is still much in demand by skilled cabinet makers. Particularly common in northern England, and especially in Scotland, the cherries were once used to produce a potent spirit with which home made wines and brandy were fortified.

There is an increasing tendency for naturalists to cultivate trees and plant out the seedlings such as this wild service tree.

Blackthorn has an even greater reputation as a home-brew plant, and sloe gin and wine have administered many a knock-out blow. I am not sure whether it is this or the use of knobbly branches by the Irish to produce a shillelagh which led to it being called a hibernian tranquilizer by Richard Mabey. The wood is dark and the blossom, which comes before the leaves, stands out against the branches like drifts of newly fallen snow. The only thing the flowers lack is perfume strong enough to be detected by human senses but once pollinated by insects the fruit begins to develop. During September the tiny, hard, bitter tasting plums ripen and although black they seem to be dusted over with a pale bloom which gives a laden tree a delightful appearance.

Blackthorn seldom grows higher than 10m (32ft) and is therefore usually classed as a shrub which has been popular with hedge-makers for centuries – the underground roots travel rapidly and put up suckers to produce a substantial thicket in a very short time. Such growths are often typical of the understorey of a woodland and are popular nesting sites for the magpie, chaffinch (*Fringilla coelebs*) and linnet (*Acanthis cannabina*). The hawfinch (*Coccothraustes coccothraustes*), a comparative rarity, can occasionally be seen cracking the tough stones with its heavy and powerful bill.

Other trees have been so important in human economy that they were cultivated like a farm crop and potential competitors removed from the environment. Willows were essential for baskets and weaving into hurdles used to confine sheep. Hornbeam, spindle and box provided wood which was so hard that machinery was made from them; dogwood provided timber for butchers' skewers and knife handles and lime was the perfect tree for providing shade and its rich honey was used by bees. Then, of course, there were the hazel woods farmed for their nuts, once one of the main foods for human beings in winter.

There are 19 species of **willow** growing wild in Britain. They are moisture loving plants and often thrive in the shrub layer of wet woodlands although the pussy willow or palm (*Salix capria*) is not quite so moisture dependent and is the one most often found thriving in woodlands. Other names for the species include great sallow and goat willow and it can grow to over 6m (nearly 20ft) in height but can become top heavy and lean over so far that it may actually fall. The species never lives long but is ideal for coppicing and when this is done it can live indefinitely. The large round, yellowish male catkins are out in March and April and are visited by bees and other early flying insects. The female catkins are larger than the males and may be recognized by their green styles. The tiny 0.6cm ($\frac{1}{4}$in) buds are red and shiny.

Blackthorn blossom.

The goat willow is an efficient pioneering tree but it will interbreed so freely with other members of the family, including sallows and oziers, that the possible combinations are bewildering. The fact that the pollen can be carried by both wind and insects adds to the confusion. Other members of the family found growing in damp woods include the white willow (*Salix alba*) and the common sallow (*Salix cinerea*), whilst the eared sallow or willow (*Salix aurita*) is a shrub of sessile oakwoods and also Highland birchwoods.

Each small nut contains only one seed and looks deceptively easy to open but if you get the chance, try this for yourself and see how tough they are. Despite this, birds such as great tits, hawfinch and chaffinches do manage to break them open, as do grey squirrels and common dormice which as the specific name implies also feed upon hazel nuts.

Britain has few woods in which **hornbeam** (*Carpinus betulus*) approaches anything like dominance but Epping Forest is a magnificent exception and there is still evidence of the extensive pollarding which once produced a regular supply of stout poles. Some damage was done to the hornbeams of Epping by a law passed in the reign of Elizabeth I allowing the people to 'top lop' the trees for winter fuel. The name Carpinus derives from the Latin carpentum meaning a chariot signifying that the Romans knew how tough the wood was and used it to make these vehicles.

When not pollarded, hornbeam can grown to an impressive 25m (82ft) having a slender grey and fluted trunk and dark green, beautifully veined leaves. In autumn the leaves first turn a rusty yellow, then brown and are often retained throughout the winter. Flowers and leaves appear together during April or May since the male and female catkins are borne on the same tree. The male catkins are larger and green until ripe when the yellow pollen then makes them very conspicuous. Each male flower within the catkin consists of a large concave scale which is pale green tipped with red, bearing a number of stamens varying from six to twelve. The female catkin consists of many green scales and in the axil of each is a pair of flowers, each being made up of a three lobed scale and bearing two long red stigmas. These collect the pollen which is carried to them on the wing.

Once the female flower has been pollinated, the catkin scales fall off but the three lobed scales enlarge and hang like a pendant on the twig. Eventually the pendant turns from green to brown and spins away on the autumnal wind to distribute the species. Hornbeam seedlings are unusual in that they lie dormant for at least a year and thrive only in dim light and can thus grow beneath the canopy of large trees such as oak and beech.

There is some argument whether the large leaved **lime**, sometimes found growing in limestone districts, is a true native of Britain although I am inclined to believe that it is. The rare, small leaved lime (*Tilia cordata*) is a true native, however, and may be identified by its heart shaped leaves. The tree commonly found in Britain is actually a cross between the two and known as *Tilia x vulgaris*. It

The sticky, succulent flesh of the berries of the rowan tree is an important food for birds and was eagerly sought by bird catchers who used it to produce bird lime. This sticky substance was smeared on to branches and perching birds were held long enough to be captured either for food or as caged pets.

There is a clump of fertile flowers in the centre of the blossom of the guelder rose, called a corymb. They are surrounded by much larger sterile flowers to attract the insects pollinating the central flowers.

Coppicing

COPPICING was one of the earliest forms of tree management and old woodlands still show obvious signs indicating the industrial history of the area. If trees have many stems rather than one single trunk then you may be sure that the woodland was once coppiced. The process involved cutting down the tree almost to ground level. The trunk does not rot but puts out a number of smaller trunks called stools which can be cut at intervals of several years depending upon the species of tree. Elms do not coppice, but grow new shoots from the roots by a process called suckering. The net effect is the same however for a large number of smaller trees are produced. The process of coppicing must be distinguished from pollarding which involves severing the trunk not at ground level but at a height of between 2 and 5m (6ft 6in to 16ft 3in). The method was not efficient in dense woodland but was employed in marshy areas with willow and in hedgerows with ash trees. Amongst the woodland coppice occasional trees called standards were allowed to grow to their full height. The coppice and standard system of management arose because of the constant demand for timber and wood which did not mean the same thing in the past. Timber was the term used for large planks suitable for building houses, ships, large items of furniture and stout posts. Wood on the other hand was the term used for smaller pieces used in the construction of smaller household items and for firewood. Coppiced timber provided faster growth for the latter purpose whilst the standards were allowed the time they needed to mature and provide the substantial timber which was so vital to the old construction industries.

The cylindrical male catkins of the hazel tree appear before the leaves and their golden green pollen is often being spread as early as February. The female organs are quite small but after fertilization they swell up to produce this edible nut.

was imported from Holland and planted out in parklands but has occasionally been found in secondary woodlands.

The tree will develop from suckers, grows fast and can live up to 500 years and the timber was popular with carvers and was a favourite of Grindling Gibbons. Although it is not a common tree in modern woodlands, lime is a member of most mixed woodlands and had many uses. Fermentations were made from the leaves to use as a hair restorer and for beautifying the skin. The nectar-rich leaves, so popular with bees, were collected, shaken with water and then drunk to treat feverish colds. Lime tea, made from the dried flowers, has a flavour resembling chocolate and the inner layers of bark were known as bast and stripped off to be used to tie up garden plants and weave mats, ropes and even clothing.

The hanging blossoms found in June and July develop into clusters of thick walled nutlets with a narrow bracteola functioning like a wing to enable the fruit to be dispersed by the autumn winds. Many of the seeds seem to be infertile – possibly due to climactic changes over many hundreds of years.

Spindle (*Euonymus europaeus*) is a delicate shrub seldom growing higher than 9m (almost 30ft) and is found in the understorey of woodlands, especially those growing on rich soils. It is more common in southern England and is absent from most of Scotland. It may well have been planted in some areas because of its hard but smooth grained timber used to make toothpicks, skewers and knitting needles and, before the invention of the spinning Jenny, it was the wood from which spindles were fashioned.

The ovate leaves burst from their buds during April and May and measure from 3cm to 12.5cm ($1\frac{1}{4}$in to 5in). The lower surface is bluish green but in autumn the colours are magnificent with delicate shades of purple, gold and red. The small greenish white flowers are found during May and June, have four petals and are pollinated by insects. The unique four sided scarlet fruits are very attractive and were once dried and used as an insecticide and when mixed with water they were used as a hair rinse to discourage nits. The fruit was also peeled and a yellow dye made from the pulp and a scarlet one from the husk.

Because it is not common in Britain, **box**, an attractive evergreen shrub, tends to be overlooked. Only two box woods now remain – one on the edge of the Chilterns and the other, appropriately enough, on Box Hill in Surrey. A glance at an Ordnance Survey map will show where the species once flourished, for example at Boxley near Maidstone and perhaps also at Buxton in Derbyshire and Boxwell in Gloucestershire. The latter may well have been planted for the timber was sought after literally to make boxes. At one time the timber was also used by wood engravers before the days of more sophisticated illustrative techniques in publishing. It is still planted today as a hedging plant.

The alternate veining on the leaves and the fact that they are evergreen make the box a popular tree – I think the golden-green of the spring leaves is particularly beautiful. There is no doubt that box is a native tree which seldom grows higher than 6m (nearly 20ft). The tiny flowers, which appear in April or May, are yellowish white and grow from the axils of the leaves (axil means armpit). It grows very slowly, however, as the timber is so heavy – it will often sink in water and at one time was appropriately called iron-wood. It was used by cabinet makers since its attractive yellow colour takes a high polish and many a Victorian child has enjoyed making words from bricks fashioned from box-wood which were much more resistant to battering than modern day plastic.

Dogwood (*Cornus sanguinea*) is most common in chalk and limestone areas but this attractive shrub, which seldom grows higher than 3m (10ft), is widely distributed throughout Britain. It is more obvious during the autumn when its blood red leaves show us clearly why it was given its scientific name of sanguinea – the red branches and hairy twigs are also conspicuous in winter. The generic name Cornus derives from the Latin cornu which means a horn, a clear reference to the tough timber which was used for mill cogs, toothpicks, arrows and children's toys. It burns easily and was also sought after because it made top quality charcoal, ideal for making gunpowder.

Dogwood begins to flower in June, the white bisexual blooms being grouped in dense groups called cymes. To the human nose the scent is unpleasant, but it seems to be attractive to the insects which pollinate them. The berries are green at first, then turn to a dark purple and are very bitter to the taste. It is said that it was named dogwood because the fruit was 'not fit for a dog'. Oil was once extracted from the fruit burning well in lamps and used in the manufacture of soap.

There are few trees with a more interesting folklore than **hazel**, which constitutes the main understorey of many of Britain's woodlands from sea level to a height of over 500m (over 1,600ft). In the south of its range, hazel is more of a tree than a shrub, can grow to over 10m (33ft) and its trunk can have a circumference of around 1m (3ft). For many years diviners have used hazel rods to indicate things hidden underground, especially water supplies, but also metals – a sort of medieval metal detector. I was once very cynical about this until a water diviner showed me the error of my ways.

Hazel leaves, which are quite hairy on the underside, resemble those of alder but have a pointed apex instead of the depression which is typical of *Alnus glutinosa*. Just below the base of a hazel leaf there is an abortive leaf called a stipule which is lacking in the alder. British hazel nuts (cobs) are produced for retailing although large quantities are also imported – the cultivated strain is usually larger and has a hairier husk called a filbert, thought to derive from a corruption of 'full-beard'. The fruit is a very important item of diet for many birds and mammals and oil can usefully be extracted from the nuts.

The tree never grows large enough to make its main trunk valuable as timber but the pliability of the twigs made it ideal for fishing rods, hoops for casks, rustic seats, hurdles and stakes. The large woody roots, often with attractive veining, were once in demand for veneering cabinets, but this was frowned upon where hazel was grown for its fruit or coppiced for its stakes.

Introduced plants

WHETHER naturalists like it or not, the planned and often gloomy forests planted by both the Forestry Commission and private landowners are likely to be with us for ever. It is, however, not the modern foresters who should be blamed but those who, for centuries past, have been felling trees without a thought for the future. Removing trees from hillsides has allowed rain to leach out the nutrients from the once rich, loamy soil and it should be remembered that almost all the present day planting is on the now infertile sites on which only a small number of tree species, all of them conifers, are capable of sturdy growth.

Another long term factor to be kept in mind, is that any sensible forest management involves the subsequent removal of the crop, the growth of which will have enriched and also stabilized the soil. At the time of felling there is an opportunity to create a much more diverse woodland and re-introduce the native trees which grew on the site many centuries ago. It is here that naturalists have a vital role to play and it is essential that they do so. It serves no useful purpose to insist on planting indigenous trees in areas where they could not possibly grow. Energies would be far better used in trying to understand the work of a modern forester and to study the wildlife which does exist among these alien conifers.

The forester's job begins by selecting his stock which is usually done by detailed consultations with a tree nurseryman. Those who provide private landowners, and perhaps even the Forestry Commission, tend to concentrate upon the production of huge numbers of trees of a limited number of species. Others confine themselves to the numerous varieties of popular ornamental species favoured by gardeners. It is the former type that concerns us here.

There are both advantages and disadvantages in planting stock raised in a nursery. There is always a danger that in the confines of a nursery, characteristics vital to survival in the wild may be bred out of the stock. The new strain may also be less attractive to wildlife, and the stock itself when planted out as a monoculture with no other species around it will be more vulnerable to attacks by one particular pest. On the credit side, however, the nurseryman is able to protect the seedlings at a vital stage in their lives. In the wild most of these are eaten by birds and animals or destroyed by disease. The seedlings can also be planted far enough apart so that they do not compete with their parents or with other seedlings.

The whole process of forestation begins with the collection of seeds. If there is already a forest containing mature trees then some natural regeneration may occur but it is considered best to locate the strongest trees which are climbed and the seeds collected. These are dried or stored in a deep freeze until required.

The natural history of the species needs to be fully understood if the seeds are to be successfully germinated. Experience has shown that some seeds need to be

OPPOSITE: **Larch cones. The leaves of the larch grow in groups of tufts and there is a rough and ready rule which often enables naturalists to assign a conifer to a family. In the spruces, the leaves usually occur singly while in the pines they are in pairs and in the larches they occur in clumps. In first year shoots, however, larch leaves are borne singly.**

soaked in hot water and others in cold, whilst it may be necessary to subject some to the abrasive action of sand to weaken the seed case and eventually allow the seedling to break out.

Recently, some foresters have begun to use a method called micropropagation, now reaching such a peak of sophistication that one single cell can be grown in a test tube and then transferred to a growing compost – many thousands of cells can potentially be produced from one specimen tree. Both these methods are a vast improvement on the more traditional grafting and cutting methods.

Hardwood cuttings are taken during the months when the tree is not using up vital energy in forming new foliage and is able to use food stores to produce new roots. With softwoods, continually in leaf, the taking of cuttings is not really reliable and the method is not popular with propagators of conifers. Layering is more often used in this case which merely involves bending the shoot of a tree over until it touches the ground, where it is secured and covered with soil. When new roots are generated following this treatment the new tree is separated from its parent.

Conifers

CONIFERS, known to scientists as the Coniferales, differ from flowering plants because they have narrow needle-like leaves as well as cones which can be seen at their best in autumn – they may, however, have taken several years to form. Cones are equivalent to the blossom and fruit of a flowering plant but there are important structural differences. Flowering plants are known as angiosperms (meaning seeds within a vessel) and have sepals to hold the flowers together. Petals to attract insects are often present, and there are always female stigmas to catch the pollen released from the male anthers. Both sexes are often present in one flower, but the male and female cones are always separate. The ovules occur at the base of a leafy scale and are not enclosed inside an ovary – for this reason they are called gymnosperms meaning 'naked seed'. Neither juniper or yew appear to bear cones but close examination will show that the red fleshy arils of yew have developed from cone scales and juniper berries are also modified scales.

In early spring, structures called primordia can be seen along the shoots of conifers which are tiny buds that can develop either into new shoots or produce a male or a female cone. The male cones contain stalkless anthers which produce copious amounts of pollen usually carried on the wind to the female cones. These latter consist of scales each containing ovules arranged around a central stalk.

The male cones are usually situated on the lower areas of the tree which prevents a tree from pollinating itself. Once the pollen has been shed the male cones die, but if a grain falls between the scales of a female cone it puts out a tube which pushes against and eventually penetrates and fertilizes the ovule. The cones develop over a period of months or years and are brown when ripe, the scales spread out and allow the winged seeds to escape. This method is typical of Scots pine as well as the hemlocks, Douglas fir, spruce and larch. Some pines have seeds spread by insects and birds whilst other species, including cedars, monkey puzzle and silver fir, only release the seeds when the dead, decaying cones disintegrate.

A specimen tree can be used in the techniques of budding and grafting using another, less useful tree, as a rootstock. A bud or a shoot of the specimen tree (called the scion) is joined to the rootstock by making incisions ensuring that the cambium of both rootstock and scion are joined to enable the two to grow together.

All these well established methods are, however, very slow compared to micropropagation which is certainly the technique of the future. Producing a seedling is one problem, but raising it through the immature stages to produce a marketable tree is quite another.

The forester's first concern when raising the young seedlings is to prepare the chosen site for planting and this can often be an awesome task. Heavy waterlogged soils have to be ploughed, drained and fenced against animals, particularly rabbits and deer which soon make short work of succulent seedlings. The access roads needed to remove the timber when mature also have to be constructed at this stage. Then comes the choice of which species to plant and this requires the forester to take careful note of the natural history of any prospective species to ensure that all environmental requirements are met.

Boles

Sweet chestnut | European larch | Austrian pine

SWEET chestnut is typified by the rugged grooves or channels in the bark running in an oblique direction producing a picturesque patterning which becomes ever more obvious with age. Older trees often seem to be composed of several trunks which appear to support the tree in the manner of the flying buttresses of cathedrals.

The Austrian pine is one of the few trees introduced for beauty rather than for the usefulness of its timber which is far too coarse to be commercially viable. It grows well on chalk and limestone, its grey fissured bark reflecting the sunlight lighting the pale rock. Larch, on the other hand, is a valuable tree to the forester. It does not provide the volume of timber typical of many other conifers, but at the thinning stage, poles can be cut which are used in the production of garden furniture, telephone poles and stout ladders. They grow very fast and the fact that they lose their leaves in winter allows light to filter through the boles and reflects from the rough, deeply furrowed bark. This bark was well known as an astringent and was also used in the tanning industry.

The young trees are then planted in lines with about two metres between each. This task has to be done by hand and using a surprising variety of spades and mattocks a skilled forester can plant more than 1,000 trees in a day. For the first four years the young trees need a great deal of help and any intruding weeds are removed by mechanical or chemical means. Some trees will still be lost and have to be replaced by a technique known as beating up.

After this period the plantation can be left until they produce a thicket although cleaning will be necessary from time to time – a labour intensive and therefore expensive operation involving the removal of self-sown plants which could affect the health of the tree crop. Some intruders are, however, often left and provide a welcome variety both for visitors and wildlife. When the forest is 20 years old, some degree of thinning will be essential, and up to 25 per cent of the original planting may have to be removed to allow the rest of the trees the room they need to grow. The thinnings are not wasted but sold for pit props, fencing, paper pulp and even for firewood: the modern forest fulfills its most ancient of roles.

By the time a conifer is 60 years old it is ready for harvesting while hardwoods may not be commercially viable until they are at least 80 years old, and it may well be twice this period before they are at their best. Many forests are now planned and organized by sophisticated computers – a trend which is likely to continue and accelerate.

If there is one group of ecologists which has been more maligned than the forester it must be the landscape architect, and even they must admit that some of the criticism has been justified. As the profession evolved during the 1960s and 1970s, large areas of scrub, rich in native wildlife, were removed and replaced with introduced species with the subsequent loss of native fauna. While some architects are still entrenched in this short-sighted philosophy, many are now keen to plant native pioneer species such as alder and birch and then allow a natural succession of vegetation to develop. Many substantial new woodlands have been planted in the 1980s and most are a good mix of native and alien species of trees and shrubs.

British naturalists are likely to find themselves in difficulties trying to identify the alien species and visits to an arboretum will overcome many difficulties. Hillier's arboretum in Hampshire, for example, has almost 10,000 types of tree growing in conditions which are much more reminiscent of a wood than of a formal garden. Some particularly attractive arboreta are listed in the gazeteer.

There are only 35 species of tree native to Britain, and from the late fifteenth century onwards explorers began to bring back exotic plants as proof of their discovery of new lands. These could not be allowed to die and collections developed, usually among the woods surrounding the country houses of the rich. During the nineteenth century the collection and display of exotic plants reached almost epidemic proportions. Some arboreta have disappeared in these cost conscious days but many nurseries and universities maintain splendid examples giving pleasure to paying visitors. They also provide an opportunity for foresters to test the hardiness and growth potential of a new species and to preserve very rare species which are almost extinct in the wild. An increasingly important function is to investigate the medicinal effects of plants which may well contain a potentially life-saving drug.

The forester, however, is not concerned with all these numerous species but concentrates his attention upon the firs, pines, western hemlock and, more especially, the larches and the spruces, economically the most important trees in Britain.

Larches are a beautiful and fascinating exception to the rule that most conifers are deciduous. They change colour from the delicate green of spring to the glorious browns and reds of autumn. In winter, the soft needles fall and thus a larch wood shows many more variations than other conifers and has been very popular with foresters who wish to compromise and produce marketable timber and yet satisfy the demands of those who enjoy changes in the landscape as the seasons progress.

Three types of larch are common in British plantations. These are the European larch (*Larix decidua*), Japanese larch (*Larix kaempferi*) and the Dunkeld or hybrid larch (*Larix x eurolepsis*) which is a cross between the two.

The European larch was probably introduced from Poland around 1620. Its creamy white timber is tough and not subject to splintering and so ideal for boat building – especially in the wooden fighting ships of the Napoleonic period.

It is particularly vulnerable to a fungal attack causing larch canker recognizable by large indentations, somewhat spoon shaped, on the trunk. The straw coloured twigs are easily distinguished from the russet red colour of those of the Japanese larch. It was once said that Japanese larch timber was inferior to that of the European species, but not all modern day foresters accept this – it is certainly far less prone to fungal attack.

By far the most popular larch planted today is the Dunkeld larch. This is a hybrid between the European and Japanese larches and was first discovered growing naturally in a forest near Dunkeld in Scotland, owned by the Duke of Athol. Here is an example of what is known as hybrid vigour where the offspring inherits the best features of both parents as well as evolving some of its own features and none of their weaknesses. The Dunkeld larch therefore grows straight, strong and fast, produces excellent timber and is canker resistant. As well as being popular with foresters, woodlands dominated by larch are in favour with naturalists because of its deciduous nature, discussed above, and also with sportsmen since the ground flora and scrub provide cover for pheasants and food for wood pigeons.

Spruces are easily recognized by their leaves growing singly on alternate sides of the twig so that they resemble a long comb. The leaves are also quite short, stand upon a stiff stalk looking like a peg and are quite often prickly to the touch. Two main species are grown in Britain, even thriving in the north and west among the high hills and coping well with the high rainfall. The Norway spruce (*Picea abies*) was introduced from northern and central Europe probably as early as the sixteenth century, but in large numbers during the nineteenth century. Its timber, known as white wood, is in great demand for the rough woodwork in cheap housing, pit props, chipboard and hardboard.

Some spruces produce fertile seed and in some woods there are self-sown trees but most are raised in nurseries. The Sitka spruce (*Picea sitchensis*) takes its name from an area in the Arctic and was introduced from North America in such numbers that the forestry commission has planted more specimens of this species than any other tree. It can be distinguished from the Norway spruce in several ways. The needles of Norway spruce are green on both surfaces whilst those of the Sitka are green on top and blue grey beneath – they are also much more pointed and prickly which means they are not really suitable for Christmas trees. The thin rough bark is much redder in the Norway spruce accounting for its vernacular name in Germany of red spruce. In contrast, the bark of the Sitka spruce is a dull grey brown and it tends to flake off. Another difference may be seen at the base of the trunk which in the Sitka spruce is often buttressed. The pale brown cones of Sitka have a crinkled edge on each scale, a feature not seen on other conifers grown in Britain. Although it tolerates wet conditions the Sitka spruce, despite its native habitat, is less resistant to frost than the Norway, and is usually grown among hills in protected frost hollows rather than on the open tops.

Spruce forests are generally dark and since the trees are usually of the same age and height they are not popular with wild life. Naturalists who complain should remember, though, that they are usually being grown in areas which were once peat moors – equally unattractive to wild life. Goldcrest, however, are common in these plantations and the occasional rarity such as the firecrest (*Regulus ignicapillus*) and nutcracker (*Nucifraga caryocatactes*) may occur.

In the spruce, the numerous male flowers are carried on catkins. Each flower can be up to 2.5cm (1in) long and are coloured yellow tipped with red, having the appearance of a small, unripe strawberry. The female flowers are carried at the tips of the branches which, when fertilized, develop into cones between 12.5cm and 17.5cm (5in to 7in) in length when ripe. The scales are rough to the touch and protect two tiny winged seeds, dispersed by wind. Foresters usually plant out these tiny seeds in beds where they remain for two years before they are considered strong enough to be transplanted into the forests.

Although **firs** are often difficult to separate from spruce one way of identifying which is which is by pulling a leaf off – if a stump is left behind looking rather like a miniature hat-peg then the tree is a spruce. By contrast, if the leaf leaves behind a small round scar the tree is a fir and may belong to one of two genera. The Douglas fir belongs to the genus Pseudotsuga and the silver firs belong to the genus Abies.

The Douglas fir (*Pseudotsuga menziesii*) was sent back from North America by the Scottish botanist David Douglas in 1827. The specific name commemorates Archibald Menzies who first described the species in 1791. The tree is tall, dark and beautiful and its soft needles smell of lemons when crushed. The dark coloured bark is covered in round bubbles which release a sticky resin when punctured. Douglas fir prefers a warm climate and deep, well drained soils and is thus planted mainly in the south and south west of Britain. The red brown resinous timber is much sought after in the construction industry and is also known as Columbian or Oregon pine.

The European silver fir (*Abies alba*) grows well in the Alps and the Pyrenees and is a true mountain tree which would seem to have been a perfect choice for foresters planning to clothe the hills of Britain with good fast growing trees. It can grow to heights of over 60m (almost 200ft) and its leaves are silvery on the under surface.

Unfortunately, the accidental introduction of the aphid (greenfly) *Adelges nordmannicanae* in 1900 proved disastrous. In the cold winters of the Alps the aphid populations were controlled, but in the mild climate of Britain numbers built up to epidemic proportions and many speculators lost a great deal of money as vast numbers of trees were killed. Some prize specimens remain, especially in Scotland, but in more recent years the North American grand fir (*Abies grandis*) has been planted which is resistant to the attacks of the aphid. Features which distinguish the grand fir from the European silver fir are needles which vary in length and lie in flat planes, and resinous buds.

Pines can be recognized by their very clean, straight trunks with branches growing in whorls from the central stem. The distance between each whorl represents a year's growth and so the age of a pine is more easily calibrated than is the case with many conifers.

The needle shaped leaves, often long and twisted, usually grow in pairs but very occasionally in threes or in fives. As we have seen the Scots pine is native to Britain, but the Corsican pine (*Pinus nigra var maritima*), which is a variety of the black pine (*Pinus nigra*), and the Austrian pine (*Pinus nigra var nigra*), which has straight needles, have both been extensively planted by foresters. Another economically valuable timber tree is the lodgepole pine (*Pinus contorta*). The latter is said to be the species used by the North American Indians in the construction of their lodges and it thrives from Alaska to as far south as California. It thrives well in the poor, damp soils of western Britain and is therefore preferred to both the native Scots and the introduced varieties of the black pine. Although it does not produce a big volume of timber at least it will thrive on exposed sites.

The needles are green, carried in pairs and are very twisted. The brown fissured bark with its typical small, square plates and heavy, bent branches also serve to distinguish the species. The pale timber is somewhat rougher than Scots pine but is widely used for pulp and rough joinery. The egg shaped cones have scales carrying prickles which does not seem to prevent birds such as the chaffinch and the Scottish crossbill (*Loxia scotica*) feeding upon the scales within. Both the red and the grey squirrel also appear to enjoy a meal from the lodgepole pine.

The Corsican pine has its grass green needles also arranged in pairs but they are up to 10cm (4in) long – considerably longer than those of the Scots pine. They are coloured grey-green and distinctively twisted. Because of its failure to cope with cool, damp conditions and its thin straggling root system this variety of black pine, so named from the very dark appearance of its foliage when viewed from a distance, is planted more often in southern Britain than on the uplands of the north.

The Corsican pine can be distinguished from both the Scots and the lodgepole by its terminal bud which ends in a sharp point, those of the other two are obviously blunt.

The monkey puzzle, or Chilean, pine (*Araucaria araucana*) was at one time grown commercially in Argentina to provide timber for railway sleepers, but it is now out of favour whilst the Parana pine (*Araucaria angustifolia*) is popular, probably because it provides a hardwood at what amounts to softwood prices.

In 1795 Archibald Menzies took some of the edible fruits and watched them grow during his long sea voyage from Chile to Britain but it was from 1843 onwards that it became increasingly popular as an ornamental tree. Its favourite conditions appear to be on the western side of Britain and there are some fine specimens in Argyll, some reaching over 40m (130ft).

There is a double layer of bark with copious resin between the layers on these trees used as a cure for headaches by applying it as a plaster to the forehead.

The sexes are on different trees. The male catkins occur in July and are ovoid in shape, around 10cm (4in) long and densely covered with lance-shaped scales. The trees cannot be distinguished until they flower, however, when the females bear bright green globular cones each being 15cm (6in) in diameter with the spines turning yellow in the second year before darkening and falling apart to release their edible seeds at the end of the third year.

Finally, the **western hemlock** (*Tsuga heterophylla*), which grows naturally on the west coast of America from California northwards, is becoming increasingly popular among British foresters because it grows so well under the shade of other trees. Its timber is used both for paper pulp and building timber. It appears to grow very well up to heights of 40m (130ft) on all soils except chalk and it copes well with the damp, cold conditions of north western Britain.

The foliage of the western hemlock has three unique features. When the lovely green leaves are crushed they smell like hemlock (*Conium maculatum*) which is a poisonous herbaceous perennial of the carrot family. The needles, which vary a great deal in length, are in crowded groups arranged at random along the twig. The first leaves to appear in conifers are usually a pair of simple leaves. Hemlock is an exception as three leaves appear following germination from the seed. The yellow male flowers are much smaller than those of the numerous pink female flowers carried on the same tree and the egg shaped cones, which develop from the female flowers, are brown when ripe. The seedlings often grow sideways at first but eventually straighten and are characterized by drooping their leading shoot.

A monkey puzzle tree. It was in a small wood near Oban that I disturbed a red squirrel feeding on acorns. The animal scuttled along the floor and attempted to climb the trunk of a Chilean pine. Its hiss of annoyance was easily heard as it gave up the attempt and sought the sanctuary of a nearby stand of larch. I therefore have first hand experience of why it was given the vernacular name of 'monkey puzzle'. Even these resourceful animals would have great difficulty in climbing through the sharp, dark evergreen long-lived leaves arranged in spirals and completely covering the branches.

Some introduced trees are now so well established that they are often thought to be native. This is certainly true of the sycamore, horse chestnut and sweet chestnut, planted in large numbers because they were not only decorative but also functional. All three provided shade in the grounds of English country house and, in addition, sycamore withstands winds so well it is ideal for shelter belts – a role shared by horse chestnut. The sweet chestnut provides tough timber and highly nutritious food.

Some botanists believe that the **sycamore**, for instance, may have been present in small numbers from the period just following the ice ages – a debate which is likely to continue for some time. The name derives from the opinion that it was the sycomorus or fig mulberry mentioned in the bible. It is, in fact, a maple and the differences between sycamore and the undisputed native species, field maple, have already been described. Basically the sycamore grows much taller and produces a greater volume of marketable timber.

Standing under the shade of a sycamore in late spring can be a joy as nectar drips from the flowers and bees, drunk with the energy-rich liquid, buzz heavily from one bloom to the next. The scent from the flowers fills the air and the ground beneath is often sticky with nectar. It is the bees, including the honey bee (*Apis mellifera*), which pollinate the blooms and the fruits develop with surprising speed.

The greyish bark of the sycamore is smooth at first, but as the tree matures the colour takes on a more brownish colour and often flakes off in plates to expose younger bark below. This enabled sycamore to thrive in the soot laden atmospheres of industrial areas since the peeling plates reveal fresh lenticels (breathing holes) in the bark.

The young shoots are stout and hairless, and the buds which are green vary in their time of bursting, but the first leaves may be present by the end of March. The deep green leaves are five lobed and shaped like an open hand (described as

An ungrazed sycamore. The trunk stands firm in even the strongest wind and this has made sycamore a popular choice around upland farms to provide a shelter belt. An old Dales farmer once told me that he could trust a sycamore, but never an elm which was inclined to drop a branch on your head when least expected.

palmate) and can be up to 20cm (8in) across, although the size varies a great deal. They are deep green and hairless above but bluish-green on the underside with a number of pale hairs along the line of the veins.

In country areas free from destructive pollution, sycamore leaves often have numbers of yellowish spots which later develop into black blotches due to the tar spot fungus *Rhytisma acerinum*. This is destroyed by the sulphur dioxide present in the atmosphere of industrial regions, but it is able to overwinter in the rotting leaves until the following spring. The black spots then release wind borne spores to infect the new crop of leaves. The damage caused to the tree by the fungus seems, however, to be very trivial.

Although sycamore does appear to be remarkably free of lethal pests some severe damage was noticed in 1945 by another fungus *Cryptostroma corticale*. This caused what has been labelled sooty bark disease, the signs of attack being blistered bark. When the bark is removed, a sooty moss of dead tissue is found beneath. From its first discovery in London's Wanstead it seemed to spread quickly, although fortunately its virulence appears to have declined to the point that it is no longer a serious threat.

Much more of a worry is the increasingly common grey squirrel which finds the peeling bark easy to chew and goes on to rip away the new sappy tissue beneath and can kill great numbers of trees.

The long flowering period of sycamore begins in late April. The greenish yellow blossom hangs in long panicles each containing from 50 to a 100 flowers of both sexes. The main stem of the panicle is quite hairy but those of each individual flower is not. Trees growing out in the open can produce viable seed when only around 20 years old and a good crop seems to be produced every year. Although sycamore can live for several hundred years the life span is usually quite short and if grown for timber it is usually cut when around a hundred years old.

The attractive looking timber is pale yellow at first but becomes gradually darker with age. It does not do well in outside conditions, but if seasoned carefully and used indoors sycamore timber is compatible with the best, including oak. Sometimes a material known as harewood is produced by dyeing the timber grey. Normally, however, it is the clean appearance of the wood which makes it popular with furniture makers and the fact that it can be scrubbed clean appeals to makers of kitchen utensils and industrial rollers, especially in the cotton and paper industries although it has been somewhat superseded by modern man-made plastic based materials. It will, I am sure, never lose its appeal as a shelter tree, and it is likely to increase to such an extent that sycamore dominated woodlands will become common.

The **horse chestnut** (*Aesculus hippocastanum*) or conker tree, was first introduced to Britain from the Balkans in 1616 as a decorative plant and has now spread to such an extent that it is a regular member of the woodland flora – especially woodlands surrounding large houses.

When the compound leaves, consisting of several leaflets originating from a stout central stalk, fall in the autumn a scar is left behind on the twig. This is shaped like a horseshoe, complete with small swellings which look like nails and this may well account for its vernacular name. Each leaflet resembles the complete leaf of the sweet chestnut (*Castanea sativa*) accounting for it being classed as a chestnut. In the spring of 1983 MJ Pearce wrote to *Country-Side* magazine:

> 'No doubt many of your readers this winter will have noticed small patches of white fluffy material covering the branches of horse chestnut and lime trees. These are likely to be wax filaments of the egg sacs of the female scale insect *Pulvinaria regalis carard*.'

The most spectacular feature of the horse chestnut are the white candle-like flowers at their best in late May and early June. The youngest flowers are found towards the tip and are described as zygomorphic meaning that they are one sided. The flowers are pollinated by bees which collect both nectar and pollen. The pale petals have patches of orange on them and these darken following pollination. During the summer the ovary develops into a spiky green protective case for the single, occasionally double, seed. Occasionally a tree is found with glorious red candles – a hybrid between the horse chestnut and the red-buckeye (*Aesculus pavia*) from North America.

The goldcrest is a species related to the warblers, which is perfectly at home in conifers.

Scale insects are related to the aphids, or greenflies, and feed by inserting their sharp mouth parts into leaves and sappy stems thus depriving the plant of essential nutrients. Scale insects differ from aphids by their round hard external surface which means that they resemble scales growing on the plants. Horse chestnut scale was first noted in the 1960s and has been spreading since. It also attacks sycamore and lime and neither the distribution or the effect on the host tree is yet fully understood.

Although sweet chestnut does not grow particularly well in Britain its fruit was such an essential item in the diet of the Roman legions that they introduced it from Italy early in the second century. In the south of England it has become naturalized in some woods but in the northern counties it has almost always been deliberately planted. The seeds keep well in moist sand and propagation is not difficult.

In the winter, chestnuts are seen at their best with their beautifully fluted boles which become even more attractive as the tree matures. The cracks between are known as shakes and can affect the quality of the timber.

The male flowers are borne in long catkins which hang downwards and are almost as long as the leaves. The female flowers are smaller than the males and after pollination develop into prickly balls which protect the brown shiny seeds within. These are familiar to us all at Christmas, but in some parts of the world, especially southern Europe, they are important items of diet rather than a luxury food.

Chestnut wood is more durable when young and was at one time used for making bedsteads – before iron became popular – and for furniture such as chairs, tables, tubs and wine casks.

Other introduced species such as cedars, cypresses, maidenhair tree, strawberry tree and the mighty redwoods are fascinating parkland trees.

Of all the **cedars** the best known is the cedar of Lebanon (*Cedrus libani*) gracing many woodlands fringing the great houses built in the eighteenth century in England and there can be little doubt that late Tudor England knew and loved the protective folds of its spreading branches. The evergreen leaves, which are replaced every two years, afford perfect cover for breeding birds such as the mistle thrush (*Turdus viscivorus*) and the goldcrest (*Regulus regulus*) whilst one huge veteran growing in a northern park housed a colony of four pairs of jackdaws each of which had sufficient space to tolerate the presence of the others.

The green, erect male catkins are up to 5cm (2in) long and seldom appear in trees younger than 25 years occurring towards the crown. The yellow pollen is usually abundant in autumn and pollinates the smaller ovoid, bright green female cones. Once pollinated the cones turn purple and develop into large barrel shaped cones up to 12.5cm (5in) across and mature in two or three years, by which time they are resinous in texture.

It is said that the timber was used in the construction of Solomon's Temple in Jerusalem and also in his magnificent palace.

Other species of cedar have been introduced into Britain's parks and woodlands in more recent times. The most notable is the deodar (*Cedrus deodara*) brought here in 1831 by W L Melville from the forests of the Junjab which it often dominates. It can be distinguished from *Cedrus libani* by its hairy, drooping, terminal shoots and longer, dark blue-green leaves. The tree can reach 50m (more than 150ft) in height (as can the equally slow growing cedar of Lebanon) and both species can live upwards of 1,000 years. The Atlas cedar (*Cedrus atlantica*) is another huge species introduced from the mountainous regions of Morocco and Algeria and can be recognized by its greyish coloured bushy needles and huge cones containing delta winged seeds. The incense cedar (*Calocedrus decurrens*) was

LEFT: **The stout angular twigs of the sweet chestnut bear substantial pinkish brown buds which burst early in the summer to produce large leaves as long sometimes as 25cm (10in) and 5cm (2in) wide. The veins on the leaf are very obvious and there is a sharp tooth-shape at the margin of the leaf.**

BELOW: **While wardening a nature trail in northern England our much loved cedar of Lebanon lost many of its branches due to the weight of snow during a particularly cold January. The fallen branches were sawn up and burned producing a delightful smell and it is no wonder that Hindus burn the timber as a type of incense. Clothes chests were once made from cedar wood and gave a lovely fresh scent to the garments they contained.**

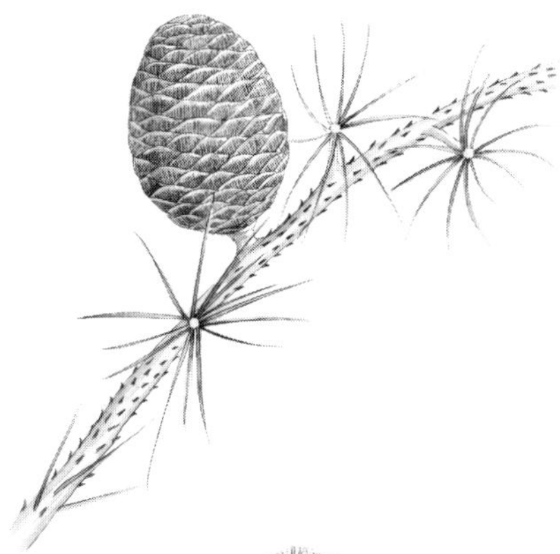

A greenfinch. Together with chaffinches, several species of tit and siskins, these birds find the seeds of cypresses very palatable.

introduced from the south western United States and when crushed the foliage emits an aroma reminiscent of turpentine.

The many species of **cypress** include the smooth Arizona (*Cupressus glabra*), nootka (*Chamaecyparis nootkatensis*), sawara (*Chamaecyparis pisifera*) and the so-called Leyland cypress (*Cupressocyparis leylandii*) which is a cross between the nootka and the monterey (*Caupressus macrocarpa*). Perhaps the most common of the cypresses used in parkland plantations is the Lawson cypress (*Chamaecyparis lawsoniana*) first brought to Britain in 1854. The abundant reddish coloured male flowers are borne on the tips of the shoots while the females are first bluish and then whitish before the cones ripen when brown and full of seeds.

The funeral, or Italian, cypress is native to the Mediterranean area, especially Cyprus from which many think it derived its name. Although planted throughout Europe it has never been popular in Britain, but does occur in some numbers in Somerset. It was planted in England from 1550, well before any other cypress.

In Roman times it was used in the art of topiary and their eminent historian Pliny noted that the timber of the doors of the Temple of Diana, then 400 years old, showed no sign of decay. A statue of Jupiter in the Capitol made of cypress wood showed no sign of decay when it was 500 years old.

Loudon described the tree as flame shaped, others prefer to call it pyramidal. In Britain it seldom grows higher than 20m (65ft) and the branches are closely covered with green overlapping and sharply pointed leaves retaining their colour for up to six years. The male cones are catkin shaped, while those of the female are of a rounded oblong shape, and much less numerous than the males. Cypress cones are produced in pairs and each can be up to 4cm (1.6in) in diameter – the scales protect the oblong shaped seeds. The dark foliage of this species accounts for its funereal associations.

OPPOSITE: **A maidenhair tree.**

Maidenhair tree (*Ginkgo biloba*) is a fascinating species that only survived in a remote corner of China because felling was prevented near monasteries which were

guaranteed a degree of solitude. It is the only living representative of a group of plants botanically placed between the cycads and the conifers which once dominated the world and have now become fossilized in coal measures.

The fleshy seeds of the maidenhair tree do not often ripen in Britain – perhaps just as well because if crushed they can cause a painful skin rash and have a most unpleasant smell. The vernacular name of maidenhair was given because of the similarity of the leaves to the frond of the rare maidenhair fern. The leaves develop in late April arising from disc shaped buds. At first they are bright green, but they quickly darken and in autumn, especially following a hot summer, the bright golden foliage is a delight just prior to its fall. One factor accounting for its survival may be that it is seldom attacked by pests, and only honey fungus (*Armillaria mellea*) seems able to live upon it.

A native of southern Europe, especially Portugal where it grows on mountain slopes the strawberry tree, or **arbutus** (*Arbutus unedo*), also seems to grow well in

Maidenhair foliage. In America the maidenhair is planted as a street tree while in Britain it has been extensively planted in the grounds of houses and parks and the odd specimen has escaped into woods. They can live a long time – the first tree was brought to Britain in 1754 and transferred to Kew in 1761 where it still grows to this day.

The sexes are carried on separate trees, the females being more shapely and slender but they are quite scarce in Britain. The male trees do not usually flower until they are much older, taller and stouter. They often reach 40m (130ft).

Ireland especially near Cork and around the lakes of Killarney. This has led to the suggestion that this evergreen tree may be a native of Ireland although many people feel that it has probably been introduced. It is the striking appearance of the fruit, appearing in late autumn, which has led to its vernacular name and also its alternative name of winter strawberry.

In Britain it seldom reaches 10m (33ft) in height but in its native setting it can be a most impressive tree. The dark green, glossy leaves are evergreen and the white, vase shaped flowers hang in racemes – clusters of blossoms arranged around a main stem, each separate flower being carried on a short stem. These are very attractive to insects such as butterflies, bees and wasps which make full use of the rich supply of nectar. The cherry shaped fruit has an insipid taste, but in Killarney it is said to have a much more pleasant taste than the cultivated forms, a characteristic said by some to support the theory that it is indeed native to Ireland. The sinuous brown bark of the trunk is very like the fur of an animal, and when it begins to peel off has an uncanny resemblance to the velvet hanging from the antlers of a maturing stag. The dark wood possesses a most attractive grain and was once used to make toys for children and ornamental boxes. The fruits can be used to produce a very potent wine and a rich spirit.

Three species of **laburnum** are found in southern Europe and western Asia two of which are now naturalized in Britain. They can be recognized by their trifoliate leaves and lovely yellow flowers which also hang in racemes. The slender twisted pods developing from the flowers should be recognized and avoided for they are very poisonous – as are all other parts of the plant.

The common laburnum (*Laburnum anagyroides*) has been grown in Britain since 1560 and although it grows quickly and is not usually long lived some specimens reach 150 years. I once spent a wonderful day in a northern wood watching bees collecting pollen from a group of laburnums which had gone wild and were growing strongly at the edge between hawthorn, ash and blackthorn. Scotch laburnum (*Laburnum alpinum*) was introduced from southern Europe in 1596, grows well in Scotland and can be distinguished from the common species by having pods with the upper seam winged. This species also has longer leaflets and racemes than the common laburnum.

The timber, although coarse grained, is quite durable and can be polished and used as a substitute for ebony. I once met a Scottish wood carver who maintained that Alpine laburnum was a native to his country and he used it to make dagger handles, bowls and noggins (small barrels) in which he kept his home made wines. He also made toys for his grand children and he even had a lovely polished table made from laburnum.

John the Baptist did not eat insects with his honey but the leaves of the thorny accaci tree, often called the locust tree. **Robinia** or false acacia (*Robinia pseudoacacia*) is a deciduous tree introduced from the south eastern states of America and is superficially similar to the accaci tree since both species have a pair of spines at the base of each leaf. The false acacia was first described in 1601 by Jean Robin a French botanist and was introduced into Europe by his son Vespasian. No other tree in Britain bears these paired spines making Robinia easy to identify.

The species grows very rapidly and its timber is oak-like, although much more brittle. It was once used for fence posts and doors, in toy manufacturing and as a substitute for box wood. The twigs are also brittle and often damaged in high winds, or broken by the weight of snow. The traditional graceful appearance is therefore often adversely affected in Britain.

The sweet scented flowers are carried in long drooping clusters of racemes, each one resembling a pea flower – both belong to the leguminaceae family. Like the rest

Laurel is more common in woodlands than is often realized, its poisonous leaves being sensibly ignored by animals.

Tree creepers find the indentations in the bark of the Wellingtonia ideal sites in which to roost.

of the family, the roots of robinia are covered in nodules containing bacteria capable of converting atmospheric nitrogen into compounds from which the plant can synthesize proteins. This means that robinia can thrive on soils deficient in nutrients. Another family characteristic is the fruit consisting of seeds carried in pods, technically called legumes. Apart from its ability to produce fertile seeds robinia can also spread by root suckers and in woodlands surrounding country houses the tree, with its attractively fluted trunk, can be quite common.

The **redwoods** are amongst the largest trees in the world and two species have been planted in British woodlands. These are the coast redwood (*Sequoia sempervirens*) and the well named giant sequoia (*Sequoia giganteum*), also known as the Wellingtonia the seeds of which were brought to Britain in 1853 two years after the Great Exhibition and the death of the Duke of Wellington. It was only discovered on the western border of the Sierra Nevada during the Californian gold rush.

Even though it is a rare tree in the wild its huge bulk makes it interesting to foresters and its rarity and longevity make it popular with those who love trees. The giant redwood can live for 3,000 years but those planted in the damp climate of Britain will never reach this age even though some specimens, including some in Scotland, have already reached heights of over 50m (nearly 165ft).

Both species have hard, tough evergreen leaves, those of the coast redwood having white bands on the undersurface whilst the colour of those of the coast redwood vary from dull blue-grey to a dark shiny green.

Whilst these trees were all introduced directly into parklands there are those, such as rhododendrons, mulberry, laurel, lilac and walnut that may have been introduced to gardens, country mansions or arboreta, subsequently dispensing their

Rhododendrons provide good cover for birds and delight the eye during spring and early summer.

seeds into areas of native woodland.

An eminent university professor – a zoologist I should point out – once exhorted his student to 'kill a rhododendron a day' and for the sake of much of our native fauna and flora we must admit that he has a point. The Victorians loved each and every one of their evergreen **rhododendrons** and their related semi-evergreen azaleas. Over 500 species were brought in, mainly from the Himalayas and south-eastern Asia by the intrepid Hookers and initially grown at Kew. The delightfully coloured funnel shaped flowers grew well under beech and provided cover for game, especially pheasants, which originated from the same geographical area.

Nest sites were also provided for our native birds and I have found several moorhens (*Gallinula chloropus*) incubating eggs some 2m ($6\frac{1}{2}$ft) above the ground in a rhododendron. Unfortunately, very few members of our ground flora can grow beneath the evergreen's lusty shrubbery and the leaves, even though they decay slowly, produce acids which run off into the streams penetrating the woodland and remove the calcium, preventing aquatic invertebrates from developing. Rhododendron tends to dominate the area, allowing few other species to flourish and looking beautiful for only a few months of the year.

Only the **black mulberry** (*Morus nigra*) really grows well in Britain although attempts are made to grow other members of the moraceae family including rubber, breadfruit, figs and the white mulberry (*Morus alba*) – the favoured food of young silkworms (*Bombyx mori*). It is, however, very difficult to grow in the British climate and is consequently very rare outside protected gardens.

The edible fruit of *Morus nigra* is cultivated in Britain tasting rather like a large juicy raspberry, but is rather darker – almost purple – when ripe. Birds find the fruit much to their liking during August and early September.

The first of the **laurels** to be introduced to Britain was the cherry laurel (*Prunus laurocerasus*) around 1580 from south eastern Europe or perhaps Asia Minor. It has spread widely to become a fairly common understorey shrub, occasionally reaching 13m (nearly 40ft). The thick, leathery, evergreen leaves can occasionally smother the native vegetation unable to survive in its dense shade.

The fragrant white flowers, often evident as early as February, grow in tall, upright species at their best during April and develop into black egg-shaped, cherry-like fruits. The Portuguese laurel (*Prunus lusitanica*) was introduced around 1650, but does not flower until the middle of June and the abundant fruits are much smaller being red at first before turning black.

Lilac (*Syringa vulgaris*) is a very common ornamental species introduced from south eastern Europe and although seldom growing over 6m (nearly 20ft) it is conspicuous during May and June because of its dense terminal panicles of scented flowers – the word panicle derives from the Latin panicula meaning a tuft. The glabrous leaves, measuring 5cm to 12.5cm (2in to 5in), are delicately veined, deep green and provide excellent cover. Lilac offers a favourite nesting site for many birds including blackbirds, song thrush, bullfinch (*Pyrrhula pyrrhula*) and greenfinch.

Lilac is yet another species which, although mainly a garden plant, is now widely dispersed and can often be found as a beautiful member of the understorey of deciduous woodlands. This spread has been aided by its winged seeds that can travel far on the wind. The tree is also able to propagate by means of suckers resulting in substantial thickets developed from a single tree. Another feature of lilac is that it can be grown on almost any soil.

The delightfully smelling lilac can sometimes provide good cover for birds and never fails to provide insects with nectar.

The botanist Loudon noted that:

> 'The first time the lilac was made known to European botanists was by a plant brought from Constantinople to Vienna by the Ambassador Busbequius towards the end of the sixteenth century . . . it soon spread rapidly throughout the gardens of Europe. In some parts of Britain and various parts of Germany it is mixed with other shrubs, or planted alone to form garden hedges; . . . Mixed with sweet briars, sloe thorns and scarlet thorns, guelder rose trees etc it forms beautiful hedges to cottage gardens when there is abundance of room.'

Several varieties of the smaller Persian lilac (*Syringa persica*) have also been introduced but are confined to gardens. Whenever I think of lilac I remember a small wood in Staffordshire where I once listened to the dawn chorus with the heady smell of lilac in my nostrils, the sound of birds blending with the fall of gentle rain on the leaves.

Only a few bird sown **walnut trees** (*Juglans regia*) grow wild in British woodlands. Its name in Anglo Saxon means a foreign nut indicating that it was probably introduced from Asia Minor by the Romans.

Superficially, the walnut resembles the ash but can be distinguished because its leaves are arranged alternately along the stem rather than in opposite pairs. The purple-black bud scales and also the leaves have an aromatic smell: a feature not present in ash.

The erect stem bears smooth grey bark in young trees, but as the tree ages, shallow fissures appear and cream coloured diamond shaped scales can be detected. The leaves burst around the middle of May, but do seem to be susceptible to late frosts. Initially the leaves are downy and bronze in colour but the hairs are soon lost as the surfaces take on a dull dark green colour above and are rather paler below. The number of pairs of leaflets making up each compound leaf varies from two to six and usually average four with a single terminal leaflet usually, but not always the largest of them all. The total length of each leaf can be up to 30cm (13in) long.

The flowers appear at the same time as the leaves. The male catkins are purple when ripe and the erect female flowers are green, and flask shaped. Green walnuts develop quickly from the fertilized flower, their wrinkled skin looking superficially like a brain. These prickled nuts were believed in medieval medicine to impart intelligence and to cure headaches. This is an example of the doctrine of signatures which postulated that plants resembling human organs were sent by God to cure us. The green husk eventually withers to reveal the brown shell and inside this are two valve shaped structures which are the food stores for the embryo plant. These kernels, known to biologists as cotyledons, are the nuts used so widely.

Walnuts in Britain seldom produce good fruit, but the timber has long been popular with carpenters.

The beautifully marked greyish brown timber has been popular with cabinet makers since the eighteenth century and there is no finer material available for the manufacture of gun stocks. For these, as well as culinary reasons, walnut has been extensively planted throughout Britain and it is no wonder that some degree of re-generation has taken place in and around predominantly native woodlands.

Fungi, lichens & non-flowering plants

AT one time living organisms were classed as either plants or animals. Plants defined as organisms made their own food from carbon dioxide from the air, water from the soil and energy from sunlight. This process would go on too slowly to support life without the pigment chlorophyll to accelerate the process: an example of a catalyst. On the other hand animals, by definition, cannot carry out this process of photosynthesis and must consume plants or other animals. Exceptions to these definitions have been, until recent years, tactfully avoided. Fungi were classified as plants despite the fact that they contained no chlorophyll, and this pigment is also lacking in bacteria. There are also some single celled organisms containing chlorophyll that are able to manage without it in the darkness, when they feed like animals. Thus it is now generally accepted that living organisms are divided into five kingdoms namely bacteria, single celled organisms, fungi, plants and animals.

This system removes many problems especially, as far as this book is concerned, with regard to **fungi**. Many fungi obtain their food from dead, decaying organisms – a method termed saprophytic – whilst others are parasites, feeding on the living bodies of plants and animals.

All fungi lack the green pigment typical of plants and must therefore absorb their nutrients through the mycelium made up of tiny tubes called hyphae. These look rather like pale spiders' webs penetrating through the soil. Microscopic examination reveals knob-like structures called hausteria penetrating the tissues of the material on which they live, known as the substrate. Digestive juices are exuded as nutrients and absorbed into the mycelium. Sometimes the hyphae may join together to form thick chords called rhizomorphs which are usually large enough to be seen without the assistance of a magnifying glass. The fruiting bodies are also formed from aggregations of hyphae. The shapes of these bodies vary a great deal, but they all produce tiny spores which can be dispersed by the wind before germinating and giving rise to a new mycelium.

Most fungi disperse their spores by relying upon the wind. For instance, the *Ascomycetes* are a class of fungi which shoot their spores into the air. They are produced inside a club shaped structure called an ascus usually containing eight spores. Species commonly found in woodlands include the stinkhorn, orange peel fungus, earth star, king Alfred's cakes and coral spot. Most of the species we usually refer to as mushrooms belong to the class of fungi called *Basidiomycetes*. They drop their spores directly onto the ground, although many are light enough to blow about in the wind especially in dry weather.

The spores, appropriately called basidiospores, are produced on club shaped

OPPOSITE: **A close look at shaggy pholiota will reveal each fruiting body to be carried on a curved yellowish stem with a dark brown ring around the middle. Below this ring the stem is as shaggy as the cap but above the ring it is quite smooth.**

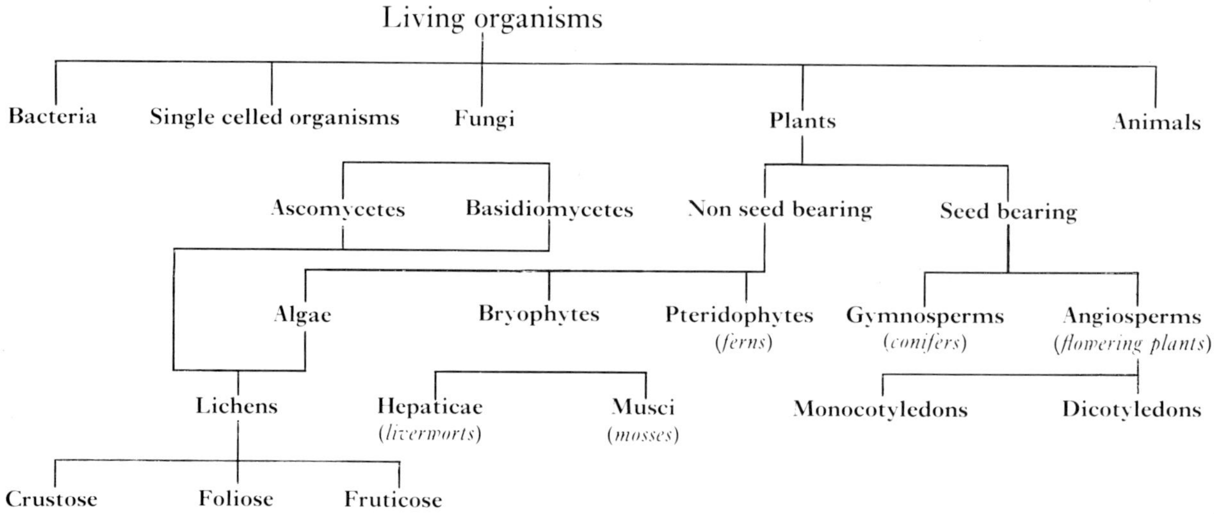

BELOW: **Detail of a typical bill fungus**

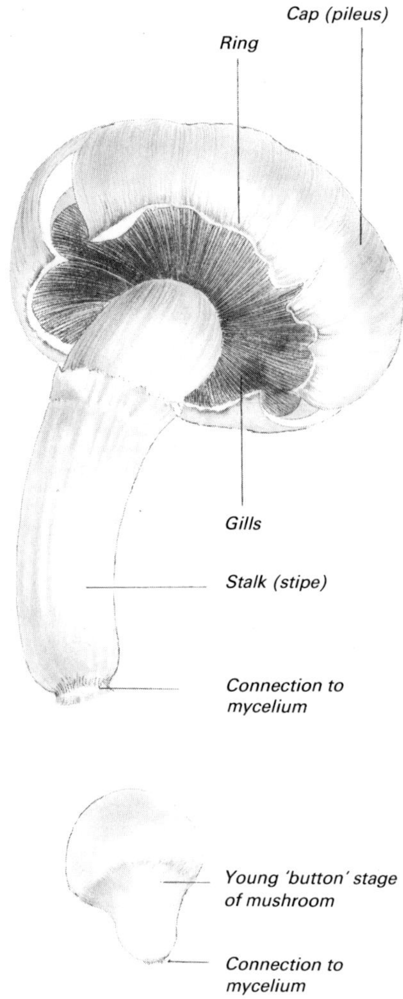

cells called basidia. The area of the fungal body carrying the basidia is called the hymenium and is usually raised into the air so that it can be blown by the wind and the seeds dispersed. The bracket fungi growing high up on tree trunks are obviously in an ideal position from which to disperse their basidiospores.

Other fungi carry the reproductive head on a long stalk called a stipe. These are classified as *agarics*, to which the edible mushroom belongs, and have an umbrella shaped cap beneath which are a large number of radically arranged gills. The hymenium producing the spores lines the gills. The boletes are similar to the agarics, except that the spores are produced on the underside of the cap inside large numbers of sponge-like tubes. Examples of agaric fungi are the fly agaric blusher, shaggy ink cap, shaggy pholiota and sulphur tuft.

Before going on to describe the common *Ascomycetes* and *Basidiomycetes* found in woodlands it must be stressed that although many fungi are edible great care should be taken over correct identification and careful cooking.

I have often found the stinkhorn (*Phallus impudicus*) by smell rather than by sight as it really does stink and the name horn refers to its resemblance to the male reproductive organ as does its generic name of Phallus.

Once the periderm (outer skin) of the stinkhorn egg ruptures, the pale phallus with its olive cap (the pileus) arises from the jelly-like interior. This can grow to a height of over 20cm (8in) in a matter of two hours – it is no wonder that the ancients thought that the Devil was at work and locked up their daughters! The smell of the pilens attracts flies which feed on the spores, but whilst they are doing so they become coated with slime and spores, which are thus distributed. The related, but smaller dog stinkhorn (*Mutinus caninus*) can be recognized by its red pileus.

Orange peel fungus (*Aleuria aurantia*) is an easily recognized species and is edible, especially when fried in butter. It grows best in woodland clearings and on paths, including those running through conifer plantations. Initially the cups are closed but when ripe can be 10cm (4in) across and when touched the spores rise like a cloud.

It always seems to me a great pity that none of the ten native species of earth stars are very common because there are few fungi to equal their beauty. *Geastrum triplex* is found in beech woods its fringed collar looking like an Elizabethan ruff.

King Alfred's cakes (*Daldinia concentrica*) are frequently found on dead

ABOVE: **The first visible sign of the erupting fruiting body of the stinkhorn is a series of oval bodies about the same size, shape and colour of hens' eggs. Some say that these eggs are a tasty morsel, but although I do eat a lot of fungi I have never plucked up enough courage to try these.**

LEFT: **King Alfred's cakes. This fungus causes ash wood to rot, the damaged areas being white, flecked with brown and called at one time calico wood.**

The orange peel fungus resembles orange peel turned inside out, but the colour is usually a little darker.

RIGHT: Sulphur tuft – although the fungus is not poisonous its waxy yellow flesh has a most unpleasant taste and it is certainly one to be left alone.

Cladonia chlorophae – a fruticose lichen that grows well both on walls and in woodland. Its reproductive structures are delicate cup-like organs carried on short stalks and hence earn their common name of cup-lichen.

ABOVE: The coral spot.

Blusher is a species of fungus with a pinkish cap and white gills which become rust coloured with age. It is common in woodlands and only edible when cooked – when raw, blusher is toxic.

branches of ash, the dark brown knobs of the fruiting bodies are about 5cm (2in) in diameter and found growing on the living tissues of *Fraxinus excelsior*. As they mature the fruiting bodies go even darker and look like burnt cakes – hence their vernacular name. They were also once called cramp balls and were gathered and carried around in pockets or hung around the neck as a cure against rheumatism.

An aggregation of spores looks like a dusting of soot and is carried by the wind, but also may be carried by the alder wood wasp of the genus *Xyphidria*. Although ash trees are the favourite habitat, king Alfred's cakes may also attack other hardwoods, including alder and willow.

A walk through a woodland, especially in autumn, will certainly lead to the discovery of coral spot (*Nectria cinnabarina*), if the dead, decaying twigs lying on the floor are turned over. The round orange to pink fruiting bodies, about 3mm ($\frac{1}{4}$in) in diameter, give the twigs a distinctly spotty appearance. As they ripen the fruit bodies become deeper in colour.

Blusher (*Amanita rubescens*) is a very common species of woodland *Basidiomycetes* and is edible, although it should not be eaten raw. Great care must be taken in its identification, too, because many near relatives, including the false death cap (*Amanita citrina*) and the death cap (*Amanita phalloides*), are very poisonous. The main point of identification is that the flesh and gills become blushing pink with increasing age or when damaged. The cap can be as much as 15cm (6in) in diameter and is initially convex in shape but flattens with age – at around the same time that it begins to blush.

The specific name of shaggy ink cap (*Coprinus comatus*) derives from comatus meaning hairy. A tall hollow stem often reaches 25cm (10in) and the torpedo shaped fruiting body can add a further 7.5cm (3in) to this. The Coprinus genus is

Initially the fruit body of the shaggy ink cap is white, compact and edible but it is most unpleasant once it begins to expand into the shape of an inverted umbrella and then breaks down into a black, sticky mass.

characterized by the possession of black spores which liquify when ripe to produce a black ink-like substance. Many years ago an imaginative scientist named Boudier suggested using this ink for important documents since the presence of spores would reveal any attempt at forgery when microscopically examined.

Shaggy pholiota (*Pholiota squarrosa*) derives its specific name from the Latin squarrosus meaning a scale because this fungus is easily recognized by its prominent covering of brown scales. The fruiting bodies occur in clusters on the base of deciduous trees, especially ash and I have often found them growing in hollow trees, each orange yellow cap being up to 5cm (2in) across. The gills are pale yellow until the dark brown spores begin to mature.

Once more the Latin name gives a clue to the pattern of growth of the sulphur tuft (*Hypholoma fasciculare*) – fascicularis means little bundles. The groups of bright yellow fruiting bodies frequently growing on old stumps can be found throughout the year except following a period of hard frost. Each cap can be up to 5cm (2in) across and is carried on a long curved slender yellow stalk. The gills are first yellow, then turn to green prior to ripening when the spores are deep violet.

At present, an acceptable classification divides plants into five classes as shown in the table. Of the **non seed bearing plants**, *Algae* are often defined as simple and of little use to us – these assumptions are, in fact, not true. Some of the unicellular algae do indeed look simple and appear to have no useful applications, although some of the large seaweeds are of enormous value both as food and in the pharmaceutical industry.

The *Algae* are restricted mainly to marine habitats in those areas where light can penetrate and where they can find a firm anchorage. The remarkable exception is

Pleurococcus vulgaris which is a single celled organism found on tree trunks and rotting branches, providing conditions are moist enough. Some *Algae*, however, can live within the body of a fungus, each partner providing the other with either essential materials or habitat – a relationship called symbiosis, and the combined organisms are called **lichens**.

Such an alga would not be able to survive in exposed conditions and lives under a thin transparent skin on the surface of the fungal body. In exchange for this protection the alga shares its food, made by photosynthesis, with the fungus which is, as we have seen, lacking in chlorophyll. This partnership of symbiosis works perfectly and although few lichens have English names many species are common, particularly in the wet woodlands of western Britain. Lichens are also very susceptible to atmospheric pollution and are important indicators used by ecologists to estimate levels of pollution. Although lichens are very variable in form it is possible to group them into three basic types namely crustose, foliose and fruticose.

Some of the crustose lichens are so thin that they seem part of the substratum on which they grow. One of the most interesting occurring in woodlands is *Leconara conizaeoides* which grows on tree trunks often in areas also populated by the alga *Pleurococcus*, typified by a much deeper green. This lichen is very tolerant of atmospheric sulphur dioxide and is often the only species to be found growing on trees affected by acid rain. The needle-like leaves of many conifers are also quite acidic compared to deciduous trees and *Lecanora conizaeoides* is frequently the only lichen to be found thriving on their trunks. Another common species found on the boles of trees is *Pertusaria albescens* which can be set so closely into the bark that it seems part of the tree itself. *Xanthoria parietina* is a delightful yellow lichen adding a bright patch of colour to the trunks of many woodland trees.

These foliose lichens get their name because they seem to be composed of large numbers of overlapping plates looking surprisingly leaf-like. I well remember, during the 1939–45 war, being sent out by my grandmother to look for 'crottles' used to move a very resistant brown dye. She used the dye to colour the sheep's wool, previously gathered, and worked it into strands on her spinning wheel. I now know the species as *Parmelia saxatilis* but even as a ten-year-old I knew that it grew best on oak and ash trees in the angles between the branches and the trunk.

The fruticose lichens are much more plant-like and are made up of a number of branches creeping over the growing area like gnarled hairy spreading fingers.

Members of the usnea genus are accurately called the beard lichens and occur in whiskery masses towards the tips of twigs. They grow in this position because the *Algae* component of the partnership is not very tolerant of shade. Neither are they happy in areas of high atmospheric pollution. Over 30 species occur in Britain and whilst they occur on deciduous trees usnea appears to prefer conifers, with larch as a particular favourite.

The next order of non-seed bearing plants are the *Bryophytes* which have not solved the problem of reproducing in the absence of water and their life cycle, like that of the ferns, demonstrates an interesting phenomenon known as alternation of generations.

The male organs are called antheridia the size and shape of which tend to be unique to a species and help considerably in the classification. Inside these delicate sac-like structures the male gametes, called spermatozoids, develop and when ripe swim through a film of water to the female organs called archegonia, being chemically attracted. The female organs do not show the variation typical of the antheridia and contain a central egg eventually fertilized by a spermatozoid. The embryo so produced develops into a spore containing a capsule carried on a stalk and ending in a structure called a seta which absorbs food from the parent plant. Eventually, often in dry weather, the spores are released and germinate into a new *Bryophyte*. The plants are half dependent upon water and it is the sexual stage which ties them to damp areas. Mosses, especially, are often dominant in areas of damp woodland even though the spore phase ensures that they can withstand periods of drought.

Bryophytes can also reproduce vegetatively when plates of tissue called gemmae break away from the parent and grow into new plants.

The liverworts (hepaticae) and the mosses (musci) make up the *Bryophytes* and their characteristics are such that they are not likely to be confused with other plant classes. The plant body of many liverworts consists of a flat thallus with no division into stem and leaves and the mosses have an axis equivalent to the stem of flowering plants on which tiny leaves are carried. The moss stem is always weak and lacks the strengthening tissue which is so typical of the more highly evolved plants.

Bryophytes are anchored to the ground or other substrata on which they may grow such as rocks, trees or rotting leaves by very delicate looking structures called rhizoids. One way in which botanists distinguish liverworts from mosses is by a microscopic investigation of the rhizoids which are unicellular in liverworts and multicellular in mosses. There are other distinctions, including the fact that anything showing differentiation into stem and leaves is a moss, while any individual with a deeply lobed thallus has to be a liverwort. It is, however, a combination rather than a single factor which enables the final separation to be made unless a microscopic examination of the rhizoid is made.

Mosses are much more common in woodlands than **liverworts** which are confined to the areas splashed by rivers or upland waterfalls. One however, is found in damp areas beneath trees and sometimes on bark and this is *Pellia epiphylla*.

Pellia is Britain's most common liverwort and is abundant in damp woods and around the base of tree trunks.

Pellia is found on banks where streams flow through wooded glades and also on loamy slopes where the water is held either by layers of clay or by fallen leaves. The shining green, flat and transluscent thallus with forked branches make it easily recognized. During February and March the very dark green capsules become obvious and are carried on almost transparent, thin stalks. As the capsules split the spores are found to be entangled in tufts of green hairy structures called elatoes. These are twisted but as they lose water in dry weather suddenly unwind and hurl the spores away from the parent plant.

The majority of Britain's woodlands are very rich in **mosses**, however, and among the most common species are *Atrichum undulatum*, *Dicranum majus*, *Hylocmium splendens*, *Hypnum cupressiforme*, *Leucobryum glaucum* and *Thuidium tamariscinum*. Although the uses found for mosses are fewer than for flowering plants there have been periods when they have been commercially valuable. Sphagnum moss, for instance, found in damp upland woodlands and more especially in coniferous areas, is able to soak up large quantities of water. It was therefore used before bandages to dress wounds inflicted on battlefields. There is some evidence to suggest that the plant may also contain a chemical which staunches blood.

The species *Atrichum undulatum* is sometimes called Catherine's moss because Friedrich Ehrhart, the eighteenth century botanist, named it after Catherine the Great of Russia. It occurs in woodland clearings and has been used by botanists as an ecological indicator of soil with a healthy humus component. Despite this, it is widely distributed although it does not grow either in highly calcareous or very acid soils. The long, narrow, pointed leaves have toothed margins and there are plate-like structures running along the nerves. The upright stems are unbranched and the capsules are carried on a long stalk projecting above the leaves. The capsule has a long, thin, beak-like lid which is almost as long as the capsule itself.

Dicranum majus is typical of mountainous woods, while its near relative *Dicranum scoparium* is more tolerant over a wide range of conditions providing those conditions are on the acid side of neutral. Areas such as tree trunks and piles of rotting leaves provide ideal habitat.

Superficially there is some resemblance to the Polytrichum genus of mosses but the very stiff stems so typical of these is lacking in the Dicranums. Both the colour and shape of *Dicranum scoparium* and *majus* varies from bright green to a yellowish tint and the stems are sometimes clothed in a pale orange coloured mat of hair-like structures making up the tomentum. The leaves of *D. scoparium* are never larger than 1.0cm ($\frac{1}{3}$in) in length and frequently much smaller whilst those of *D. major* are always longer than this, up to a maximum of 1.5cm ($\frac{2}{3}$in). The tufts of scoparium are also much denser than those of majus and thus the two species are easily separated. (A hand lens is essential if mosses are to be mastered and a ×5 or better still a ×10, lens can be purchased very cheaply.)

Hylocomium splendens is very much at home in acid woodlands, often forming extensive carpets in conifer woods or lying concealed beneath grass or heather. It needs to be a robust plant and is recognized both by its bright glossy shoots and red stems branching regularly accounting for the occasional vernacular name of ostrich plume moss. The oval leaves are up to 3mm ($\frac{1}{4}$in) long, are toothed and terminate in a long point. Viewing with a lens will reveal tiny scale-like structures called paraphyllia between the leaves.

A regularly branched mat-like moss called *Hypnum cupressiforme* is commonly found covering fallen logs or tree bases. There are several varieties which botanists have recognized growing in different habitats. The *laconusun* variety, for example, grows on limestone whilst the *ericetorum* species grows on heather. All have overlapping leaves curving downwards and tapering to a point. The leaves also lack nerves and the margins are slightly toothed.

Dicranum sceparium

A walk through a beechwood or among conifers in early spring will often reveal cushions of an unusual moss which, like the sphagnum of the uplands, looks white when dry but has a most absorbent texture. Like sphagnum, *Leucobryum glaucum* was used as a wound dressing and also contains an astringent which troops in the First World War used in preference to bandages. It is a large moss growing to heights of 10cm (4in), the bottom part of the stem being white and dead looking while the tip remains a succulent green. The species is unique in being the only British moss with cell walls more than one cell thick, although this can only be observed through a microscope.

The cushions of the moss are only loosely attached and can be rolled about and broken up. This does not matter because the fragments, especially those bearing the dull purple rhizoids, divide vegetatively to produce new plants. What does matter, however, is its popularity as the matrix for hanging baskets causing the extinction of *Leucobryum glaucum* in some areas – particularly those near to garden centres.

Thuidium tamariscinum is a species more common in the north and west of Britain. It has bright green leaves and dark green, almost black stems. They are clothed in long triangular pointed leaves between which are tiny branches, hair-like structures called paraphyllia. Other recognizable features are the three branched main stems and leaves carried on the branches which are narrower and smaller than those on the main stem.

The woodland moss hunter would also do well to look out for *Mnium hornum* which can be the dominant species on the bark of trees growing in tufts. If the separate plants can be teased out, the upright branches may be seen to rise from a tangle of reddish brown rhizoids. The main stem also branches at the tip to produce a plant looking remarkably like a miniature palm tree.

The third order of non seed bearing plants are the *Pteridophytes* – **ferns**. They are larger and more conspicuous plants and all non-flowering. In the past they were thought to bloom briefly each mid-summer eve and for the rest of the year were invisible. Therefore fern extract was thought to produce invisibility useful in avoiding the Devil and spying on suspected lovers – a considerable folklore has consequently built up around the ferns.

Ferns also show an alternation of generations in their life cycle, the asexual spores being carried in structures called sori arranged on the back of the fronds. The number and positions of these sori can often be used to separate the species.

Ferns are not a difficult group to get to know since there are only some 46 species native to Britain and not all of these occur regularly in woodlands. Among those likely to be encountered are bracken (*Pteridium aquilinum*), mountain fern (*Thelyp-*

Ferns

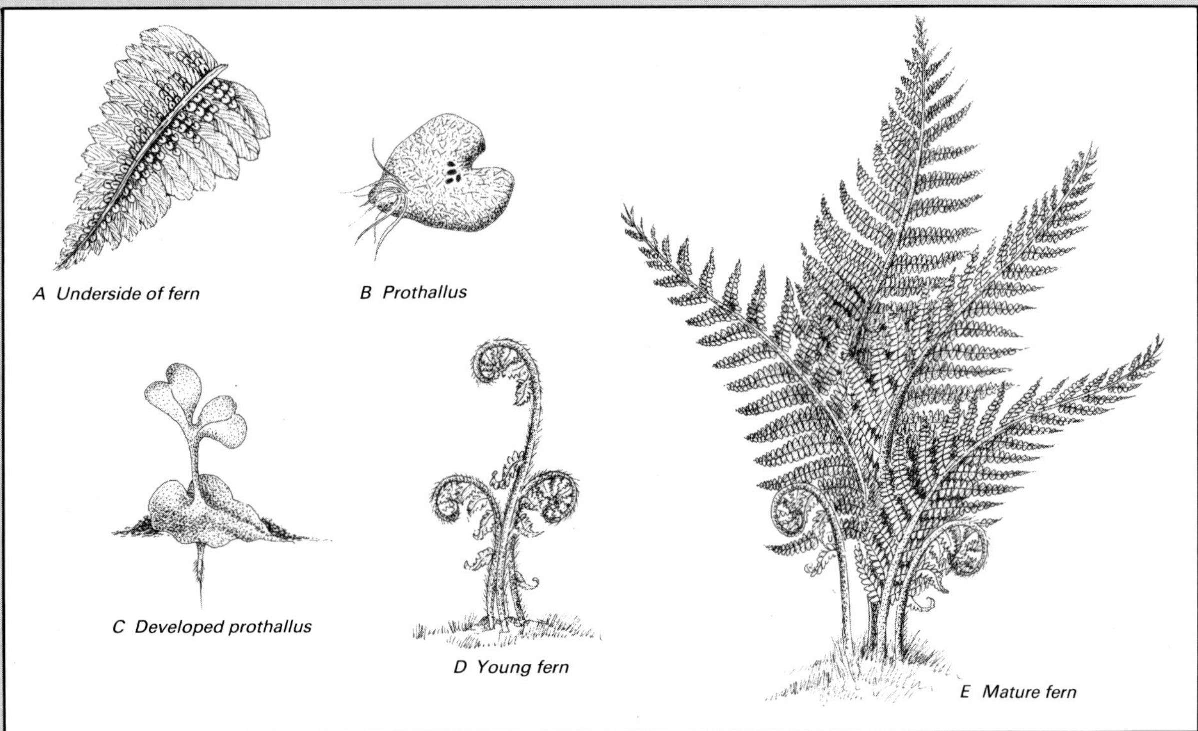

A Underside of fern
B Prothallus
C Developed prothallus
D Young fern
E Mature fern

FERNS consist of an aerial portion called the frond growing from an underground stem called a rhizome. The clear distinction between root, stem and leaf only occurs in the seed bearing plants. This plant reproduces by spores and is therefore referred to as the sporophyte generation. **A.** There are tiny structures called sori (the singular is sorus) on the underside of the frond. These produce spores which are so tiny and light that they easily blow about in the wind, and certainly do not require water. **B.** Millions of spores are spread randomly and when a suitable habitat is found they germinate to produce a small, flat and very delicate structure called the prothallus or gametophyte which is usually less than 1 cm (0.4in) across, and on it there are male and female reproductive organs. **C.** The male cells swim towards the female and this is the phase which needs water and explains why ferns are still restricted to damp habitats. The gametophyte generation, as it is called, comes to end when the fertilized female cell grows by feeding on its parent rather like a parasite. **D.** Eventually the gametophyte withers and the sporophyte by this time can photosynthesise and is self supporting. **E.** A mature fern. The life cycle then begins again.

OPPOSITE: **Horsetails are among the most ancient plants found in Britain and are related to the ferns. They grow in most deciduous woodlands.**

teris limbosperma), hard fern (*Blechnum spicant*), male fern (*Dryopteris felix-mas*), lady fern (*Athyrium felix-femina*) and common polypody (*Polypodium vulgare*).

Among the old, common names for bracken were eagle fern and brakes – when the stem is sectioned and the two slices placed side by side they give the appearance of an eagle with spread wings. To some eyes it resembles a branch of a spreading old oak. Bracken is unpopular with foresters because of its hard, tough rhizomes buried deep in the soil, but it used to have many uses, a few of which were listed in Phoebe Lancaster's fascinating book *A plain and Easy Account of the British Ferns* published in 1854. She points out that bracken was economically important and that:

> 'As a manure it is largely consumed in some places: and in the western parts of Scotland is a profitable source of alkaline ash for the glass and soap maker. As a litter for horses it it in great request in some parts of Wales, Ireland and Scotland. The stalks are used as material for thatching, and this seems to be a very ancient practice – as early as the year 1349. In the Forest of Dean, pigs are fed upon the fronds. A botanical friend of our own, rather given to speculative devices, sent us one day a dish, consisting of the lower parts of the stem of this fern cut off just below the ground so as to return the delicate appearance of underground growth, assuring us that it was quite equal to asparagus. It was accordingly cooked and served as seakale or asparagus and pronounced to be quite palatable, though not equal to either of the other named vegetables. It might, however, well form a substitute for them, and, being so easily and inexpensively obtained, it is surprising that it does not oftener find its way to the poor man's table.'

RIGHT: **Bracken, found in every continent except Antarctica often dominates our woodlands, the fronds frequently growing higher than 2m (6ft 6in). Each year new fronds arise from the stout underground rhizome and are initially covered with brown hairy scales, although these soon fall off. As the fronds begin to uncoil they look surprisingly like a collection of bishop's crosiers. Soon after this, glands in the axils of the fronds produce a liquid so like that of flowering plants that the structures are referred to as 'extra-floral nectaries' and are much appreciated by insects, particularly ants. Mature fronds have channelled stems with divided triangular blades which are folded backwards. The sori occur in a row along the underside of the margins of the lobe and protected both by hair-like structures and by the tendency of the pinnae (leaflets) to roll inwards.**

The mountain fern. The sori are protected by folded scales called indusia arranged around the edges of the pinnae – a feature enabling the species to be easily identified during the reproductive phase.

Despite its dense cover often shading out the other members of the herb layer, especially the flowers, bracken has some useful part to play in woodland ecology. Few plants provide better cover for ground nesting birds and nocturnal animals which wish to hide from their predators during the day.

Mountain fern is also known as the lemon scented fern because of the smell of the crushed plant. This lovely fern is a feature of many upland woods, especially those graced by towering waterfalls hurling spray into the undergrowth. The species appears to avoid areas of chalk and limestone and since it can also be found at low levels I prefer to call it the lemon scented fern. The rootstock is short and from this the fronds arise in tufts clothed with a light layer of yellowish glandular hairs. It is these hairs which provide the lemony scent.

The hard fern is another species found in many British woodlands, except those on chalk and limestone. It is an evergreen which also has separate reproductive fronds rather than sori on the vegetative fronds. The stiff, erect reproductive stalk is much narrower and the oblong shaped sori are found in pairs on the undersurface of the pinnae. Because of this shape the hard fern is often called the herring bone fern. After the dispersal of the spores the reproductive fronds die, but the vegetative fronds remain throughout the year and deep greenery can add succulent colour to the dark, winter woodland.

Common throughout Britain in all types of woodlands the male fern can be recognized by its sori which are found in groups on the underside of the frond. These are protected when ripe by a grey kidney-shaped indusium which distinguishes the species from all others. The fronds are carried on very stout stalks and covered in orange-brown scales. If each lobe of the male fern is examined it will be found to be made up of smaller lobes each with a toothed margin – each plant may have as many as 30 fronds arising from a single root stock.

The lady fern is found in damp woodlands, often close to the male fern – it was once thought that this more delicate looking species was the mate of the male fern, but they have long been recognized as separate species. Lady fern has an almost worldwide distribution but varies a great deal depending upon the conditions in which it is growing. When found in damp woodlands they can grow up to 1.5m (almost 5ft) high and 0.5m ($1\frac{1}{2}$ft) across the frond. It has a soft texture and arises from a stout, often upright rhizome clothed in rusty coloured scales. The new fronds unroll with surprising speed during April and May being initially covered with red brown scales which have a strong smell, but they soon wither and fall off. Lady fern is deciduous and the fronds wither after the first frosts of autumn.

One of the most easily recognized ferns is the common polypody. The fronds are oblong-oval but, like the lady fern it varies considerably according to the habitat in which it is growing. It is often found growing high in a tree with its fleshy rhizome embedded in a cushion of mosses between the main trunk and a stout branch. Such species can be as small as 7.5cm (3in) but those growing beneath the tree in a layer of leaf mould overlying a fertile soil can be as high as 60cm (2ft). The rootstock was at one time avidly searched for and was said to be a sure remedy in the treatment of lung diseases and also of whooping cough.

The tough frond is evergreen and extremely resistant to frost and is therefore often found by winter walkers – yet another reason why naturalists should never hibernate during this season. The frond is surprisingly un-fern like and is lobed, rather than divided, into large numbers of smaller pinnae. The large circular sori are also unusual, having no indusium to protect and cover them but the sori are bright orange in colour. They can be found in a ripe condition from early June to late October and are arranged in regular rows on either side of the mid-rib.

No account of woodland ferns would be complete without some mention of the horsetails which, although they have some distant relationship to the ferns, are placed in their own family – the equisetaceae – of which there are around 25 species although only seven occur in Britain. All have jointed underground rhizomes (or rootstocks) from which erect, jointed stems arise. Horsetails are among the most primitive plants living at the present time and may well have been present 400 million years ago. They are interesting to the biologist because they were the first plants to develop a vascular support system strong enough to make them at least partially independent of water.

During the carboniferous period approximately 300 million years ago horsetails may have been the dominant plants which were gradually crushed to form vast coal deposits: some of these truly giant horsetails were almost 30m (100ft) high! In the woodlands of today we find only a pale shadow of these dinosaurs of the plant world and the horsetail (*Equisetum telemateia*) is common in damp areas. This fern can grow to a height of 1.5m (about 5ft) and is easily recognized by the slender branches drooping delicately from the white jointed stem, almost woodlike in its texture. At the end of the stem is a cone-like structure called a strobilus in which the globular spores are produced. These are catapulted out by elators similar to those of mosses described above. In the horsetails, however, each spore contains chlorophyll and the prothallus soon manufactures its own food. Another unique feature of the horsetail is that there are separate male and female prothalli carried on the same body. When the sperm cells are released they must have a film of water in order to swim to the female cell to which they are chemically attracted.

The stems are hollow, but they have solid joints called nodes and the surface of the stem is marked by a series of ridges and grooves, each species having its own unique pattern.

Of the seed bearing plants only **conifers** are non flowering and have been discussed already. They have made one most significant advance over the lower plants by making their reproductive process independent of water although the reproductive generations are still present. The visible part of the conifer, which we call the tree, is the sporophyte while the gametophyte is very much reduced, represented only by parts of the pollen grain and the ovule. The male gamete is in the pollen grain carried either by wind or animal to the female cell, and is therefore independent of water. Too often the woodland walker's eyes are dazzled by the banks of coloured flowers and foliage of the lower plants is lost in a sea of green. The occasional flash of colour is provided by the lichens and fungi – a welcome reminder of just how important these organisms are in the ecology of British woodlands.

Once the female ovule has been fertilized by the male gamete contained in the pollen, the young plant develops but is not protected, unlike the embryo of flowering plants which have fruits enclosing the seeds. The seeds of conifers, in contrast, have no surrounding fruit and are therefore termed naked explaining why they are called gymnosperms – gymnos is Greek for naked.

Flowers

DECIDUOUS trees produce blossoms which are, of course, flowers and usually called woody perennials. There are also herbs which are commonly called flowers which die down and are not obvious during the cold weather. The whole basis of evolution is variation and one of the greatest thrills for a natural historian is in the study and understanding of these often subtle differences. Within the family groups of flowering plants the number of sepals in the calyx will vary as will the number of petals in the corolla, stamens in the androecium, carpels in the gynoecium and egg cells in the ovule. The possible variations are infinite, but a basic knowledge of flower structure is obviously the key to identification.

The buttercup for example, has a large number of carpels each of which has a single ovule. The petals are all of the same shape and the flower can therefore be described as radially symmetrical. The buttercup is a typical member of the ranunculacea family and this contrasts sharply with the rose family (to which, incidentally, the hawthorn belongs) and to the clover and pea family – leguminosae. A legume means a pod and typical leguminous plants are the broom, gorse, the vetches, sweet pea, and the clovers. Such flowers have only a single carpel but this contains a row of ovules. The petals are not all the same shape, either the top and bottom petals differing from those on either side – an arrangement described as bilaterally symmetrical.

Obviously, there are many other variations in flower shape – the petals may be actually fused together as in the trumpets in the daffodil, and the arrangement of the flowers along the stem may also vary. The various ways that the flowers are grouped on the shoot is called the inflorescence.

Whatever the arrangement of the flower may be, they all have one thing in common – to ensure that ripe pollen from the male anthers reaches a receptive stigma of the female, the process being called pollination. Cross pollination is the transfer of pollen from one flower to the stigma of a different flower of the same species. This ensures that the genus which determine the plant's characteristics are given a good shake-up and there is no chance of in-breeding weaknesses, the case during self-pollination, giving evolution much less raw material to work upon. Cross pollination may be carried out by either wind or insects and whichever method is employed will result in differences in the design of both pollen grain and in the stigma which receives it.

Insect pollinated flowers are large and brightly coloured so that they can be seen, and a strong – but not necessarily attractive to the human senses – scent is also typical. The insects need a reason, other than philanthropy, to visit a flower and nectar is produced for this purpose although some species, including bees may also eat some pollen. The anthers tend to produce large pollen grains which are either

OPPOSITE:

It is not easy to understand why Solomon's seal is so named since it has absolutely no connection with the wise old King. The Victorian naturalist Prior offered the following explanation in his book *Popular Names of British Plants*:

> **'From the flat round scars of the root-stock resembling what is called a Solomon's seal, a name given by the Arabs to a six pointed star, formed by two equilateral triangles intersecting each other, and of frequent occurrence in Oriental tales.'**

After the flowering period is over the plant becomes less easy to see until autumn when the fertilized flowers on the column develop into berries which are green at first but later a succulent scarlet. They are poisonous to man, but birds, especially pheasants, find them a valuable food.

Flower structure

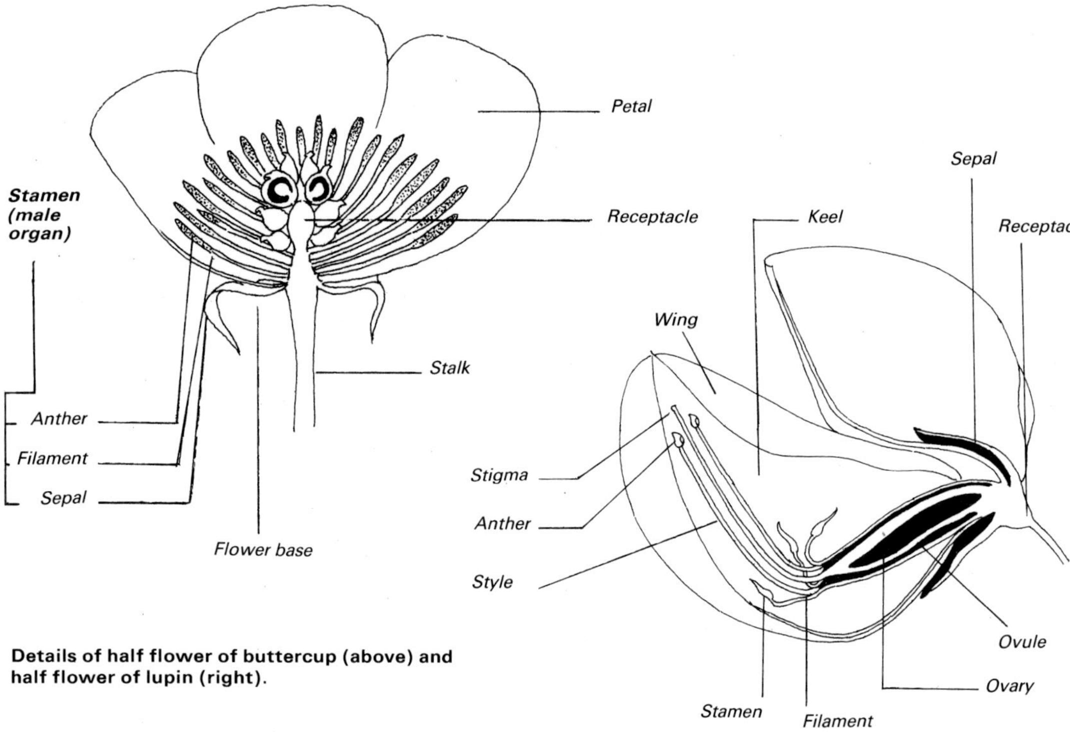

Details of half flower of buttercup (above) and half flower of lupin (right).

ALL flowers have the same basic design, but there are obviously many and various diversions from this theme. Simple flowers are found in such useful plants as hawthorn, damson and cherry. The flower is supported on a pedicel the end of which is swollen into a drum-like structure called the receptacle. This supports the rest of the flower, the parts of which are organized in a series of rings.

The outer ring consists of green, leaf-like (indeed they are modified leaves) structures called sepals. The collective name for the sepals is the calyx and its function is to fold around and protect the rest of the flower while it is still in bud. Inside the calyx is a ring of petals, together known as the corolla which may be brightly coloured – especially in flowers which are insect pollinated. At the base of the petals of insect pollinated flowers you can find a hollow but thickened area containing nectar which is a solution of sugar and is the fuel which fires the insects. An even closer look at a petal will reveal a series of lines running towards the nectary, called honey guides.

In the centre of the flower is the androecium which is the male portion of the structure. It is made up of a varying number of stamens, each consisting of a stalk called the filament and a knob-like structure called pollen sacs holding the pollen grains which are equivalent to the sperm cells of a male animal.

The pollen must join with the female cells produced in the gynoecium situated in the centre of the flower and made up of varying number of carpels, each of which consists of three parts. At the top is a swollen structure called the stigma and this leads, via a long style, to another swollen structure at the base called the ovary. Within this ovary are ovules attached to the wall by means of a short stem and within which there is a tiny egg cell. This cannot be seen without a microscope and around each egg cell is an embryo sac. Very high magnification is required to see a tiny hole in the wall of the ovule. This is called the microphyle and it is through this that the growing pollen grain passes in order to reach the egg.

Once the pollen grain has arrived on the stigma the completion of the reproductive cycle depends upon its growth through the stigma down the style and its fusion with the female nucleus. Why cannot any pollen grain achieve this instead of only those of the same species? It seems that the food for this growth is provided by the tissues of the stigma and each species of flowering plant has its own unique strength of fluid within the organ.

Although fertilization follows pollination, the interval between them can vary considerably from as little as a few hours to almost a whole year. The pollen grain produces a tube which grows down towards and then into an ovule through the

Details of a flower (top) and flower stalk (bottom).

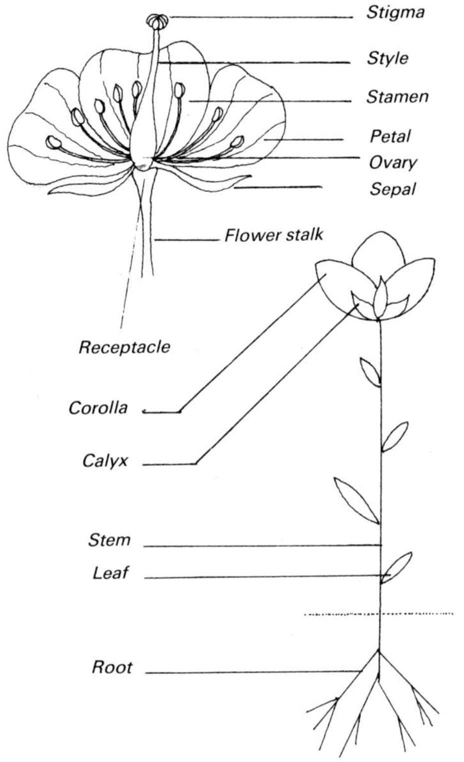

Examples of inflorescences.

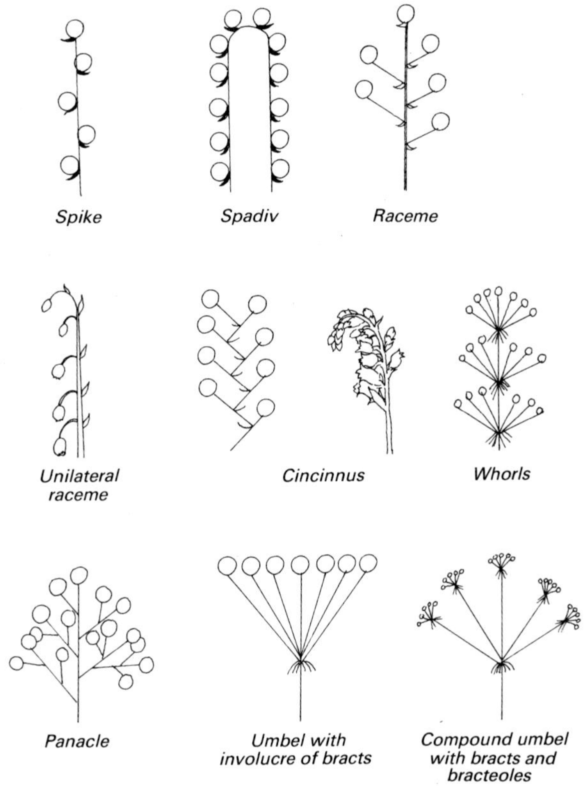

micropyle. Once the pollen tube is inside the ovule the end breaks open and the male nucleus enters and fertilizes the female cell. Following the successful union, the petals and the female parts, all now redundant, wither and fall off although the petals sometimes remain attached but usually dry and shrivelled.

The fertile egg cell now begins to divide and produce an embryo made up of a tiny root called the radicle, another small shoot called the plumule and one or two primitive leaves called cotyledons which usually contain food reserves. In other seeds the food reserves are stored on a special tissue called the endosperm. Flowering plants are classified either as monocotyledons or dicotyledons depending upon the number of these embryo leaves – the former being the more primitive condition.

The integuments of the ovules gradually thicken and harden to produce the protective testa of the seed and in the final stages of seed formation most of the water is removed in which condition the structure can survive both extremes of heat and cold. In addition to this, the enclosing ovary wall may become dry and hard, as in the poppy family, or it may become succulent and fleshy, as in a gooseberry or a plum. After fertilization the whole ovary is called the fruit with the embryo plus its protective case being the seed.

Insect pollinated plants include honeysuckle, dog rose and primrose. As the insect pokes its head inside in search of nectar its hairy body is dusted with pollen. When the insect visits the next flower the pollen in its body is rubbed onto its stigma and new pollen is collected. Self pollination is usually prevented by the male and female organs ripening at different times – some species have separate male and female flowers, however, and others have developed complex arrangements to keep the sexes apart. As man's involvement with, and dependence on, plants developed, methods of ensuring cross pollination artificially have been perfected.

Dog roses – an example of an insect pollinated plant.

spikey or sticky to become attached to the insect's body. In order to receive the pollen the stigmas of insect pollinated flowers tend to be situated inside the flower and to be large and sticky themselves.

Ingenious experiments have shown that insects, bees in particular, are attracted to flowers by shape, colour and smell accounting for the wonderfully attractive flowers which grace our countryside. Without bees there would have been no colourful flowers, and vice versa, since the evolution of one stimulated that of the other – a perfect example of nature's intricate yet fundamental harmonies. On occasions the connection between flowers is even more intimate – literally! Some orchids have flowers which resemble the females of the species – the bee orchid for example, but there are also fly, spider, wasp and butterfly orchids – and the male insect becomes coated with pollen when he tries to copulate with the flower. Some flowers have even evolved a scent resembling the sexual attractant of the insect (a pheromone) ensuring many male visitors and successful pollination.

On the other hand, wind pollinated flowers tend to be small, not very colourful, have no smell and do not produce nectar – indeed it would be wasteful to do so. The pollen grains are produced in far larger numbers and are smaller, lighter and smoother so that they are not slowed down by weight or friction. The pollen has to be caught and so the stigmas tend to be very much branched and feathery.

As in all other habitats, the wildlife in a woodland is battling for survival, the weakest species dying out. This battle is very obvious among the animals when the vole is hunted by the weasel, woodcock by fox, squirrel by pine marten and the small birds doing their best to avoid the owl by night and the sparrowhawk by day. A much more subtle fight, however, is being waged among the plants as they struggle for the light from which they make their food. The best period for obtaining light is during the long summer days and the trees such as oak and beech produce their leaves during this period. Their dense foliage prevents light reaching the smaller plants growing below them and this is why shrubs such as elder, hawthorn and hazel come into leaf during May building up their food reserves prior to the period of summer shade. The flowers such as bluebell, violet, dog's mercury, primrose and wood sorrel are therefore forced to flower early in the spring in order to prevent their being shaded out by the shrubs. Finally plants such as liverworts and mosses which grow on the woodland floor must have their peak period of activity during the winter when there are no larger species in leaf. Thus a typical British deciduous woodland has four distinct layers called the ground layer, herb layer, shrub layer and canopy layer. Naturalists wishing to study a woodland properly must make regular visits throughout the year and it will soon be realized that winter is far from a dead season – there are plants making use of every shaft of cold winter sunshine.

It is the colourful spring flowers, however, which splendidly remind us all that warm days are ahead. In summer the shady depths of the woodlands support fewer species and flowers must make use of the clearings and edges. Finally as the leaves fall from the trees a number of late blooming flowers come into their own.

Early one **February** morning, with an icy breeze rustling the branches of a gnarled old ash festooned wity ivy, I shivered in the shelter of the tree watching a hungry rabbit searching among the frozen leaf litter for some morsel of greenery. I noticed that the dog's mercury (*Mercurialis perennis*) was already peeping through and earning its reputation as one of the earliest flowers to appear. The rabbit, however, carefully avoided nibbling the leaves – a very wise move since the plant is related to the spurges and shares their poisonous properties. This may be one reason why

A cranesbill showing the honey guides. Although we have colour vision it does not entirely equate with that of insects which are able to detect ultra-violet light. When viewed in ultra-violet the honey guides can be seen clearly, showing the route taken from the top of the petal to the nectary gland at the base and functions in a similar manner to the landing lights marking an airport runway.

this plant dominates large areas of our woodlands. There are two species of mercury growing in Britain, the other being the less poisonous common annual mercury (*Mercurialis annua*) which does not flower until July. Surprisingly both species have been used by herbalists in times past, and annual mercury was once a popular pot herb. The seventeenth century herbal compiled by John Gerard recommended annual mercury, which he called French mercury, for preparing enemas. Dog's mercury, so named because it was very common, is so fierce a purgative that it is dangerous, and many old woodlanders associated it with the Devil – one of its old names being boggart's (meaning a demon) plant.

Both species grow on erect stems about 30cm (1ft) in height, arising from a perennial underground creeping stem called a rhizome. The male flowers are separate from the females, but both are tiny and seldom measure more than 0.5cm ($\frac{1}{4}$in) across. The yellow-green male flowers are borne on slender racemes often containing over 20 blooms at the end of a long stalk, whilst the female blooms are carried on a shorter spike containing only two or three flowers which are also greenish. In Britain there seem to be far fewer female flowers meaning that the pollen carried on the wind has little chance of achieving a successful pollination. The spread is therefore mainly by vegetative means and some botanists believe that whenever dog's mercury is found growing in the open it is indicative that the area under study was once part of an ancient woodland. The use of plants as indicator species is becoming increasingly common and there is no doubt that the technique being developed will soon be a vital tool of the natural historian.

The word primrose means the first rose and is an accurate description of this delightful flower's delicate scent even though it is not a member of the rose family. It was only when speaking to my herbalist grandmother who was well versed in the

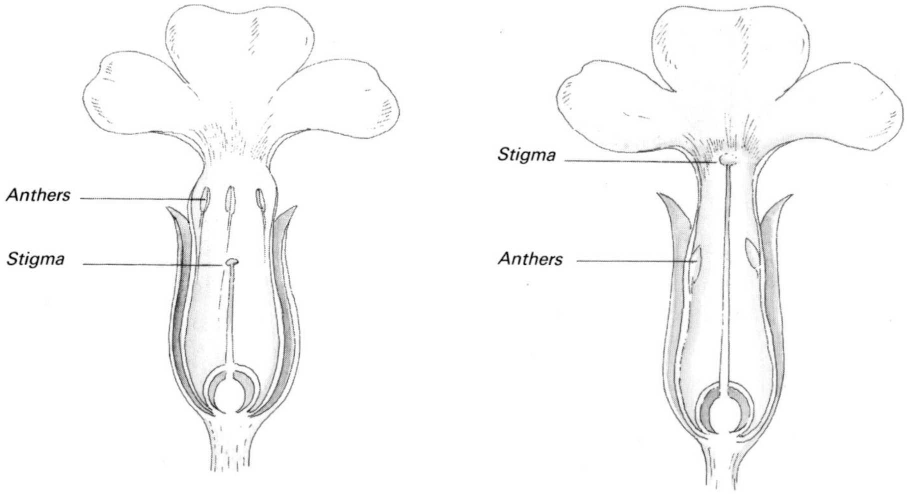

Details of the thrum eyed (left) and pin eyed (right) primroses. Both are composed of yellow petals joined into a tube below and opening out into a spreading disc. In the centre of the pin eyed flowers there is the green head of the stigma looking just like a pin's head. In the thrum eyed variety it is not the female stigma which takes the eye but five male anthers arranged in a ring round the tube. If the two flowers are split down the centre and compared, the pin eyed flower is seen to have five anthers looking like little sacs hanging on the wall of the tube, while the thrum eyed variety has a stigma knob situated low down inside the flower. In both varieties the ovary is found at the base of the stigma stalk and around it are the nectaries. It is for this that the insects visit the primroses and during their search for honey pollinate the plant.

country crafts that I discovered that primrose ointment was used in the treatment of sceptic and often green wounds – hence Parkinson's description of the 'green primrose'. The ointment is made by gently warming the flowers of primrose with animal fat – I have used it ever since with good effect.

Primroses illuminate the south facing banks of open woodlands by the end of **March** and can dominate the area throughout April. They grow from thick underground stems called a rhizome containing vast stores of food, made by the leaves of spring and early summer.

A close look at a bank of primroses will reveal that there are two basic types of flower called thrum eyed and pin eyed – carried on different plants. It was Charles Darwin in the middle of the nineteenth century who first let us into the secret of the primrose. The corolla tube formed from the base of the petals is deep inside the flower and only a long tongued insect can reach the honey. He believed that moths were the chief agents in the cross pollination of the primrose and the pale flowers are certainly very conspicuous in the fading light of evening. It is at this time that the scent is so strong and the whole woodland is filled with its delicate sweetness.

If an insect starts by collecting honey from a pin eyed flower it gets pollen on the central area of its tongue – called the proboscis. This comes from the anthers half way down the tube. In nature there are about the same numbers of both pin eyed and thrum eyed flowers and the insect is quite likely to come across a thrum eyed flower next. The pollen on the proboscis is now just at the right position to rub off on the stigma of the thrum eye. In the meantime, the head at the base of the proboscis receives pollen from the long stamens which is deposited on the prominent stigma of the next pin eyed flower providing the moth with nectar.

It is fascinating to find that the pollen grains of the two flowers differ. The grain from the thrum eyed flower is much larger and the stigma of the pin eyed flower is rougher in order to receive it. This is obviously because the grains from the thrum eyed flower fall on the long stigma of the pin eyed flower and have further to grow before they reach the ovary. They therefore need more food stores and are consequently larger. Not only has the primrose evolved these differences in order to be pollinated by moths but the development of the moth has also been profoundly influenced by availability of nectar.

I remember being taken by an old Cumbrian naturalist into our local wood to look for St Peter's keys and it was only much later that I learned to call the nodding heads of this lovely plant by the name of cowslip. It's quite strange how the association with keys has followed the cowslip through many cultures. In both

Sweden and Holland cowslips were called the Keys of May and were thought to have belonged to the goddess Hulda and to open the gates of her palace which was loaded with treasure. The Norse culture also had their key to spring, in this case dedicated to the goddess Freyer. Obviously the Christian missionaries had to overcome these green religions and they simply re-dedicated the cowslip to St Peter or on occasion to the Virgin Mary.

Cowslips begin to come into leaf early in spring each appearing as a member of a rosette above ground looking like a coiled spring. Each resembles a primrose but rather shorter and more rounded. At one time the very young leaves, whilst still tender, were used as a constituent of a salad.

The rosette is thought to be of value to the plant in the sense that it serves to funnel water down to the root. From the centre of the rosette rises the long flower stalk and at the tip appears the flower buds resembling green crinkled bags. As the bags open the golden blooms burst and droop to produce the typical shape of the cowslip. Like the primrose, the flowers are of the pin and thrum eyed type and are pollinated by bees, which combine to increase the chance of hybrids arising.

In the wild windy days of March and early April the delicate looking blooms of wood anemone (*Anemone nemorosa*) swing from their slender yet pliable stems, and defy the strongest storm. The white, star-like flowers glint from their brown bed of dead leaves and withered bracken. They grow so quickly from a tough root stock running horizontal to, and just below, the ground that vast carpets of wood anemones dominate many woodlands. The flower stalks have an arrangement of three leaf-like structures situated just below the flower head, their function being initially to protect the developing bud during the bitter weather of late winter. Once the flower has burst, these leaf-like organs prevent insects crawling up the stem to eat the blossoms.

The main characteristic of the flower is that it has entirely dispensed with petals, and the sepals make the plant so beautiful. Although the occasional flying insect lands on the blooms there is no apparent reason for the visit since there is little, if any, scent and no nectar at all. It seems likely that the plant is usually self-pollinated or vegetatively propagated with the occasional crossing bringing in new genes to prevent the in-breeding of weaknesses.

The unusual orchid twayblade (*Listera ovata*) grows commonly in damp woodlands throughout Britain but is often overlooked because the flower is usually obscured by the pair of ribbed leaves from which its name derives – it was also once known by the equally descriptive name of bifoil. Twayblade's scientific name Listera is in memory of the English botanist Dr Martin Lister who died in 1711 and ovata derives from the egg shape of the rounded leaves.

A wood anemone.

A child's sense of right and wrong is often quite disarming as I discovered on a blustery day in **April** as I guided a group of young naturalists through a wood. When I told them that toothwort (*Lathraea squamaria*) was a most unusual plant which did not make its own food but lived as a parasite two little girls refused point blank either to draw it, look at it or write about it!

Toothwort develops disc like suckers which grow into the roots of trees and soak up their vital juices – it does not seem to be too particular about its choice of trees, but conifers are seldom attacked. Hazel is a particular favourite and I have noticed an increasing number of sycamores attacked by the parasite. The flowering shoots pushing above ground are ivory-like (hence tooth wort) and covered by thick scales overlapping like roof tiles. The word squamaria derives from the Latin word meaning a scale. There is no green about the plant at all indicating its reliance on parasitism and in recent years scientists have suggested that the toothwort might

ABOVE: **Broomrape (*Orobanchaceae*). This plant is a close relative of toothwort and is rather an uncommon species living as a complete parasite. The semi-parasitic common cow-wheat (*Melampyrum pratense*) and wood cow-wheat (*Melampyrum sylvaticum*) are also related, the latter being less common but found in mountainous woodlands between Yorkshire and Inverness.**

OPPOSITE: **The blooms of the cowslip also possess red spots which were at one time thought to be a sign that the fairies had kindly removed the freckles from some unfortunate girl. For this reason many old herbalists recommended cowslip water for skin lotions. Cowslip wine was also thought to be a good skin tonic.**

also be insectivorous. However, this opinion is not so new. Whilst reading *Wild Flowers as they Grow* by H Essenhigh Corke and G Clarke Nuttall – published in 1912 – I came across the following:

> 'But the toothwort is something more than an ordinary parasite, and has another source of supply for its needs, though for long this was not suspected, and indeed it takes a very careful examination to reveal this side of its character. The mystery lies in the apparently solid-looking thick white scales, for they are not so solid as they appear at first sight. If we remove one we find that on its under surface near the junction with the stem, is a little canal running across it, and into this canal open, by very minute apertures, some extraordinary winding chambers which are hollowed out in the flesh of the scale. These chambers vary in number, but the average number is ten, and, if we examine them closely with the microscope, we find that they have all over their interior two sorts of peculiar structures, one set looking like little mushrooms and the other like small domes.
>
> Now the question comes, what can be the purpose of these most mysterious chambers? And the answer is that they are ingenious animal traps of a kind that is probably unique in the whole realm of plant life. Of course, they can only entrap animals of the most minute description – the tiniest flies, infusoria, and the like – but such as these creep into the canals from the soil and eventually slip through into the chambers. Directly they get inside they come into contact with the little mushroom and dome-like structures on the walls, and these immediately send out long filaments like tentacles, which seize and hold their prey. And very soon all that remains of the intruder, if he be a fly, is his bristles, legs and hair; if he be merely a jelly-like amoeba – nothing! All has been absorbed by the white fleshy scales. We do not know what lures the insects into these death chambers; perhaps it is adventurous exploration, but more probably it is a search for food. When we remember that there are some ten chambers in every scale, and a very large number of scales on the many branching thick stems, we can realize that the annual "catch" of insect life is comparatively very great, and moreover, since the scales do not fall off in winter-time nor are greatly affected by the frost in their under-ground seclusion, the process goes on all the year round. In this way it differs from the parasitic habit of the plant, for the suckers on the roots only work when the tree is in full leaf in summer-time. When the leaves fall and the tree hibernates, the suckers wither away and sever the connection. When spring comes and the sap once more begins to flow new suckers form and the old routine commences afresh. Thus in summer-time the plant is both insectivorous and parasitic, and may be considered a gross feeder.'

What we see above the ground are the straight flowering fleshy branches reaching heights of up to 30cm (1ft). The flowers themselves have a slightly bluish tint and are covered by glistening white hairs. There are four sepals and inside these are four petals, both sets being united to form tubes concealing and protecting the male and female organs. At the base of the ovary is a yellow cushion-like structure full of nectar serving to attract the bees which pollinate the toothwort. Should an insect fail to pay a visit the stamens grow longer and the pollen is spread by the wind.

Tucked in the sheltered slopes of south-facing woodlands the first flowers of the delicate common violet (*Viola riviniana*) can be found in February, but are seen at their best in March and April. The leaves, still succulent from June onwards, are the essential food plant of five species of woodland based fritillary butterflies. These are the small pearl-bordered (*Boloria selene*), pearl bordered (*Boloria euphrosyne*), high brown (*Argynnis adippe*), dark green, (*Argynnis aglaia*) and the silver-washed fritillary (*Argynnis paphia*). These species will also eat dog violet (*Viola canina*), which blooms later in the year and maintains a continual supply of leaves until the late autumn.

Violets are very variable and individual species are difficult to classify. The plant

is usually rather smooth and arises from a short central rhizome. The broad leaves are arranged in a rosette and flowers branch from it, each backed by a short broad spur. In the dog violet the rhizome merges into a distinct stem carrying the flowers and the sepals are narrower and more pointed than those of the common violet. Both species are, however, very common – to appreciate this, one needs to examine the field layer very closely and part the taller vegetation.

Although the Moschatel (*Adoxa moschatellina*) is not uncommon, the colonies of this tiny green flower are often overlooked as they grow tucked away in the dark confines beneath the shade of tree stumps, of which ash seems to be a particular favourite. The flowers appear early in March, but are at their best in mid-April. During the short growing season, food is passed down from the leaves into a system of corms and runners which break apart when the parent decays. This method accounts for the appearance of large colonies of moschatel but it also has a sexual method to ensure that there is some mixing of the genes.

Pollination of the plant is effected by small insects. Each stem bears flowers that point in four directions with yet another flower pointing upwards – this accounts for its alternative name of town hall clock, the old woodlanders believing that the 'clock' pointing upwards was to acquaint the Almighty with the stem. Insects are attracted to the 'town hall' by the very faint smell of rotting meat and the generous supply of nectar.

The versatile flower is also able to pollinate itself if the insect supply dries up by closing its petals which serves to squeeze the reproductive parts together. In time berries develop which are eaten, and so dispersed, by small birds. It also seems that moschatel seeds germinate best only after exposure to low winter temperatures.

Nearly 600 years ago, St Patrick used the three part leaves of the wood sorrel (*Oxalis acetosella*) to explain the Holy Trinity to the Irish and it has been used as the shamrock ever since. I have been taken to task many times by Irish friends who insist that the Shamrock used on the Saints day on 17th March is either a separate plant or a type of clover. Surely, however, it must be the common wood sorrel that he used because it is in leaf on this day in the shady areas of damp woodlands throughout Britain. The clovers only come into leaf much later in the year.

The leaves are rich in oxalic acid once known as binoxalate of potash or salts of sorrel. Although mildly poisonous this substance gives a pleasantly sharp flavour to the leaves and made them popular in salads and used to produce a green sauce, served with fish. Wood sorrel leaves were also brewed into a concoction which was used to quench thirst, reduce high fever and to ease ulcerated mouths.

The delicate flowers resemble the cranesbill family to which they are related and have five sepals joined to produce a cup-like calyx. There are also five white petals, delicately veined with purple honey guides and joined at their bases and there are ten stamens of which five are long and five short. There are also five styles arising from an ovary containing five chambers.

The honey guides, as their name implies, lead to a nectary but few insects appear to avail themselves of it and the wood sorrel is therefore obliged to make some provision for self-pollination. It does this in two ways. First, the flower closes up so tightly at night that the male and female parts are pressed together. Secondly, and much more intriguingly, very tiny flowers of a special type are produced. They are concealed by the leaves and the tiny twisted petals never open out but retain the shape of a tiny cup which eventually falls off. Inside this the male and female parts touch and fertile seeds are produced by these cleistogamous (hidden) flowers. The unusual reproduction arrangements of the wood sorrel does not end here and its method of seed dispersal is equally fascinating.

When pollinated, both types of flower head bend over and become tucked in under the leaves. As the seed within matures, the stalk straightens and a very remarkable thing happens within the capsule. The seed capsule has five chambers arranged spirally around a central column, each chamber containing two comparatively large seeds attached to the central column. The wall of the capsule opposite these seeds is so thin that it eventually ruptures. Each seed has two coats, the outer of which is transparent and quite thin, whilst the inner coat is black and hard. The space between the two coats gradually fills with sap and pushes with such force that the whole seed jerks inside out, bursts out of its dual skin and is hurtled several metres away from the parent. When ripe plants are shaken this bursting can be observed and as a boy I can remember them being called catapult fruits – another old country name was sling fruit.

In the days before the Wildlife and Countryside Act protected our flowers I remember my father visiting a local wood and bringing home lily of the valley the scent of which filled the house. When my father was called up in 1940 I went to the wood to search for my mother's favourite flower. I remembered the broad flat leaves and it was only on my arrival home that the stench of wild garlic, or ramsons (*Allium ursinum*), told me that the leaves of the two plants are so much alike.

The white star-like flowers are very attractive especially when they dominate the whole of a damp woodland between late April and early June. Some say that the stench is intolerable but I find it pleasant especially when wafted on the breeze from a distant wood. The flowers are carried in groups called umbels on a triangular shaped stem. Storing food in an underground corm, wild garlic has been used as a substitute for the culinary herb, but it is usually far too strong.

The lily of the valley, on the other hand, prefers dry woodlands, especially those dominated by ash when quite large areas can be so covered with lily of the valley that they can be located by scent alone.

The scent is so strong that the bees have no trouble in finding the white flowers with six stamens situated at the top of a bell formed by the union of the sepals and petals. The main pollinators are the bees and the resultant cherry red fruits hang down giving rise to another vernacular name – our lady's tears. Although these seeds are fertile its most effective method of reproduction is through vegetative propagation.

Despite the fact that lily of the valley contains poisonous compounds it was once very popular with herbalists. There was supposed to be a special virtue contained in water distilled from the flowers and was known as golden water (*Aqua aurea*) – it was so valuable that it was kept only in vessels of silver or gold. In Coles' herbal, written in 1657, the recipe is given:

> 'Take the flowers and steep them in New Wine for the space of a month; which, being finished, take them out again and distill the Wine three times over in a Limbeck. This Wine is more precious than gold; for if anyone that is troubled with Apoplexy drink thereof with six grains of pepper and a little Lavander water they shall not need to fear it that moneth.'

A century before this, the German physician wrote that:

> 'a Glasse being filled with the flowers of May Lilies and set in an Ant Hill with the mouth close stopped for a month's space, and then taken out, ye shall find a liquor in the glass which being outwardly applied helps the gout very much.'

It was also reputed to be useful in the treatment of nervous disorders and headaches, being used with some success in the First World War to treat victims of gas poisoning.

ABOVE: **The leaves of wood sorrel arise from the slender creeping rhizome and are usually bright green above, tending to be purplish on the undersurface. Each of the three leaflets is folded along its mid-rib and are very sensitive only fully extending when in deep shade. As soon as the leaflets are struck by the sun they fold up tightly into a pyramidal structure. The leaflets also fold during the night but along the mid-ribs.**

OPPOSITE: **Haslemere Wood in the winter.**

Although herbal cures fascinate me it cannot be stressed too often that such cures can often create more problems than they solve. In any event, the distribution of lily of the valley is local and many populations are shrinking and require strict protection.

One of the earliest and most delightful flowers of the early spring is the lesser celandine which is yet another example of a species so common that it is too often overlooked or taken for granted. During the summer and autumn the shiny, deep green heart-shaped leaves are manufacturing food to pass back to the storage organs – in this case, root tubers. If these tubers are dug up and washed they can be seen to be like a hanging bunch of figs accounting for its old country name of figwort. As soon as the winter frosts become less extreme, the golden starry blooms reflect each shaft of sunlight to illuminate the dreariness of the winter woodlands.

Because the flowers appear so early in the year when there are very few insects about, even the bright coloured petals and plentiful nectar do not produce a high rate of successful pollination and few fertile seeds are produced. The celandine overcomes this by having developed a fascinating reproductive strategy. Look at the point where the upper leaves join the stem and you will find a tiny rounded growth about the size of a wheat grain. When the leaves begin to die down in the summer these growths fall off. During heavy rain the growths float away and after lying dormant give rise to a new plant.

Despite its faint smell of 'tom-cat' few flowers of the spring are more attractive than the early purple orchid (*Orchis mascula*). The flower spikes can be up to 20cm (8in) high, arise as a stout column from a rosette of leaves and other strap-shaped leaves surround the flower. Low down on the flower spike there are one or more almost transparent and very delicate structures called bracts. When these catch the light just a hint of both green and purple can be detected. Higher up the stem and twisted around it is another bract which is more deeply dyed.

Once the early purple orchid is mature its pollination mechanism can be easily studied and the ingenious mechanism appreciated. A sharpened pencil is pushed into the flower and when removed two sticky pear-shaped pollinia are seen attached to the upper surface of the pencil. Bees searching for sugary juices found in the tissues of the big petal push their proboscis into the orchid and the pollinia become attached. Eventually the bee searches into another orchid by which time the sticky substance has become less effective and as the ripe female stigma is also sticky the pollen is transferred.

The flowers of the orchid are thus remarkable, but the underground portions are even more fascinating. There are two egg-shaped tubers fed by a series of pale, stout rootlets. One of the swellings provide food for the plant's immediate needs whilst the other swells up with reserves providing a store for the future. Because of the superficial resemblance to the testicle it is not surprising that orchids were used as aphrodisiacs and had sexual overtones. The fresh tuber was thought to promote true love and the withered one was helpful in the control of 'wrong passions'.

Despite being one of the commonest plants in damp woodlands the golden saxifrage (*Chrysosplenium oppositifolium*) is one of the least known, its tiny yellow flowers tucked in beneath taller plants or in the shade of a stream or tree trunk.

The round, spoon-shaped leaves are about 2.5cm (1in) across and are arranged in pairs accounting for the specific name of oppositifolium and distinguishing it from *Chrysosplenium alternifolium* – the alternate leaved golden saxifrage. This flowers earlier, often in February, has unbranched stems, a more tufted form of growth and the kidney-shaped leaves are, as the name implies, arranged alternately along the stem. The opposite leaved golden saxifrage was used by the old woodlanders to treat disorders of the spleen, explaining its scientific name of Chry-

An early purple orchid. Orchids are complex flowers and a close look at a single flower will reveal three sepals and three petals. Two of the sepals look like wings, the third forming an arch over the back of the lower. Two of the petals are small and pale being protected by the sepals, while the third is large and in the main part of the flower. The whole structure is quite stiff and is wrapped firmly around the stem forming a tube, which can be up to 1.25cm (½in) in length.

sosplenium, deriving from the Greek chrusos meaning gold and splen meaning spleen. The golden spleenwort, once known as rock-cress and eaten in salads, is in flower from April to June by which time the woodlands are beginning to be dominated by flowers able to tolerate greater degrees of shade.

Mention a British woodland to any naturalist and the picture conjured up will be one of tall trees surrounding open glades, full of the nodding heads and heady perfume of the bluebells in May. Look more closely and the white blooms of greater stitchwort blend into the red of campion and the yellow of herb bennet, whilst in the damp areas yellow iris and golden marsh marigold add to the riot of colour. Barren and edible wild strawberries are also found on shady banks whilst searchers after unusual plants will find comparative rarities such as herb Paris, Solomon's seal and orchids such as the lady's slipper. Those who find plants once used by country-folk and herbalists fascinating will not be disappointed either since lords and ladies, burdock, bugle and betony grow in most woodlands and even the ubiquitous nettle has played its part in botanical history.

At one time the scientist's name for the bluebell was *Hyacinthus non-scriptus* and in truth its delicately sweet perfume is very reminiscent of hyacinth. As scientific classification became more precise, however, it was found that all members of the hyacinth family had scribbling on the petals which looked as if someone had tried to form the initials A L. This writing was missing on the bluebell petals and accounts for its name non-scriptus (no-writing). Later it was discovered to have anatomical and physiological differences from the hyacinth and was removed from that family, given the name Endymion and assigned to the lily family.

Keats called the bluebell Sapphire, Queen of the mid-May and who could argue with this. Bluebells grow from an underground bulb – that is, a swollen stem protected by scale leaves and with a tuft of roots growing from its base. This bulb is a storehouse of energy which can be drawn upon when the bluebell comes into bloom only to be replaced when the long lance-shaped leaves soak up the rays of the late spring sunshine.

The strap-like leaves curl inwards and when it rains they channel the water straight down into the bulb and the roots below. Bluebell sap is very sticky and at one time was used to gum the leaves into books and the fletchers also used bluebell glue to stick the feathered flights onto the shafts of arrows. As a boy just after the war I used bluebell glue to stick pictures into a scrap book and they are still firmly stuck nearly 40 years later.

Each flower has six floral leaves – the petals – which are all alike and at first glance appear to be united into a bell from which the flower derives its name. A closer look, however, shows that the petals are separate and only joined at the base. Inside the bluebell the stamens are arranged one per segment with a long one alternating with a short one. In the centre is the ovary divided into three chambers each containing two columns of ovules around which arises the stigma catching the pollen. The rich nectar produced by bluebells serves to attract the butterflies pollinating them.

After fertilization the flowers wither and the ovaries become dry and feel like paper. The ovary walls become even thinner and as the flower heads shake in the wind the seeds are spread and the next generation of bluebells is assured.

The Victorian naturalist Richard Jefferies obviously loved the greater stitchwort (*Stellaria holustea*) and knew that its square, brittle, grass-like stems needs the support of other more sturdy plants to be seen at its most attractive. The long narrow leaves which taper to a point arise in pair directly from the stem:

'There shone on the banks white stars among the grass. Petals delicately white in a whorl of rays – light that had started radiating from a centre and become fixed – shining among the flowerless green'.

Stitchwort is pollinated by bees, moths, butterflies, beetles and flies which are provided with good supplies of nectar and attracted by the large stands of flowers which form patches of white as easily seen as drifts of late lying snow. The blossoms react to rain by closing and bending over so that the rain does not flush out the fertile pollen.

The old name for the plant was 'all bones' which obviously related to its jointed stems which are easily fragmented whilst prior to 1900 in the north of England, stitchwort was known as 'deadmen's bones'. The name stitchwort itself owes its origins to the belief that when brewed up with powdered acorns it was a sure remedy against a pain in the side.

The red campion (*Silene dioica*) is a perennial plant which can dominate areas of damp woodlands from **June** until September, but flowers can be found much later in the year. In 1984, for instance, I found several specimens on Christmas Day. The leaves found on the stem can reach 1m (3¼ft) in height and are quite narrow, whilst the ground-hugging rosette leaves, from the middle of which the flower arises, are egg-shaped. The five sepals are dark red, in contrast to the rosy pink petals, of which there appear to be ten, but close examination reveal only five each deeply cleft and appearing to be double. Within the ring of petals we do not find both stamens and stigmas but either one or the other since the sexes are carried on separate flowers – dioica which means two sexes.

Once the ovules have been fertilized in the campion family, the ovary of the female flower develops into an egg-shaped structure called a capsule functioning rather like a pepper pot. It splits into five at the narrow end, each segment curving outwards. The head of the plant swings in the wind and the seeds ejected.

Herb bennet (*Geum urbanum*) is a perennial plant also known as wood avens. It puts out only a few, almost hairless, straggling stems from an underground rhizome reaching 1m (3ft) in height, although half of this is more usual. Stipules – leaf-like structures at the junction of the true leaves and the stem – are in the avens and are very large round structures. Even the leaves themselves show great variation in shape depending upon where they are found. Those near the top of the stem are made up of three long, narrow leaflets. The centrally situated leaves are also divided into three but each is round in shape. The lower leaves are carried on long stems, along which are a series of small leaflets ending in a terminal leaflet much larger than any of the others.

The rose-like flowers are around 1.25cm (½in) across, look small compared to the rest of the plant and the deep yellow colour has a delicate attraction. The fruit is dark crimson in colour and made up of several parts each ending in a hook which enables the structure to stick to the fur of passing animals.

The derivation of the name is from the old herb-bene meaning the good herb and, mistakenly it seems, it was thought to be a medieval cure-all. The word Geum comes from the Greek meaning aromatic, and this is certainly a true description of the roots. They are a mild astringent and have also been used to flavour ale. This feature is also part of the make up of the closely related water avens (*Geum rivale*), also found in damp woodlands. The roots of the latter have a taste rather like cloves and are used to give the traditional flavour to Augsburg beer. It is a shorter, stouter and more hairy plant than wood avens and the drooping flowers are also very different – the combination of purple calyx and orange petals when looked at closely are startlingly attractive. It is only when the hooked fruits are in evidence that the close resemblance between the wood and water avens can be appreciated.

OVER: **Hazel woodlands on Islay. The trunks are distorted by wind and covered with moss.**

Although normally associated with swamps and river banks, the yellow flag iris (*Iris pseudacorus*) is a frequent member of damp woodlands especially alder-carr and woodlands fringing moorlands. It illumines the dark, damp areas of woodland from May until mid-July, often in the company of the equally colourful kingcup. At one time it was called the segg which had the same origin as sedge deriving from the Anglo-Saxon word meaning a small sword. This obviously relates to the long sharp leaves which arise from the stout underground rhizome. The flowers do indeed look flag-like, especially when waving in the breeze and it was also known as the fleur-de-lys, although several other plants have been suggested as the inspiration for the gallic heraldic device. The scientific name is interesting – Iris is Greek for a rainbow, an ideal choice for a genus of plants containing so many colourful species. The specific name pseudocorus is also Greek and indicates that it has a resemblance to another plant (pseudo) and acorus is the generic name for the sweet sedge.

When growing in wet open meadows or by riversides the marsh marigold (*Caltha palustris*) earns its Italian name of Sposa di Sole meaning bride of the sun. It is also found deep in the damp hollows of woodlands and alongside any tiny streams which trickle down the steep banks. The thick green stems, which may be 30cm (1ft) high, lift the simple flowers away from the heart-shaped leaves. The flowers lack petals and it is the sepals, of which there are five or six, which attract the insects to pollinate them. There are no obvious nectaries, but there is plenty of pollen to be found in the carpels, and hordes of flies, beetles, moths and bees soon learn where the supply can be tapped.

Only damp woodlands are suitable for kingcups since the stems soon wither in dry conditions and in the south west of England they were known as drunkards.

Marsh marigolds add a splash of spring colour to damp woodlands.

Barren (*Potentilla sterilis*) and wild strawberry (*Fragaria vesca*) are two delightful little plants found in woodlands and despite many differences it is easy to see why they are confused. Barren strawberry flowers earlier but is rather less common than the wild strawberry. It arises from a rhizome and has silky leaves covered with hairs. The upper surface of the barren strawberry leaves have no obvious veining whilst those of *Fragaria vesca* are also deeply grooved. The petals of the barren strawberry are notched – those of the wild strawberry lack this feature. Yet another difference is that the runners so typical of strawberry plants are never found in *Potentilla sterilis*, which also lacks the juicy, sweet-tasting fruits and has to make do, instead, with a cluster of dry seeds called achenes.

No member of the genus Solomon's seal is common in Britain, but the one most likely to be encountered is *Polygonatum multiflorum*, which typically flowers during June. It is found occasionally in a number of English woods and also a few in Scotland, but many people think that it is not indigenous north of the border. The stems of *P. multiflorum* are round distinguishing them from those of the well-named angular Solomon's seal (*Polygonatum officinale*), a much rarer plant confined to limestone woodlands.

Solomon's seal is a perennial, arising to a height of 60cm (2ft) from a stout rhizome, the first leaves being obvious from the middle of May. The large oval leaves, each with a pointed apex are very obviously ridged and grow alternately along the stem and partially clasp it by their bases. The leaves all face one direction and the flowers, arising in clusters in the axils of the foliage, droop in the opposite direction. These are creamy white and have an unusually waxy consistency particularly apparent near the tips which have a yellowish tinge. The fruits are bluish-black berries.

The generic name Polygonatum means many angled which may well relate to the jointed stem and multiflorum is also easily understood since the stem bears large numbers of flowers. This distinguishes this species from *P. officinale* where the flowers are mainly solitary.

Lady's slipper (*Cypripedium calceolus*) is a lovely orchid recognized by its large inflated lip and is one of Britain's rarest plants now found growing only in northern limestone woodlands and needing all the protection it can get. It is something of an indictment of our society that despite the accent on conservation and the existence of the Wildlife and Countryside Act that Our Lady's slipper has to be surrounded by sophisticated trip wires and guarded by a vigilant warden spending the flowering period on guard and living in a tent.

At one time the underground rhizome of the commonly occurring but unusual looking lords and ladies (*Arum maculatum*) was dug up and the starch contained within it dried and powdered. It was used for starching clothes and for powdering wigs and was thus always in demand – the old country name of starchwort has now all but died out.

The word maculatum means spotted and refers to the leaves which are deep shining green and shaped like arrows. Not all the leaves bear the purple spots and blotches giving the specific name, and botanists have not been able to discover whether the marks are inherited or merely occur by chance. This is but one of many examples of how much is left for us to discover of nature's secrets.

About a month after the leaves appear, usually in late March or early April, the uniquely shaped flower begins to develop consisting of a large green sheath. Gerard accurately described it as being 'in proportion to the ear of a hare'.

Within this spathe, the flower stalk appears resembling an erect male organ leading to many suggestive country names including wake robin, pop lady, cuckoo-baby and the equally saucy lords and ladies. In their book *Wild Flowers – Where They Grow* Cork and Nuttall provide us with a delightful description of the flower and fruits as well as considerable food for thought:

> 'The upper part of the flower spike is plain, purple and fleshy; below this, and just where the "waist" of the spathe occurs is a ring of hairs all pointing downwards; each of these hairs represents a tiny aborted flower. Below them again comes a circular group of yellow male flowers, each flower reduced to a single stamen only; beneath all is a broad ring of round knobs, each a female flower represented merely by a single ovary. Therefore, why is the plant sometimes called Ladies Finger. – "because of its rings", explain the children.
>
> 'A large number of small flies, either lying on or crawling about the walls of the enclosure would probably next strike our notice. Now the arrangements which the plant has contrived out of the above material, though rather complicated, are most interesting to work out.
>
> 'At the outset, when the spathe unfolds, the midges, attracted by the purple column – possibly, too, there may be a slight foetid odour – enter and crawl downwards past the "waist" into the hollow chamber, the downward-pointing hairs affording them every facility. They have probably come from another similar plant – if so they are covered with pollen dust. At this moment the female flowers are in a receptive state, and the flies, crawling about, necessarily rub them with their dusty bodies. It should be noticed that the midges cannot escape for in this lobster-pot-like enclosure the previously accommodating hairs now stand as an imposing and impossible barrier to departure. Each stigma, thoughtfully secretes a drop of honey which sweetens the detention.
>
> Meanwhile, the male flowers above have opened their pollen boxes and showered out the pollen, covering the little flies and forming a thick carpet in which they can roll and eat. Shortly afterwards the hairs wither, and as there is now no barrier the flies depart to seek fresh woods and pastures and, incidentally, cross-fertilize the arum. One hundred or more of these midges are often enclosed in one spathe.
>
> There is one particularly curious feature about all these processes, and that is that considerable heat is given out by the flower-spikes during their course. By carefully

The square stem of the soft, hairy red dead nettle grows up to 30cm (12in) in height and the heart-shaped leaves, which are concentrated mainly at the top of the stem, grow in pairs, are deeply veined and have serrated edges. Each leaf, but especially the upper ones, are tinged with purple – an impression increased by the reddish purple flowers which grow in whorls close to the upper leaves.

The white dead nettle is a much larger and coarser plant than the red, often reaching 60cm (2ft). The leaves are similarly heart shaped and serrated but each pair is set at right angles to the next. A further difference is that the creamy-white flowers are placed at intervals up the stem instead of being crowded together at the top.

inserting a thermometer into the chamber and keeping it there this can be detected by any observer.

Fertilization completed, the upper part of the spathe withers and falls forward, completely shutting up the opening and serving as a sign to flies of all kinds that proceedings there are completed. From this peculiarity the country folk have originated two more for the plant – Priest's Hood and Friar's Cowl – thus incidentally recalling the days when hooded Religions were a common feature of the time.'

Some people have suggested that the Arum may well be able to 'digest' some of the insects and thus, like the toothwort described above, be able to supplement its food in this manner.

Great Burdock (*Arctium lappa*) is a large, erect, branching biennial flowering in **August** which can grow to almost 2m ($6\frac{1}{2}$ft) in height and is common in clearings and hedges. The heart-shaped lower leaves are up to 30cm (12in) long and almost as wide. The leaves higher up the stem are somewhat smaller but both types are covered on the lower surface with white down. This was at one time, prior to the invention of matches, scraped off the leaves and soaked in salt petre before being dried and used in tinder boxes.

The leaves of the coltsfoot (*Tussilago farfara*) are also covered in cottony material and were collected for the same purpose. Although coltsfoot is now associated with open ground its original habitat must have been on the open banks overlooking woodland clearings or along the sides of streams running through the forest – a habitat also suitable for butterbur (*Petasites hybridus*) whose huge umbrella-like leaves provide shelter for many a woodland rodent.

Bugle (*Ajuga reptans*) grows in profusion, although it never becomes totally dominant, and the blue blooms delight the woodland visitor during June, July and, in some moist northern woodlands, until well into August. Arising from a rhizome

The flowers of the wild strawberry look like tiny white roses, a little less than 2.5cm (1in) across. The lobes of the sepals of the barren strawberry – unlike the wild – can be seen between the petals.

each square flowering stem is unbranched, smooth and hollow, often growing up to 30cm (12in) high, although most are between 15cm (6in) and 20cm (8in). In areas where the competing vegetation is tall, bugle can grow almost 60cm (24in) in an effort to reach the light. The leaves are found in pairs and are smooth and oval in shape, those at the top of the stem having a distinctly purple appearance. The flowers occur in whorls around the stem forming a long pointed spike at the top of the stem, and in Austria it is often referred to as the blue steeple. The old herbalists were convinced of its value and used extracts to treat ulcers, wounds and bruises.

Flowering in woodlands throughout Britain from late June until well into September betony (*Betonica officinalis*) was another plant held in high esteem by the herbalists. Antonius Musa, who was physician to the Emperor Augustus, wrote a whole book on the uses of the plant which he was sure would cure 47 different complaints. In Italy there was once a complimentary saying used to make friends and influence people which suggested that 'You have more virtues than betony'. It would stop bleeding, cure colds, reduce temperatures and it was an absolute winner in the treatment of the 'bloody flux'. I don't know about the bloody flux, but when camping I once used the leaves to good effect when I cut myself shaving. A better astyptic it would be hard to find.

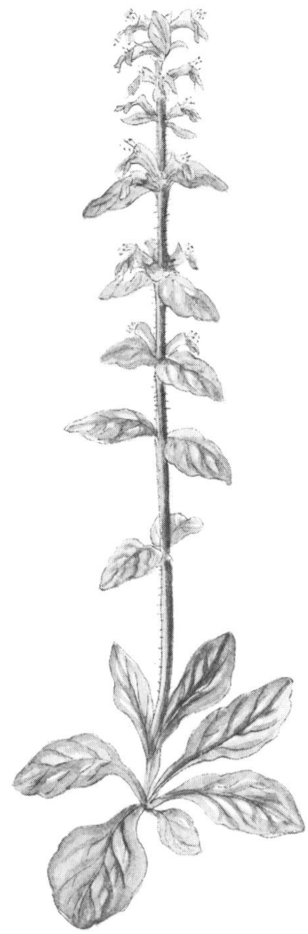

The bugle. The origin of its name is somewhat obscure but some have suggested that it derives from the Latin 'to drive away' – a clear reference to its medicinal properties.

The square, erect stem of betony grows up to 30cm (12in) high and the lance shaped lower leaves are on foot stalks and are somewhat wrinkled and hairy with very prominent veins. The upper leaves are a great deal narrower and grow opposite one another in pairs. At the top of the stem is a whorl of flowers and beneath each whorl is a modified leaf called a bract. The sepals form a tubular calyx divided at the edge into five narrow teeth. The petals also make a tubular corolla with an upper lip which is erect and round while the lower one is clearly divided into three segments of which the middle one is far the broadest. There are two long and two short stamens with purple arches producing pollen and the central part of the flower consists of a single pistil longer than any of the stamens.

Once known as the great nettle (*Urtica dioica*), this perennial plant with the powerful sting is dominant in many a clearing and edge and flowers from June to September. The erect stems grow from an underground rhizome and can be over a metre (3ft) in height. When heated, the plant loses its stinging juice and the young shoots were used as a vegetable. The fresh leaves are an important source of food for many insects, especially butterflies such as the small tortoishell and the peacock. The lower leaves are heart shaped and tapering whilst those towards the top of the stem are narrower. The whole of the plant is quite downy although not too many naturalists are prepared to touch the stems to find out! The flowers growing together in long clusters are greenish and a close look reveals them to be either male or female, a condition known as dioecious, giving the plant its specific name.

In many ways the late summer and autumn is a fascinating time for the botanist since many flowers are able to grow in clearings and woodland edges adding their mosaic of colours to those of ripening berries and dying leaves. The deadnettles, woundworts, agrimony, bittersweet, bryony and purple loostrife all play their part as do the foxgloves one of the most beautiful, if dangerous of British plants.

The deadnettles belong to the labiatae family and although their leaves bear a superficial resemblance to the stinging nettle there is no scientific relationship whatever. As their name indicates neither the red dead nettle (*Lamium purpureum*) nor the white dead nettle (*Lamium album*) can inflict a painful sting but I know of more than one otherwise competent naturalist who remains reluctant to take a firm grip on either. Both species are in flower for most of the year but are seen at their best, in my view, from **September** on.

Sylvatica really means wood and this is a more fitting name for hedge woundwort (*Stachys sylvatica*) which evolved in woodland clearings and open glades before becoming well adapted to life in the hedgerow. The erect, square stem can grow up to a metre (3ft) high and puts off pairs of branches which are hairy and, as with the rest of the plant, give off a most disagreeable smell when crushed. Despite this the leaves were once used, with some degree of success, as a wound dressing. They occur in pairs – each being heart-shaped, notched at the edges and feel like a piece of flannel.

The dark, purple-red flowers grow in whorls along the stem each separated from the other by intervals of bare stalk and beneath each whorl is a pair of small leaves called bracts.

Agrimony (*Agrimonia eupatoria*) is a cure for snake-bite, according to the ancient Greek Dioscorides, a Holy Salve against goblins and other divers evils, all ensuring agrimony a place in herbal history. There are, however, few plants so graceful, its long flowering stems rising to a height of 60cm (2ft) and terminating in a long spike of yellow blossoms. A spike is a botanical term indicating that a series of stemless flowers arise from a central stalk common to them all. Each flower is said to be sessile – a term meaning sitting.

Bittersweet (*Solanum dulcamara*) is also called woody nightshade and this species is the most common of the three nightshades occurring in Britain. The other two are the dwale, deadly nightshade or bella donna (*Atropa belladonna*) and the black nightshade (*Solanum nigrum*). Enchanter's nightshade (*Circaea lutetiana*), occurs in abundance in British woodlands and is not, in fact, a nightshade but a harmless member of the willowherb family.

The foxglove is a delightful looking, if poisonous, plant with a long history of medicinal use.

Woody nightshade is a slender plant needing a great deal of support from other stronger plants if its angular brittle stem is to reach a height of 2m (6ft). It is substantial enough to have a bark which is ash coloured, apart from in young specimens the branches of which have a purplish tint. The oval pointed leaves are dark green and veined and the leaves at the apex of the branches have two obvious lobes at the base.

Both the roots and stems, if chewed first give a taste of bitterness followed by a sickly sweetness, a practice to be discouraged. It was once, however, recommended as a cure for skin diseases, rheumatism, and also a purgative. The latter is certainly a valid use although its effect is far too dramatic to have any degree of application these days!

Another delightful looking plant which is poisonous is black bryony (*Tamus communis*) – it is common in the woods of England and Wales, but rather uncommon in Scotland. Black bryony is a climbing species found at considerable height gaining support from other, more sturdy trees – much as the woody nightshade. The annual shoots appear early in the spring and bear distinctive glossy heart-shaped leaves. The pale green flowers grow inconspicuously on small branching stems and it is not until late summer or autumn that the full glory of black bryony berries can be seen. At first they are green but soon turn red and are ignored by the birds to such an extent that they often continue to festoon the supporting tree and to grace the hedgrow long after the stems and leaves of the plant have withered away. The berries are so poisonous that they can cause a skin rash even if only handled.

Black bryony is the only member of the dioscoraceae family growing wild in Britain and is not related to the white bryony (*Bryonia diocia*) which, strangely enough, is the only native British member of the cucurbitaceae family. White bryony, as its name implies, has male and female flowers on different plants and the berries turn brighter red than those of black bryony. The leaves of white bryony are large, hairy, and lobed and grow alternately along the stem. It is much more common in the south of England than in the north.

An abundant species throughout Britain and thriving in damp woodlands purple loosestrife (*Lythrum salicaria*) earns its generic name of Lythrum meaning blood by imparting a gory looking blanket over damp areas during July and August. These stands, especially when growing in alder woods, prove that the area has only just developed from marshland which is the favourite habitat of the purple loostrife.

As already noted, the primrose has two different types of flower each up to 2.5cm (1in) in diameter – a condition known as dimorphic. The purple loosestrife carries this one stage further by having three ways of arranging the relative positions of the styles and stigmas. This condition is known as trimorphic and there are types with long styles, others with short styles and others where the styles are of an intermediate length. The pollen grains also vary in size and since there are so many ways in which pollination can occur it is easy to see why the species is so successful, since no flower can be self-fertilized.

Stems of up to 1m (3¼ft) arise from a perennial rhizome each carrying stout lance-shaped leaves which can be arranged either in opposite pairs or in whorls around the stem. These prove popular with the caterpillars of the elephant hawk moth (*Deilephila elpenor*) which also feeds upon bramble (*Rubus fruticosus*) and rosebay willow herb (*Chamaenerion angustifolium*) both of which are common in woodlands. There is some debate among botanists regarding the true status of the latter. Most are of the opinion that it was introduced from north America and spread along railway lines since it is an early colonizer of disturbed ground. Others think that there have been a few resident plants since the days of the early wildwood but they have only become dominant in the last century. In any event, many clearings are now completely dominated by clumps of the well named fireweed, and the feathery seeds floating in the gentle breezes of later summer are a familiar sight.

Providing there is no lime in the soil the biennial foxglove (*Digitalis purpurea*) will grow almost anywhere throughout the British Isles and is particularly beautiful in the birch woodlands overlooking the lochs of Scotland. The erect tapering stem can reach heights of almost 2m (6½ft) and are covered with fine downy hairs. The large oval leaves are serrated becoming narrower towards the points, show distinct veining and are downy. The purple flowers grow in a long terminal spike marked on the inside with dark coloured spots surrounded by white rings. They appear in June but are thriving in July and August with the odd stand still dominant at the end of September. There are two pairs of stamens one pair longer than the other and ripening first. The stigma is never mature until the pollen has been shed and a number of hairs in the mouth of the corolla prevents excess pollen escaping and keeps out small insects. Fertilization is effected by stronger insects especially bumble bees whose hairy bodies become yellow with pollen and carry it away to another plant with a mature stigma.

Agrimony – each flower has five spreading yellow flowers making up the corolla while the greenish sepals, once pollination has occurred, wither and become covered with bristly hairs. Tiny burrs are then formed which stick to the fur of passing animals – just like those of burdock.

Invertebrates

ALL animals can, broadly speaking, be divided into those which have backbones – the vertebrates, and those which don't – the invertebrates. The latter are far more numerous and ecologically important than the vertebrates. Because of the microscopic size of the great majority – living either in the hidden depths of the soil or burrowed away in decaying leaves or rotting branches, invertebrates are often not given full recognition. Indeed, it is very difficult to do so.

Many invertebrates are microscopic protozoans and tiny nematodes either living as parasites feeding upon living organisms or as saphrophytes, feeding upon the decaying remains of animals and, more usually, plants. They may conveniently be grouped under the heading of *Cryptozoa* – meaning hidden away. Although this word has no taxonomic value it is a most useful umbrella under which the naturalist can place animals which cannot be seen without a microscope. However, there are also many invertebrate animals which are visible to the naked eye, for those who have the patience and skill to look. These are the *Annelids*, *Arthropods* and *Molluscs*.

The *Annelids* are an important and interesting phylum comprising of around 9,000, mainly aquatic, species. The most obvious characteristic is that the body is divided into segments – indeed, the name of the phylum derives from the word annulus meaning a little ring.

The *Annelids* are divided into three main sub-phyllum. Firstly there are the *Polychaets*, a largely marine group of 5,500 species with segmentally arranged appendages – *Polychaet* means many bristles. Then there are the leeches (*Hirudinea*) of which there are around 500 species mainly based in freshwater, with a few marine species and a tiny minority are land based, none occurring in Britain. However, it is the third class of *Annelids*, the *Oligochaets* which are of primary interest. They have no appendages and comparatively few bristles enabling their long thin bodies to slide between soil particles with a minimum of friction. Oligo means few and the bristles are indeed reduced in number, especially in the terrestrial species. Two other characteristics are typical of *Oligochaets*. The head is very much reduced and lacks external sensory and feeding appendages – obviously another adaptation designed to cut down resistance to movement through soil. There is also a structure called the clitellum, concerned with reproduction, situated at the anterior end formed by the swelling of several adjacent segments.

The common earthworm (*Lumbricus terrestris*), is a hermaphrodite and copulation tends to occur on wet nights when two individuals come together to exchange sperm by pressing their ventral surfaces together. Their position is such

OPPOSITE: **The elephant hawk moth larva on rosebay willow herb.**

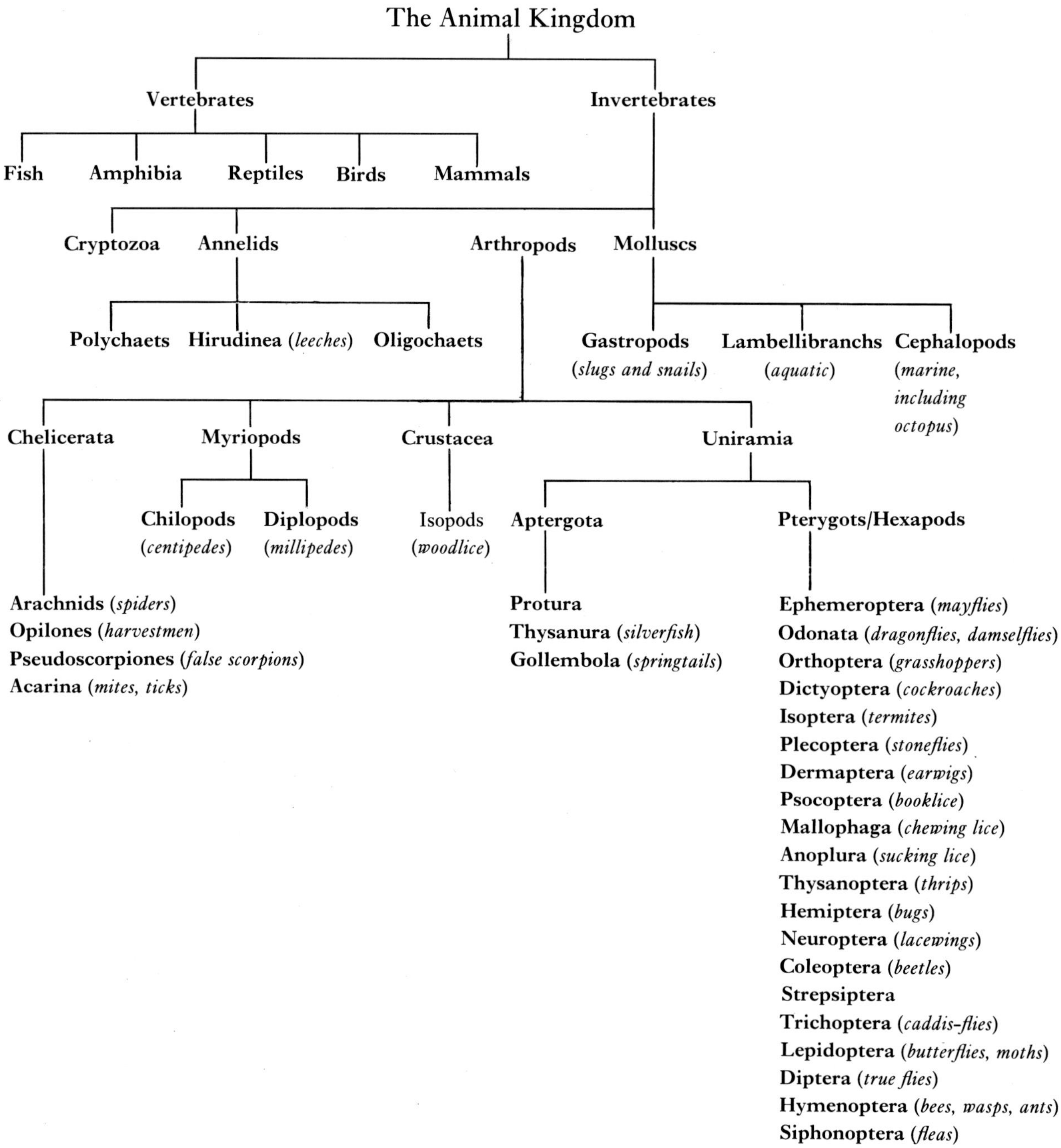

that the sperm openings situated on segments nine to eleven are pressed against the clitellum occupying segments 32 to 36 of the other. Each animal pushes its chaetae into the skin of the other, secreting a thick layer of mucus and sperm is exchanged. The eggs are eventually laid in cocoons, formed as a result of a complex of secretions from the clitellum and the segments immediately in front of it. The cocoon then passes backwards over the sperm stores and the eggs are fertilized. Although as many as 16 eggs are laid in each cocoon not all survive, and in the case of *Lumbricus terrestris* only a single young worm emerges. Just prior to the cocoon being deposited under stones or in the soil it shrinks to an oval pea sized structure.

Earthworms are usually herbivores dragging plant material, especially leaves, down into their burrows assisting in the breakdown of dead material and are important re-cycling agents. In woodland ecology these animated ploughs play a vital role, and the improvement in soil texture, aeration and drainage was realized way back in 1837 by Charles Darwin. He worked out that there were as many as 50,000 worms in each acre of soil producing between ten and 18 tons of worm casts each year. Modern biologists have calculated earthworm efficiency in terms of weight, in grams, in each square metre of soil. Farmland yields between 50 and 100 grams per square metre. The figure for coniferous forests can be as low as 11 grams per square metre, while a rich deciduous woodland is 120 grams per square metre – the value of worms in woodland ecology is very clear.

Pardosa amentata

Araneus umbraticus

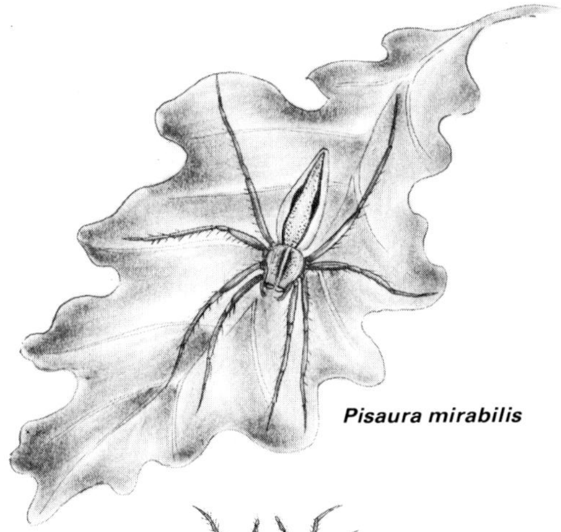

Pisaura mirabilis

Araneus cucurbitinus

Zebra spider

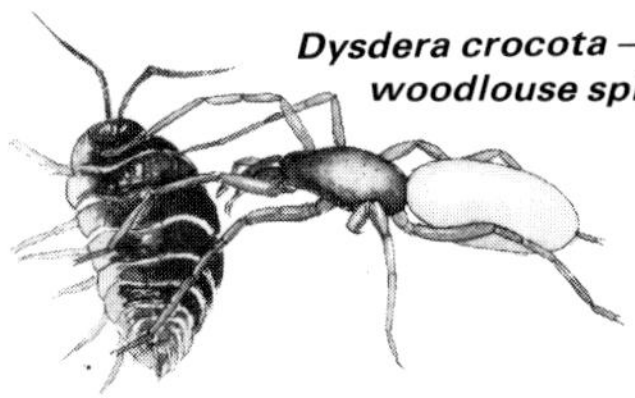

Dysdera crocota – the woodlouse spider

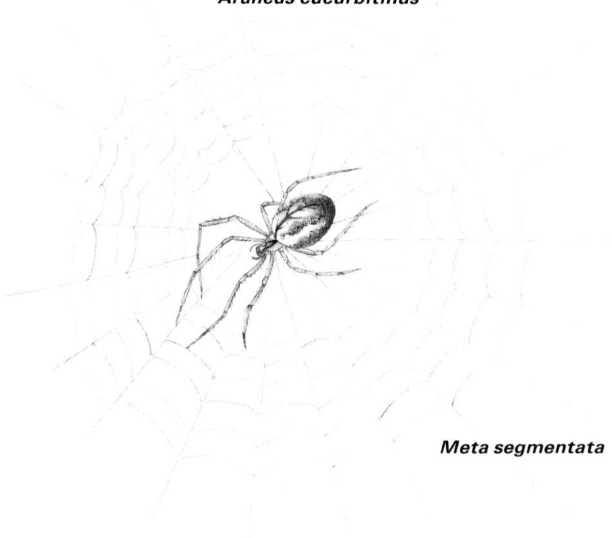

Meta segmentata

There are several genera of earthworms but two – *Lumbricus* and *Allolobophora* – are common in Britain and both are represented in woodland. *Lumbricus* lines its burrows with its own faeces and although it can tolerate a wide range of pH conditions it tends to avoid soils which are really wet.

The pH scale is a measure of the acidity or alkalinity between two extremes of 0 and 14. Neutral conditions are 7 whilst any reading below 7 is acid and those above 7 are alkaline. *Allolobophora* is found commonly in compact dry soils but also wetter areas where the pH can fall quite low – perhaps towards 5. The earthworms of the family enchytraeids can survive Ph levels below this and are one of the few to be found in coniferous woodlands. The various species of earthworms are not easily distinguished but the position of the clitellum and the number of body segments are useful in classification.

The third group of invertebrates are the *Arthropods* of which there are more than 80,000 alive in the world today – around 80 per cent of the animal kingdom. Modern taxonomists now recognize four sub-phyla of this group. The **Chelicerata** include spiders, harvestmen, false scorpions and mites; the **Myriopods** centipedes and millipedes; the **Crustacea** woodlice and the **Uniramia** insects.

Spiders (*Arachnids*), of which there are around 630 species in Britain, fascinated biologists for many years for several reasons. These are the production of silk, the presence of poison fangs and their strange courtship behaviour. Not all spiders spin webs, but they all produce silk which is used for wrapping up their eggs and also their prey. Silk is a liquid protein produced by large glands at the front of the abdomen. It is squeezed out of six spinnerets and immediately hardens on exposure to the air. The prey, usually an insect, is either trapped in the web or actively hunted by the spider. It is then bitten by powerful fangs and injected with poison. The spider may retreat to allow the poison to take effect and digestive enzymes are pumped in and the prey sucked dry. If a spider's web is examined, the dried hulks of the prey can be seen suspended in the threads. No British spider has fangs powerful enough to penetrate human skin.

The third characteristic of the spiders is their bizarre courtship behaviour. Males are usually recognized by the swollen palps used during pairing. Of the orb-web spiders – so called because of the shape of their web – the web building spider *Araneus diadematus* is identified by a white cross on its dorsal surface from which it gets one of its vernacular names – cross spider. It is also sometimes called the garden spider, even though it frequently occurs in woodlands, which was doubtlessly its original habitat. The male transforms his sperm to his palps during mating and then swings on his web of silk towards the web of the female. He has the good sense to leave a safety line behind him because spiders are predatory animals and the female is quite likely to eat her mate. He plucks the female's web sending a sort of morse signal which he hopes will allow him to transfer his sperm to her storage pouches called spermathecae. Egg laying follows copulation with each female laying several hundred and securing them to a solid surface with silk. After this the female dies. The eggs overwinter in the cocoon and hatch into spiderlings moulting several times before becoming sexually mature at about 18 months.

Meta segmentata is another fascinating species of orb-web spider found in woodlands – especially those with open glades and plenty of tall plants such as nettle, rosebay willow herb or burdock. It can sling its web among these plants, and may be recognized by the lack of central platform. This spider has a rather slender shape that shows quite a lot of variation in both colour and the relative proportions of the body zones. Unlike many species, the male is rather larger than his mate but he is just as sly and often goes to the trouble of depositing a fly, neatly wrapped in

A garden spider. Spiders have often been confused with insects, but are actually quite different. Insects' bodies are divided into three sections – head, thorax and abdomen, and there are also three pairs of five jointed legs, one pair situated on each of the three thoracic segments. Spiders, on the other hand, have their bodies divided into two regions and they have four pairs of legs. Spiders never have wings or antennae but have a pair of sensory palps bearing superficial resemblance to antennae. Also included in the *Arachnids* are mites, false scorpions and harvestmen. These can be distinguished from spiders because their cephalothorax is fused to the abdomen. They also lack the typical spider's waist.

silk, on her web. Whilst she is busy tucking-in, the crafty male nips in, mates with her and makes his escape before she turns her ever-hungry eye on him.

Among the most common and easily found group of woodland spiders are the hammock, or lace webbed spiders which belong to the amaurobiidae family. They are characterized by stout bodies and a prominent black area towards the front of the abdomen.

The bluish, wool-like silk of this species is very sticky and is combed out from the spinnerets by hair-like structures growing on the fourth pair of legs. These spiders are active web makers throughout the year and I once had a black Labrador who had a talent for creeping into woodland thickets and emerging with his coat festooned with untidy hammock webs. The glue-like nature of the silk is reinforced by globules of thick dew-like liquid.

The crevices in tree bark are ideal areas to site the webs and a single spider may have several such traps, each with a single thread leading to the hiding place of the spinner. Like a crafty angler, the trapping of a fly or other small invertebrate leads to the rapid appearance of the spider. *Amaurobius ferox* is a very evil looking character with a skull and crossbone pattern on its almost black abdomen and is very common in damp woodlands.

A look at the trees during a warm summer's day will reveal many leaves that are curled and within them you may well find a real tough-guy of a spider. This is *Enoplagnatha ovata* which belongs to the theridiidae family and I have found it to be common in oak woodlands, especially in damp areas with high growths of nettle. The web also has globules of glue which is so strong that insects as large as butterflies, moths, wasps and bees can be captured, wrapped in silk and consumed. The species almost always has red patterning on its abdomen making it instantly recognizable.

Close relatives of the lace-webs are the tiny spiders of the family linyphia which are usually known as money spiders. They seldom exceed 3mm ($\frac{1}{9}$in) and are dark in colour making them difficult to see. The best time to hunt them out is during the early morning when the jewels of early dew hanging from the webs festooning the woodland grasses reflect the first rays of dawn sunlight.

Species like *Linyphia triangularis* have another method of despatching prey which does not depend upon a sticky web. The spider waits beneath the hammock and when the prey literally 'falls into the trap', part of its body sticks through the mesh and the crafty spider jabs its poison fangs into this vulnerable area!

Money spiders do not spin webs but actively hunt out their prey and wait in ambush ready to pounce. Some are active by day whilst others are purely nocturnal – naturalists really do need to be active both by day and night and throughout the four seasons.

Wolf spiders are diurnal hunters belonging to the family lycosidae. There are some 37 species in Britain many of which are found in woodlands. Typical of the genus is *Pardosa amentata*. The female carries her egg sac around with her attached to the spinnerets which have worked a blanket of silk to protect the eggs. After the spiderlings hatch, they quickly make their way round to the back of the female and are carried around with her for some time before becoming independent.

The 33 species of jumping spiders belonging to the family salticidae are diurnal spiders with huge, highly efficient eyes who hunt by slow stalking followed by a quick pounce – they are rightly called the cats of the invertebrate world. One of the best known is the zebra spider (*Salticus scenicus*) which is commonly seen lying in wait around the boundary fences of woodlands.

There are 38 species of crab spiders making up the thomisidae family which have evolved their own particular niche. They derive their name from their squat appearance and sideways walk – an ideal adaptation for creatures hiding among flower heads waiting for insects to land in search of pollen. The various species, of which those of the genus *Xysticus* are most common, have evolved colour variations to match the background and there is evidence to suggest that they are able to change their colour as the blossoms begin to fade. The first two pairs of legs, which are very much longer than the other two, enable crab spiders to be identified in the field. Precise identification, however, is never easy and field guides will certainly be needed to identify some of the rarer species.

Once the sun has set the daytime spiders need to select a safe refuge for there are nocturnal species such as *Ero furcata* which specialize in eating spiders. Although they are only some 4mm ($\frac{1}{8}$in) long, they can inflict a lethal bite on the largest of the web spiders and eat them with surprising speed. The woodlouse spider (*Dysdera crocata*), as its name implies, specializes in feeding upon woodlice which are also nocturnal and extremely common in the rotting trees and leaf litter of a deciduous woodland. Although woodlice have a powerful exoskeleton the huge powerful jaws of *Dysdera crocata* is more than a match for it. The species is very colourful having a dark cephalothorax, pinkish yellow abdomen and red legs.

The 23 species of **harvestmen**, making up the opilones order of the *Chelicerata*, have no narrow waist, only two eyes and are usually active at night. Their diet is also different to that of spiders since they are scavengers hunting for rotting material. If the leaf litter is examined closely during the late summer and early autumn, large numbers of these fascinating long-legged creatures will be found, the most common being *Phalangium opilio* and *Leiobunum rotundum*. The latter has very long black legs arising from a relatively small round brown body.

There is little preliminary courtship behaviour shown by the males which usually mate with the female soon after initial contact. Perhaps this is because poison fangs are not necessary in harvestmen. Although the male has a very long penis with which sperm is transferred to the female, most of the time it is not possible to distinguish the sexes externally. There is a difference in jaw structure, however, between males and females of the species *Phalangium opilio*. Unlike spiders harvestmen have a permeable body cuticle and are very vulnerable to dessication.

False scorpions, another order of *Chelicerata*, obviously derive their common name from a superficial resemblance to scorpions. These small carnivorous animals are found in the leaf litter of woodlands and seldom grow larger than 4mm ($\frac{1}{8}$in). They have poisonous glands at the tip of their claws which enable them to deal effectively with other small invertebrates, including spiders. The little-studied animals are grouped in the order *Pseudoscorpiones*.

Lastly, the **mites and ticks** are placed in the order *Acarina* and there are more than 32,000 species in the world, many of which are important in terms of human health and as pests on both wild and domesticated animals. In woodlands they are extremely common in the leaf litter where they are important as decomposers, especially in well-drained woodlands. The red earth mite (*Tromdibium holocericeum*) is a predatory species very common in deciduous woodlands. It occasionally bores into mammalian skin including that of humans, causing a rather unpleasant rash. It is strange that larval mites have only six legs, whilst the adults have eight.

Crustaceans are basically aquatic and their exoskeleton is not suitable for life on dry land. For this reason one order, the woodlice (*Isopods*), tend to seek out damp, dark areas of woodland under rotting logs or behind peeling bark – a habitat they often share with millipedes and centipedes.

Woodlice play a vital role in the woodland cycle as they feed upon partially decayed material and break it down so well that the nutrients become available once more for growing plants. Actually they are not lice at all but relatives of crabs and crayfish. All woodlice are flattened in shape and have seven pairs of legs. The colour is usually greyish brown but occasionally red and even white specimens are found. In Britain there are over 40 species but two are particularly common. *Oniscus asellus* is found in damp woodlands and in drier woods *Pocellio scaber* is the species most likely to be encountered. The pill-bugs of the genus *Armadillium* may also be found – when danger threatens they curl into a tight ball.

Woodlice, on the other hand, either play possum and pretend to be dead; produce a foul smelling and tasting chemical; clamp themselves down hard to a solid object or, if all else fails, scuttle away quickly on their surprisingly long legs.

As it grows, the woodlouse tends to burst its exoskeleton and must therefore moult. This is a strange and potentially dangerous business since the animals is immobile and vulnerable at this time. Only half the skeleton is usually moulted at one time and this can result in a strange looking beast. One end is of the normal body colour whilst the other has a milky appearance.

After a series of moults the animals become sexually mature and the life span is thought to be not much longer than two years. Mating is a rather quick affair, the male mounting the female after some nibbling. The female has a brood patch within which the eggs develop and hatch into tiny replicas of the adult.

As already mentioned the fourth sub-phylum of *Arthropods* are called *Uniramia* – the insects. They can be instantly distinguished from all other *Arthropods* by the presence of the three pairs of five-jointed legs, accounting for the alternative name of *Hexapoda*. There are over 750,000 different species, with more being identified each day. There is no way of providing a detailed description of all the insects present in a wood and it has been necessary to be very selective.

Whenever **butterflies** or **moths** are roughly handled or become entangled in a spider's web a fine dust may be seen to rub off the wings. When examined under a hand lens or, better still, under a microscope this can be seen to be tiny scales which in a living insect overlap rather like the roof tiles on a house. It is this feature which allows us to separate butterflies and moths into a separate order of insects called the *Lepidoptera* which literally means scales-winged.

At one time, especially on the continent butterflies and moths were simply divided into day-time *Lepidoptera* (the butterflies) and night-time *Lepidoptera* (the moths). This, however, is not sufficient since a number of moths, especially the six spot burnet (*Zyganena filipendulae*) which is seen around ragwort (*Senecio jacobaea*) in woodland clearings, is very active during the day. Butterflies, however, are generally diurnal but have several other reliable points of distinction.

Butterflies at rest usually raise their wings vertically above their body whilst moths hold their wings flat down against the surface on which they settle. While this distinction holds true most of the time, butterflies which have been cold during the night often spread their wings to catch the warming rays of the early sun building up their strength to fly – photographers who realize this will obtain their best butterfly photographs just after dawn. A further difference is that butterflies have a clearly marked waist line between the thorax and abdomen, a feature lacking in moths.

Padosa lugubris is a regular member of the woodland fauna often seen out hunting among the litter.

Life history of the butterfly

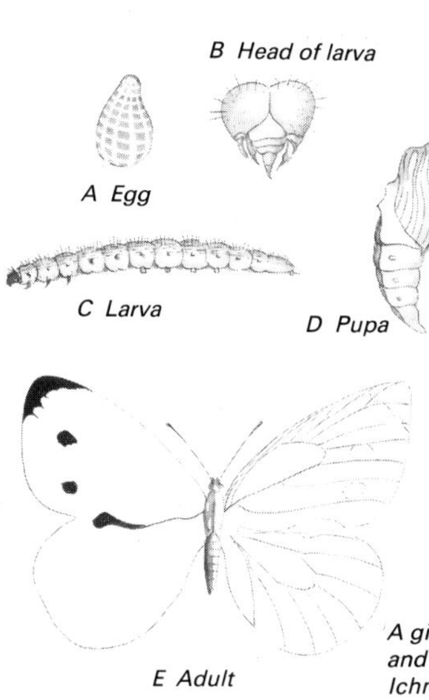

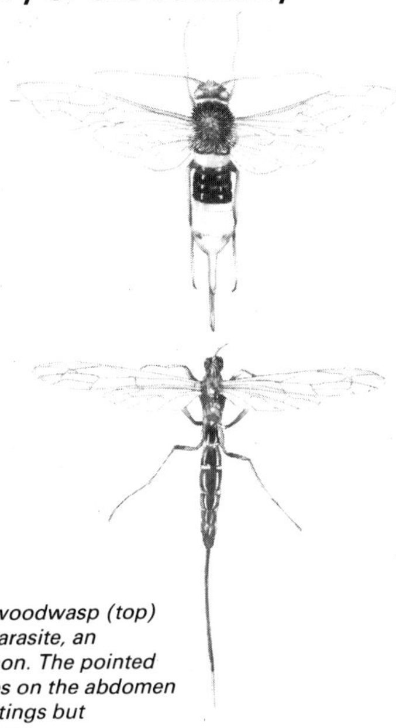

A giant woodwasp (top) and its parasite, an Ichneumon. The pointed structures on the abdomen are not stings but ovipositors

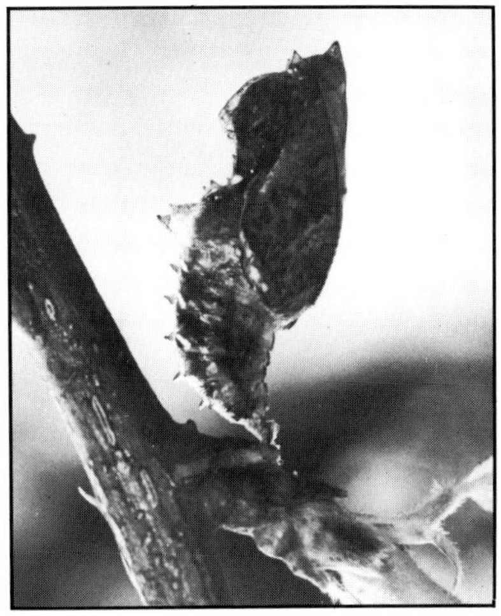

An oak eggar pupa.

ALL *Lepidoptera* pass through what is known as a complete metamorphosis involving a life history of four stages. First an impregnated female lays her eggs onto the leaves of the plant species used by the larva to feed upon. The number of eggs, shape, developmental time and, of course, favoured plant varies from species to species, but eventually larvae (often called caterpillars) emerge and their sole role in life is to feed and grow by means of a series of moults.

The chief destroyers of caterpillars are almost certainly the ichneumon flies which, despite their name, are not flies but parasitic wasps. The female ichneumon has a sharp ovipositor which penetrates the skin of the host caterpillar and a number of eggs, from one to 50, are deposited deep in its tissues. When the ichneumon grubs hatch they proceed to eat their host alive. Once they are fully developed the parasites eat their way out through the host's skin and spin themselves a cocoon of silk, within which they pupate. When the adults emerge from their cocoon, usually the following spring or summer, they mate and are ready to begin their destructive life cycle all over again.

Those caterpillars which escape their predators eventually reach full size and then change into a chrysalis which, again depending upon the species in question, can take as long as several days or as little time as a few hours. Many larvae bore into the ground prior to pupation, while others push into crevices under logs in walls or hollow trees. The duration of the pupal stage may last a few days or, in some cases, for several years. *Lepidoptera* may hibernate as eggs, larvae or pupae while a few – the small tortoishell for example – overwinter as adults. Illustrated here is the silver washed fritillary pupa prior to the butterfly's emergence – the wing pattern can be distinguished.

When the adult first emerges from its crysalis it is not the beautiful creature which we see illustrated in the books, but dull and wet, with its wings seen as mere stumps. At this stage the creature is very vulnerable but air is soon pumped into wings and body, the bright colours appear and the adult is ready to reproduce. At this state *Lepidoptera* do not grow, but visit flowers to obtain nectar which provides them with the fuel they need to fly and maintain vital body functions.

The main difference between the two groups, however, is in the nature of the antennae for those of the butterfly are obviously club-shaped. This accounts for the scientific name of Rhaphalocera which derives from the Greek rhapalon meaning a club and keras meaning a horn. The moths are classed as Heterocerag, again having Greek roots as heteras means different. The antennae of moths are never club-shaped but can be bristly, comb-shaped, toothed or plumed.

Both butterflies and moths are such mobile creatures that it is possible for almost every species to appear in a woodland from time to time. Some, however, are typically associated with this habitat.

No group of butterflies are more typical of woodlands than the fritillaries which are supposed to have been given their name because of the resemblance between the flowers of fritillary and the dappled upper surface of the butterflies.

The pearl bordered fritillary (*Boloria euphrosyne*) can be distinguished from the small pearl bordered fritillary (*Boloria selene*) not only by its slightly larger size (which is never reliable unless you see the two together), but by the fact that the small species has six or seven silver patches on the underside of the hind wings, while *Boloria euphrosyne* has only two. The small pearl bordered is more typical of the damp woodlands of northern Britain often venturing out onto the moorlands, while the pearl bordered is more at home in the drier warmer areas typical of the south of Britain. Both species prefer to lay their eggs on the leaves of dog violet (*Viola canina*) although other species of violet can also be used.

The largest of the British fritillaries is the silver-washed, the caterpillars of which also feed on dog violets. The eggs are invariably laid during July and August on the moss covering the bark of a tree as high as 2m (6½ft) from the ground. As soon as the larvae hatch they make their way down the trunk and onto the violets so often growing at the foot. A feature of the fritillaries is the delightfully patterned larvae bearing prominent spines. In the case of the silver-washed, two horn-like spikes stick out in front of the head. Their pupae are also interesting and hang suspended by the tail, but surprisingly it also has two spikes and a number of other projections thought to act as shock absorbers whenever the insect swings in the wind and bumps against its support. Its light colour, with brown markings ensure that the pupa is well camouflaged against a background of withered leaves.

Woodlands with open areas and damp spots are favoured by the Duke of Bergundy fritillary. Despite its common name and superficial resemblance this butterfly does not belong to the fritillary family. It belongs, rather, to the metal mark family of butterflies and is the only one to occur in Britain, its larvae feeding upon cowslips and primroses. The Duke of Bergundy occurs mainly in the southern and central counties but there has been some loss of habitat due to thoughtless people transferring clumps of its food plant from woodlands to estate gardens.

The interesting woodland butterflies the large tortoishell (*Nymphalis polychloros*) and the comma (*Polygonia c-album*) are two of only seven British species of vanessids which over-winter as adults. Few butterflies are as difficult to census at the present time as the large tortoishell which has suffered badly because of the ravages of Dutch elm disease. Although the larvae will feed upon willow, whitebeam, cherry and a few other species there is a distinct preference for elm. It is also difficult to be sure whether the individual sweeping along the woodland edge is an over-wintering adult or a migrant from the continent.

Butterfly migration is much more common than is often realized and species such as the red admiral (*Vanessa atalanta*), clouded yellow (*Colias crocea*) and the very rare Scandinavian based Camberwell beauty (*Nymphalis antiopa*) are all well documented migrants.

The comma, however, is much more widely distributed and accepts a wider

Butterflies

THE male silver-washed (top left) tends to be brighter than the female the overall ground colour being yellowish red and although both sexes are patterned with black the male alone has a heavy covering of black scales. When squeezed these give off a scent which may well stimulate the female to mate.

The Duke of Bergundy (top right) over-winters as a pupa and is on the wing from the middle of May to coincide with the peak growth of cowslips. It is a very fast flying butterfly, but a census can be taken by keeping an eye on areas of wet mud where several may collect to drink.

The brown hairstreak (above) is the only British butterfly with green scales but the white hairstreak on the underside of the wing is quite variable and in some individuals this feature may be absent altogether. The eggs are laid singly onto the shoots or flowers of the food plant and after their first moult they are cannibals which is obviously why evolutionary pressure has determined that they are laid singly. All the hairstreaks, except the green, over-winter as an egg. They hibernate in the soil as a pupa from which the adult emerges during May.

choice of food plants including sallow and stinging nettle thriving in damp lowland woods. The adult spends the winter hanging upside down beneath a tree branch and its wings, which have jagged edges, show a remarkable resemblance to a dead leaf. Even the white legs function perfectly to break up the outline.

It is heartening to report that this species is more common today than it was at the turn of the century and it is also slowly extending its range. The comma is certainly unusual in this respect because British butterflies have faired very badly in recent times.

The hairstreaks are a family with five British species, all of which are totally associated with woodlands or dependent upon areas of shrubs suitable for food plants. The name hairstreak is given because of a thin white mark running across the underside of the wing. The five species are the brown (*Thecla betulae*), green (*Callophyrs rubi*), purple (*Quercusia quercus*), black (*Strymonidia pruni*), and white letter hairstreak (*Strymonidia w-album*).

The most widely distributed species is the green hairstreak and it is found both in woodlands and adjoining scrub and heathland. I am sure that its wide distribution is due to the large variety of plants eaten by the larvae. They feed upon heather (*Calluna vulgaris*) found in coniferous woodlands with rides and clearings populated by the plant, and there will often be whortleberry (*Vaccinium vitis idaea*) and bilberry (*Vaccinium myrtillus*) present, also eaten by the caterpillars. Rock rose (*Helianthemum nummularium*) is an acceptable food allowing the green hairstreak to adapt to limestone areas where rock rose grows particularly well. Bramble, oak and mouse eared hawkweed (*Hieracium pilosella*) are also accepted by the larvae.

The distribution of the brown hairstreak depends upon the presence or absence of the larvae food plant which is blackthorn. The purple hairstreak is truly a forest butterfly and the larvae are almost totally dependent upon oak, although the occasional brood may survive on a diet of sallow. The white letter hairstreak has been very much associated with elms, especially the wych elm, but there is no doubt that, much like the tortoishell, it has suffered in some areas as a result of Dutch elm disease. Even more restricted in distribution is the black hairstreak now found only in a narrow band leading from the Oxford area towards the Wash. Woods containing blackthorn have been very much reduced in recent years as this area has been built up. The white hairstreak populations will have to be watched very carefully if this species is not to become extinct.

Taxonomists seem fairly well agreed that butterflies and moths had a common ancestor – a sort of missing link of the lepidoptera. There also appears to be agreement that the skippers, the most primitive and the satyridae family usually referred to as the browns, are the most highly evolved.

The ground colour of the upper surfaces of the wings is brown and there are a number of eye spots adding to the efficiency of the butterfly's camouflage. The main food is sheep's fescue grass (*Festuca ovina*) but the larvae will also accept cock's foot (*Dactylis glomerata*) and annual meadow grass (*Poa pratensis*).

Several of the brown family are much more intimately associated with woodlands, including the speckled wood. This has many spots on its wings giving it a very dappled appearance which is a perfect design for a butterfly among the mosaic of woodland leaves. Some of the spots resemble eyes and are situated on the less vital areas of the butterfly and predators, especially small birds, will strike at these eyes first allowing the only slightly injured insect to escape.

The speckled wood is unique among British butterflies in that it can spend the winter either as a crysalis or a half grown caterpillar feeding upon grass. The distribution of the speckled wood is rather strange being very common in Wales and the southern counties of England as well as in a number of woods throughout

OPPOSITE: **The only member of the satyridae family which has no eye spots is the marbled white. Although a mainly grassland species restricted to the south and midland counties of Britain this butterfly does occur in woodlands growing on chalk and limestone.**

Ireland. In the north and east of Britain it becomes less and less common, but is found in one or two isolated spots on the west coast of Scotland. It is thought that the ancestors of these populations were cut off as the Ice Age ground to a halt, but managed to survive in a few isolated, relatively hot areas. No doubt the presence of salt-laden sea breezes wafting through the woods fringing the sea lochs helped those primitive populations.

The Scotch argus (*Erebia aethiops*), on the other hand, is restricted to the woodlands and hills of Scotland, especially those which face the warming rays of the early morning sun. The larvae will eat several grass species but prefers purple moor grass (*Molinia caerulea*). This often dominates the floor of the native highland pine and birch woods as well as some of the conifer plantations where wide rides have been left to prevent the spread of fire. The brown, upper surfaces of the wings are broken up by eye spots ringed with an attractive hoop of deep orange.

The ringlet (*Aphantopus hyperanthus*) is one of the most widespread of the woodland browns although it does become less common the further north you go. The comparatively wide distribution is no doubt due to the larvae being prepared to feed upon a variety of coarse grasses including couch (*Agropyrum repens*), cock's foot and false brome (*Brachypodium sylvaticum*). The female does not lay her eggs directly onto the food plants but scatters them at random. Once caterpillars they lose no time in finding a suitable larder. The larvae survive the winter in partial hibernation, but are able to find enough to eat during the warmer days of winter.

A small hammock of silk is constructed before the creature goes through its pupal stage which seldom lasts longer than a couple of weeks. The adults are on the wing from June to August, when they eagerly seek out nectar from such plants as red campion (*Silene dioica*), wild thyme (*Thymus drucei*) and especially bramble.

The pieridae family are among the most widespread and common of British butterflies and includes the well named wood white (*Leptidea sinapis*), a very localized species whose larvae feed upon the leaves of the leguminosae (pea family) – especially the vetches. It has a very feeble flight and may account for its preference for sheltered woodlands, although there are a few coastal sites in Devon where the wood white now survives.

Much tougher species are the large white (*Pieris brassicae*), small white (*Pieris rapae*) and the green veined white (*Pieris napi*). They are all gardener's pests since their larvae feed greedily on cruciferous plants which include cabbage, cauliflowers and nasturtium. In a woodland, however, they feed on their natural diet of native plants, including garlic mustard (*Alliaria petiolata*) and lady's smock, also known as cuckoo flower (*Cardamine pratensis*). These two flowers are also the food plants of the orange tip (*Anthocharis cardamines*), one of the most delightful of the butterflies to be seen in Britain.

Woodland moths are much more numerous than butterflies and this section is therefore even more selective. Since many moths are nocturnal their true beauty can only be appreciated by trapping or photographing using flash. Caterpillars may be seen feeding on the leaves of many trees during the day but the true woodland naturalist must spend some time on night patrol. I use two methods to obtain moths which should always be unharmed and released. These methods are sugaring, and making use of the moth's often fatal attraction to light.

Each moth fancier has their own favourite recipe to attract the insects, but I like to warm a bottle of stout and stir into it a tin of syrup or treacle plus two tablespoons of sherry. This is painted on the boles of trees during the early evening using a large paint brush. Soon after dark moths are attracted to this rich smelling brew for it is so full of intoxicating nectar that they are unable to resist it. Photographing drunken moths with flash is then relatively easy. It should be realized, though, that not all species are so attracted and may more conveniently be caught in a moth trap.

These are relatively expensive since moths respond best to ultra-violet light. Portable types functioning well from a car battery can, however, be purchased. The use of a sheet spread on the ground beneath the branches of a tree which is then shaken can be a valuable source of moth larvae.

Woodland species include Kentish glory, three hawk moths, buff tip, clouded magpie, clouded border and vapourer.

Despite its name the species Kentish glory (*Endromis versicolora*) is now widely distributed, although never very commonly, throughout England and parts of Scotland as far north as Aberdeenshire. The food plants of the larvae, which are seen from June to August, include birch and alder especially those surrounding heathland over which the adults may be seen flying strongly. The male is often seen on the wing during the day, but the female is much more nocturnal and can be captured in a moth trap rather than brought to sugar.

The adults vary from 5cm to 9cm (2in to 3½in), the females being larger than the males. The latter can be attracted by keeping a mature female in a cage where she will produce a chemical called pheromone which carries on the wind and attracts the males. This method is known as sembling.

The caterpillar of the Kentish glory is green but with oblique stripes of a darker green and yellow. In May, when they first hatch, they are gregarious and groups of caterpillars construct a silk web under which they all shelter. They prefer birch but will also feed upon hazel and alder and by the end of July they are fully grown and descend to the leaf litter where they pupate until the following spring.

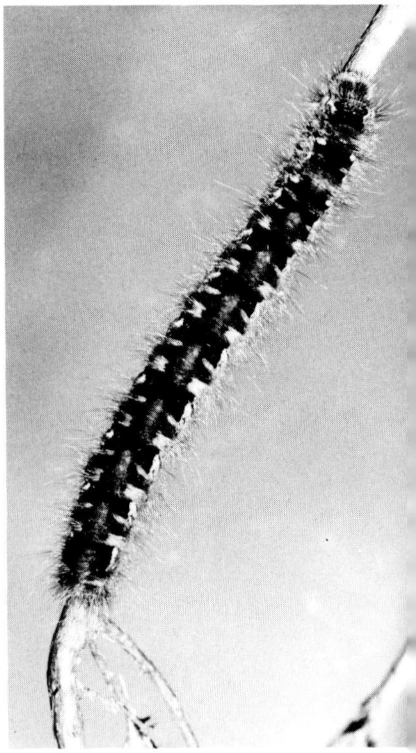

An oak eggar caterpillar.

Two other species in which the female is larger than the male are the drinker moth (*Philudoria potatoria*) and the oak eggar (*Lasiocampa quercus*). The larvae of the former feed upon grasses, especially the cock's foot often growing in profusion in woodland rides. The larvae of the oak eggar feed on a wide range of trees and shrubs in addition to the oak including bramble, sloe, hazel and willow.

The hawk moths are placed in the sphingidae family which includes around 60 species, of which only nine are native to Britain. Eight others occur as occasional migrants. The larvae are invariably brightly coloured, lacking in hairs and have a hook-like projection on the twelfth segment. The pine hawk moth (*Hyloicus pinastri*) is mainly confined to south eastern England which perhaps is just as well as far as commercial foresters are concerned. The green caterpillar has a reddish line edged with yellow along the centre of the dorsal surface and also red rings around the spinacles (breathing holes), a pattern giving it perfect camouflage among the leaves of the Scots pine and the spruce on which it feeds. Some continental forests have been considerably damaged by plagues of pine hawks. The privet hawk (*Sphinx ligustri*) larvae feeds not only on privet but also upon ash, while those of the lime hawk (*Mimas tiliae*) feed upon elm, alder and birch. The adults of all three species are attracted to light and overwinter as pupae.

The buff-tip (*Phalera bucephala*) is a true night moth attracted towards light although few specimens are caught before midnight. It is particularly common in England and Wales and I once caught over a hundred on a calm July night in a Dorset woodland of which only two came to the trap before midnight. The buff-tip adults have a curious habit while at rest of wrapping their wings around them like a cloak so that they resemble a piece of dry stick, the buff tip at the end looking like the cut end of the twig.

The moth's basic colour is purplish grey, but when the body is highlighted by shafts of light there is a lovely silvery glint making the buff-tip one of Britain's most attractive woodland insects. The gregarious caterpillars are hairy and mustard yellow, with many black bars across them making them hard to pick out against the branches of the trees on which they feed. When fully grown they can be over 7.5cm (3in) long and cause considerable damage by defoliating trees including oak, elm, sallow, hazel, beech, birch, lime and alder. When they are ready to pupate the caterpillars descend the tree and march away in search of soft earth in which to over-winter.

The clouded magpie (*Abraxas sylvata*) species is best described as local rather than widespread and has certainly suffered as a result of the demise of its larval food plant – almost exclusively English. Because it also feeds on wych elm, both have declined due to Dutch elm disease. Occasionally hazel and beech may be eaten which helps the moth to survive in those areas particularly hard hit by Dutch elm disease. The adults are easily attracted to a light and are on the wing from May until well into August.

The English name clouded moth probably arose because of its more suffused colouration when compared to the magpie moth (*Abraxas grossulariata*) also occurring in woodlands. The latter's larvae feed on blackthorn, hazel, hawthorn and wild gooseberry (*Ribes uva-crispa*). The mottled magpie is popular with collectors, however, because it shows many variations in colour and is easily caught in nets, having a slow fluttering flight and is readily attracted to a light. When there was a craze for collecting moths in Victorian times this particular moth was called the Yorkshire magpie because there was a variety in that county with dark grey on the wings which brought a good price on the market.

Another member of the same family showing similar variations in the adult phase is the clouded border (*Lomaspilis marginata*). The adults are found on the wing from May to August with the caterpillars feeding on hazel, willow and sallow. Damp woodlands are therefore ideal habitats for the yellow-green caterpillar with their distinctive trio of double dark green lines running down the back.

The larval period of the orange tip coincides with the peak flowering periods of its main food plants and tends to be short. The slender, pale green larvae have a tendency to eat each other but are protected from other predators by their resemblance to the stems and developing fruits of the cruciferous plants. They overwinter as chrysalids which show an uncanny resemblance to the withered plant pods. It should be remembered that only the male has the lovely orange tips, but both sexes look alike when they close their wings. These are mottled with green and provide a very efficient camouflage when the butterflies are settled on garlic mustard.

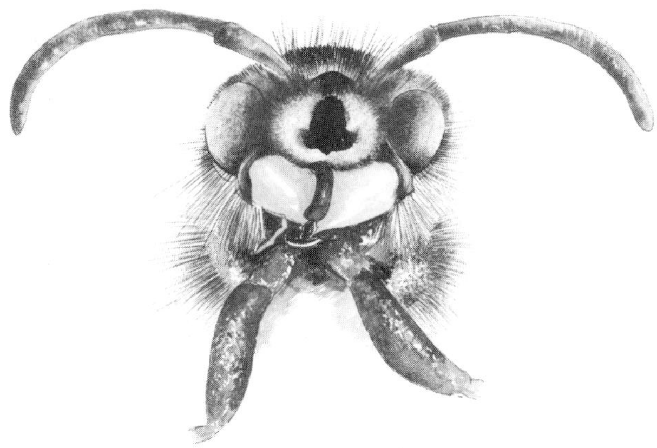

The common wasp invariably chooses an underground site for its globular nest. The insect can often be seen chewing away at the bark of a tree or a rotting log. Its powerful jaws grind this into a fine grained greyish paper from which the nest is made – wasps have been making good quality paper from wood pulp since carboniferous times almost 350 million years ago.

The interesting species vapourer (*Orgyia antiqua*) over-winters as an egg and the emerging smokey-grey caterpillars feed on almost any deciduous tree and also upon heather in upland areas. The males can measure up to 4cm (1⅔in) across the wings, but the females are flightless and rely upon air-borne pheromones to attract a mate. Males following the scent trail are often seen in flight during the day. The female is often mated by several males as soon as she emerges from her cocoon and the eggs may be laid on the outside of this structure lying dormant until the following spring.

The role played by the ichneumons going about their secretive business has already been mentioned, but there are other more obvious species in the order and the *Hymenoptera* are more feared by woodland picknickers than any other group of invertebrates. Many a happy gathering has been disrupted by the heavy drone of a bumble bee looking for a landing pad or the uncomfortable presence of ants.

In early spring moths are no problem but by September **wasps** seem to be everywhere, a real sign of the egg-laying efficiency of their queen. Many of the *Hymenoptera* are social insects living together in huge congregations of which the hive of the honey bee is perhaps the best known, but 'wasp cities' are equally efficient. There are seven species of social wasp, only two found commonly in our woodlands, namely the German (*Vespula germanica*), and common (*Vespula vulgaris*) but it is the much less common hornet (*Vespa crabro*) which generates the most fear.

Although superficially similar the German wasp can be distinguished from the common wasp by the patterning on the abdomen and the fact that *vulgaris* is much less bulky. Both species have dark bands across the yellow abdomen segments, but each band in the German wasp has a triangular black pattern almost reaching to the next band. In the common wasp this only occurs on the first band. Although the German wasp will use woodland nest sites such as rabbit holes and hollow trees it seems to show a preference for human habitations and suspends its almost circular nest under eaves.

The queen of both species is usually the only member of the colony to survive the winter and with the return of the first shafts of warming spring sunshine she begins nest building and egg laying. She has an ample store of eggs and by midsummer she has raised enough workers to enable her to assume the role of what amounts to an egg laying machine. This is also the pattern followed by the bees and ants. It has been estimated that from the start of the season a single queen can spawn up to 30,000 wasps.

Activity within the hive is hectic but surprisingly well organized. There are nursery wasps to look after the grubs, cleaners, entrance guards and those which forage for food. Just like an aeroplane, adult wasps in active flight need fuel, gathering nectar from a variety of plants, but seem to show a preference for umbelliferous species including wild carrot (*Daucas carota*), introduced giant hogweed (*Heracleum mantegazzianum*) and the native common hogweed (*Heracleum sphondylium*) as well as a number of other plants including heather, lesser knapweed (*Centaurea nigra*) and sycamore. These fuel sources may also be used by bees which need to keep a wary eye open for wasps because the latter do not stock their nests with honey but feed their larvae on other insects, including bees.

Their method of feeding the young is unique. The adult approaches the larval cell and knocks on the wall with its head. The larva raises its head and exudes a drop of digestive fluid onto which the prey is placed. Once digestion has taken place the fluid is sucked up by the grub.

The hornet, because it is a much larger size is more feared but there is no doubt that it is far less aggressive than its smaller relatives. It is a true woodland creature prefering to site its nest within a hollow tree. It is far less common than it used to be, a fact which is rather surprising in view of the fact that the trend has not been followed by other species of wasp.

If the hornet is maligned because of its size rather than its 'evil' temperament, then we should feel even more sorry for the wood wasp (*Urocerus gigas*). This is a member of the horntails, or wood-boring, family. The huge sting-like structure is an egg laying organ called the ovipositor which bores into tree trunks and deposits the egg deep into the tissues. The larvae feed on the wood and pupate within it before emerging as adults. Horntails can be over 10cm (4in) long and inflict considerable damage on valuable timber but they have no sting and are totally harmless to us. Wood wasps can reach lengths of almost 15cm (6in) and are the largest of the British *Hymenoptera* – at the other end of the scale we have the gall wasps.

Amaurobius ferox

Few animals have been so difficult to study as gall wasps. They are not so much gall makers as gall causers, the growths being formed by the plant after invasion by the insect. Most galls are caused by wasps – of the cynipid family – laying their eggs in the tissues of plants, but they can also be caused by mites, beetles and moths. They have been used by mankind since the days of Ancient Greece for they are all rich in tannic acid and were used in the treatment of hides. From the Middle Ages onwards galls were ground up and added to the ink made from fungi to make it more stable.

Enoplognatha ovata is even prepared to tackle a wasp

The life history of the wasps have proved very difficult to unravel and some have not been worked out at all. The oak marble gall wasp (*Cynips kollari*) has been found to have two generations spent on different hosts and the growths they stimulate are so unalike they were once thought to be separate species. This alternation of generations involves the production of a unisexual generation in which only females are produced and the bisexual generation which contains both males and females. After mating, only the females survive the winter and the following spring they give rise to the all female generation. Prior to the autumn the bisexual generation occurs again. *Cynips kollari* occurs on both the common oaks and the turkey oak (*Quercus cerris*) and, incidentally, the oak apple gall *Biorhiza pallida* shows alternation of generations too.

Linyphia triangularis

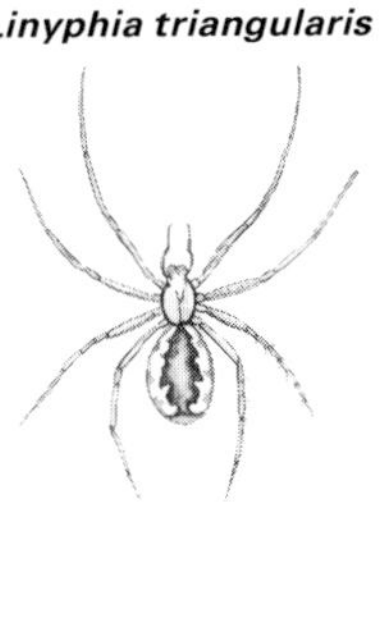

The oak marble galls are best collected in December and kept in a jam jar with damp cotton wool in the bottom and a perforated lid. Only entire galls should be collected since those with large holes in them will have been battered open by birds in search of the juicy grub within them. Those with tiny round holes are no good either since the adult will have escaped via this aperture and gone off to find another oak bud on which to lay its eggs. The wasps will eventually emerge from the galls and any amateur studying galls is more than likely to make new discoveries since there is much research yet to be done.

It is no accident that **bees** and flowers evolved at the same time since each depends upon the other. Bees fuel themselves and feed their young on either pollen or nectar or, which is more likely, on a combination of both. The flowers depend upon the bee for transfering the pollen allowing it to reproduce efficiently. While other insects are also associated with flowers it is the bees which have carried the process to the peak of perfection. The honey bee has been of such value as a human source of food that we often forget that not all bees are organized into large hives and there are several woodland-based species of solitary bee.

The leafbee (*Megachile centucularis*) is so named because of its habit of cutting up leaves to make shelters beneath which its young can develop. A crevice in an old tree trunk is an ideal site filled with honey before being sealed in with a circular lid of leaf. The body of the leaf cutting bee is black but covered with a layer of fine grey hairs and the edges of the abdominal segments and the head are yellow contrasting sharply with the dark body.

The carpenter bee (*Osmia aurulenta*) is also common and can be distinguished from the hive bee by its brownish-grey abdomen with a pale gold band on each segment and there is also a golden cast on the central portion of the thorax. The nest is constructed at the end of a 15cm (6in) long tunnel, often in the soil but also under the roots of a tree. Honey and pollen are provided for the larvae hatching from the three or four eggs the female leaves in the burrow. Carpenter bees have also been known to use discarded snail shells as nurseries.

The humble bees appear to steer the middle course between the solitary bees and the densely populated hives of the honey bee. The buff-tailed humble bee (*Bombus terrestris*) is also known as the bumble bee and its large body with very small wings beating vigorously accounts for the loud humming sound which are so much a part of country walks. The body is covered with long, silky hairs and there are two conspicuous yellow bands across the abdomen. The nest is usually some way below ground and the females, which hibernate in its tunnels, can often be seen foraging for early spring nectar which they often find on ivy.

The large red tailed humble bee (*Bombus lapidarius*) is the most common of the humbles in the south of England coming out of hibernation comparatively late, often not being active until June. The body is also covered in long black hairs but there is no mistaking the bright red lower abdomen. The nest is reached via a tunnel which can be more than a metre ($3\frac{1}{4}$ft) in length.

The largest of our native **ants** is the wood ant which, as its name implies, is confined to woodlands, often prefering coniferous areas.

The presence of the wood ant is easy to detect because of the huge piles of dried grass, twigs and dry earth constructed by the workers, at their most active from April to September. By altering the quantity of vegetation, the temperature and water content of the nest can be controlled. The young are fed on other insects while aphids are carried into the nest and 'milked' to provide workers with energy. Nests are common in alien conifer plantations the needles making ideal nesting material.

The workers are over 6mm ($\frac{1}{4}$in) in length and the rusty red thorax stands out clearly from the black abdomen. Periodically, slightly larger winged females and males are produced and during a spectacular nuptual flight the females are fertilized and are then capable of starting a new colony. Like the social bees and wasps the female ant is an egg laying factory and once she has produced the first workers this is all she is expected to do. Attracted by her individual scent the workers provide her and her offspring with food.

Hogweed produces lots of nectar providing insects with an ideal feeding station.

RIGHT: **The bumble bee plays a vital role in woodland life, without it many of the early blossoms would never be pollinated.**

ABOVE: ***Diastrophus rubi*, has no common name but is found on bramble. The gall can measure up to 15cm (6in) and looks like a shrivelled peanut, each containing as many as 100 larvae.**

Other species warranting close attention are the robin's pincushion or rose-bedeguar gall wasp, the oak apple gall and oak spangle gall. In the oak apple gall the unisexual generation is found on the roots of oak while the bisexual generation occurs on the leaves.

A wood ant's nest may have as many as 100,000 individual workers, each of which will vigorously defend the nest. Ants do not sting like bees and wasps, but have powerful jaws which can pierce human skin, and they then turn around and squirt formic acid into the cut – a most painful experience. The jets of formic acid can give the whole of a woodland the smell of vinegar when the nests have been disturbed by hungry birds such as jays or woodpeckers, or mammals like the badger. These latter seem capable of feeding on the wood ant but there is no doubt that most potential predators are quickly discouraged.

In the world there are as many as 275,000 species of **beetle** making up the *Coleoptera* while in Britain there are over 4,000 species. Beetles are easily identified by their hardened fore-wings folding over the body protecting both the thorax and the abdomen. These elytra, as they are called, are joined together along the back producing a prominent line down the dorsal surface which is only found in beetles. Although beetles do have a pair of functional wings they spend most of their time buried in the soil, hunting around in the leaf litter, climbing vegetation or hiding beneath the bark. Their mouth-parts are tough making beetles most formidable predators.

There are about 40 species of ladybirds in Britain, but the most common is the seven spot (*Coccinella septempunctata*), whose larvae can often be found feeding upon aphids on trees, especially dog rose. The wing cases are bright red with seven black spots. Under this bright cover is a pair of shiny dark brown wings which are efficient but the insect does not always choose to use them.

The stag beetle (*Lucanus cervus*) is the largest and most magnificent of British beetles, the male having horn-like structures from which its English name derives. The female is somewhat smaller and lacks the antlers. Both sexes are very shiny brown and have long pointed brown wings making their flight very powerful and enabling the stag beetle to travel long distances. The larvae feed on dead wood and rotting piles of twigs.

The female nut weevil (*Curculio nucum*) is able to pierce developing hazel nuts whilst they are still soft. The egg she deposits develops inside the nut, feeds on the kernel and then bites through the hard shell before burying itself in the soil prior to pupation. An examination of autumn nuts will reveal many with a small hole to show where the insect escaped. The nut weevil is light brown in colour and its body is around 6mm ($\frac{1}{4}$in) long but the prominent snout doubles this length.

The **bugs** making up the order *Hemiptera* are typified by having two pairs of wings, the front pair are horny and the hind pair transparent. The mouth parts are well adapted for sucking fluids from plants. Greenfly are common but the species most likely to be encountered in woodlands is the froghopper (*Philaenus spumarius*). This small insect produces the froth-like globes which stick to vegetation, known as cuckoo spit. In the early stages this spit prevents the animal from drying up while it sucks the sap from plant stems. They are mostly greyish-brown in colour but some individuals are grey and others black. The wing cases covering the whole body are hard and shiny, the head is small and their eyes are black. The most astounding feature of froghoppers is their ability to jump fantastic distances accounting for the common name.

Although the true **flies** have two pairs of membranous wings, the hind pair have become modified to form balancing organs called halteres. They are grouped into the order *Diptera* meaning two pairs of wings. All adult flies have sucking mouth parts and there are over 5,000 British species – no doubt others await identification. The midges which are such a nuisance, the gad flies or clegs (*Tabanus bovinus*) which can inflict a really painful bite and the housefly (*Musca domestica*) are all common in woodlands. Precise identification of the *Diptera*, however, requires a specialist text.

The cardinal beetles get their names from their bright red colour rather like a cardinals hat. Two species occur in Britain – *Pyrochrea coccinea* which has a red body with a contrasting black head, and *Pyrochrea serraticornis* whose head and body are both of brilliant scarlet. The cardinals are sluggish animals which are found climbing on woodland flowers and under the flaking bark of trees. Their unpleasant taste seems to repel potential predators and so there is no need for the beetles to go anywhere in a hurry. The flattened, yellowish-brown larvae are also sufficiently destructive to be easily recognized.

The last phylum of the invertebrates are the *Molluscs* of which there are over 100,000 species in the world the majority of which live either in the sea or in fresh water. The word mollusc means soft bodied and this is a true definition even though the delicate flesh is often protected by a shell. Of the three main classes of *Mollusc* only the *Gastropods* are terrestrial and slugs and snails are common among the leaf litter and damp vegetation. The high humidity and shelter typical of these areas make the perfect habitat, providing that the soil is sufficiently lime rich to allow the snails in particular to build up their shells. Apart from the absence of a shell the body of slugs is very similar to that of the snail and they all chew their food with a rasp-like organ called the radula.

The two species of woodland **slug** most likely to be encountered are the great grey slug (*Limax maximus*) and the even larger black slug (*Limax cinereoniger*). Both species can reach a length of 20cm (8in). *Limax maximus* is usually, as its name implies, grey but many specimens are pale brown with two or three lateral bands of a rather darker shade. These lines may not always be continuous but can be broken into spots or dotted lines.

The courtship of this species, and of most land *Molluscs*, is very unusual. Each individual is an hermaphrodite having both male and female reproductive organs, but neither is self fertilizing. The pair circle touching each other gently with their tentacles for periods of up to two hours. They create an appreciable amount of slime (mucus) during this time and finally mate whilst suspended in mid-air on a rope of the mucus. They can sometimes be seen twined around each other hanging from beech twigs and exchanging sperm.

The great grey slug feeds almost exclusively on dead plants and fungi and is not particularly upset by disturbance. *Limax cinereoniger*, on the other hand, lives deeper in the woodland and is much shyer. Specimens of up to 40cm (16in) have

Unless the weather is very wet the black slug waits until the humidity builds up during the night when it emerges from beneath logs to feed mainly on fungi.

been recorded but most are half this size – the body is so elastic that precise measurement is not easy.

Snails found in woodlands may either be pulmonates or operculates. The pulmonates breathe through a primitive lung between the shell and the body, a sure sign that they are adapting well to life on land.

Woodland pulmonates includes the garden snail (*Helix aspera*), which no doubt began life as a forest dweller but has proved adaptable enough to live easily in gardens, town parks and even on sea cliffs.

The plaited door snail (*Cochlodina laminata*) is an attractive species of pulmonate confined to woods thriving mainly in those dominated by beech and ash. It seeks out sheltered spots in the leaf litter and its long, club-shaped shell has a 'door' which the snail can pull tightly across the opening when it is at rest excluding most predators, the most persistent being the beetles. A further degree of protection is also afforded by the shell entrance being folded to form a series of sharp, tooth-like structures.

A woodland species defying the rule which says that snails are confined to areas rich in lime, is the carnivorous hollowed glass snail (*Zonitoides excavatus*) feeding on invertebrates including worms and other snails. The shell is only 6mm ($\frac{1}{4}$in) high but it is worth searching for since Britain is one of the few countries in which it is found. It occurs in areas containing no lime and how it manages to successfully form its shell is still something of a mystery. It has been suggested that it chooses such areas because it avoids competition with other snails for space and food.

The operculate snails, however, are much less adapted to life on land and retain many features typical of their marine ancestors. They can be identified by the presence of a disc called the operculum used to seal the shell when the animal is resting and keeps predators out and essential moisture in – this can be seen clearly in the periwinkle family.

In British woodlands only two operculate snails occur. *Pomatias elegans*, or the land winkle, can be very common in some lime rich areas, but is absent from others where conditions would appear to be ideal. The tough shell can be almost 2cm ($\frac{3}{4}$in) high and is found on woodland edges and alongside paths running through the trees. Fossil evidence suggests that it was once much more common than at present. Although its range is still shrinking it is not yet in any danger of extinction. Neither is the tiny *Acicula fusca* which is common but needs searching for in old beechwoods. The cylindrical shell is only 2mm ($\frac{1}{9}$in) high but it is well worth searching for in the leaf litter. Operculates differ from pulmonates by having separate sexes and the eyes are not borne at the tips of the tentacles but stand upon separate little stumps at the base. This can be seen by the use of an inexpensive binocular microscope. Such a purchase would open up a whole new and fascinating world by enabling a deeper and more detailed study of woodland invertebrates.

At night ladybirds do tend to fly but if they are disturbed in the daytime they prefer to drop to the ground and scuttle away. The larvae are much less active and prefer to stay among the greenfly but if they run out of food they crawl about until they find a fresh supply of aphids.

Woodland birds

Woodlands of today are an often confusing mixture of the ancient and modern as introduced species struggle to intrude into the world of the native dominants such as oak, beech, ash and alder. Careful research in recent years has satisfactorily proved the obvious – the more varied the woodland the more species of bird it will support. It is, however, not just the species of tree which determines the birds present, but where these trees are located. The pedunculate oak trees of south eastern England for example, provide quite a different environment to that of the sessile oak woods growing on the slopes of Wales or the Lake District. Similarly the birches of a lowland valley will attract a more varied population of birds than those overhanging a Highland loch.

The seasons also influence the birds which will be seen in our woodlands. The beech woods of south eastern England are filled with a shimmering green haze during June and July as the summer sunlight filters through the mosaic of overlapping leaves. The wood warbler (*Phylloscopus sibilatrix*) loves these conditions and flits from the foliage of one tree to another, its *stip-stip-stip, shreeee* call echoing across the glades. This species also has a second equally distinctive call consisting of a high pitched, piping call when the syllable *piu* is repeated.

By the time the glowing bronzes of the autumn beechwoods have replaced the succulent greens of summer, the warblers have departed for the warmer climate of Africa and the wintering finches have arrived to seek refuge from the icy climate of northern Europe. Chaffinches (*Fringilla coelebs*) are the first to arrive and swell the already large resident population in British woodlands, but they are soon joined by the brambling (*Fringilla montifringilla*), a truly northern finch.

The smooth undulating flight of the chaffinch is easily distinguished from the much less agile more erratic flight of the brambling. There are also obvious physical differences, especially between the males. Cock chaffinches have an olive-brown back with a chestnut mantle, and a delicate pink flush on the underparts while the head and nape are slate blue. The bird is at its most attractive when caught by shafts of sunlight and in flight, when the set of double white wing bars and creamy-white outer tail feathers show up clearly. Chaffinches are around 15cm (6in) long in contrast to the 14cm (5¾in) of the brambling although, once again, this is not obvious in the field. Bramblings, on the other hand, have a white rump, while that of the chaffinch is green, and there is also far less white on the tail and wings of the brambling. The real feature of the cock brambling is the orange breast, very obvious patches of orange on the shoulders and the brown mantle which as the winter draws to a close changes to the black of the breeding plumage.

The females of the two species are more difficult to distinguish, but the hen brambling has a white rump and dark stripes on the head both of which are lacking

OPPOSITE: **Although the pheasant is an introduced bird it is now around in many of our deciduous woodlands.**

in the chaffinch. Although male bramblings have been observed singing in the mixed birch and Scots pine woods of Scotland and one female has been seen in summer with a brood patch, breeding is not firmly established in Britain and the species is a bird of winter woodlands. Literally millions of chaffinches from northern Europe winter in Britain and many also breed throughout the country with perhaps as many as seven million pairs!

Many professional ornithologists have worked on woodland bird populations, but in recent years the British Trust for Ornithology has co-ordinated the work of amateurs in their ambitious Common Bird Census which has proved a resounding success.

Following a tentative start in 1961, the census really took off in 1964 and has gone on from strength to strength. The observer is provided with a large scale map of the area from which the census is to be taken and a sheet detailing the shorthand to be used. The presence of blackbirds for example is indicated by (B), song thrush by (ST) and chaffinch by (C). If two males are seen fighting over territory then the symbol is BB, when a bird gives the alarm call the symbol is *B* and if a nest is found, the sign used in B*.

The observer makes several visits during the breeding season keeping a separate map for each visit – the route followed through the habitat is the same on each occasion. This method, apart from adding to the interest of the walk, may well have an important conservation role to play in the future. When the results of all the woodland plots are compared it is possible to work out not only which species dominate each type of woodland but also how much space each pair of breeding birds require. It is also possible to show how the bird life is affected when woodlands are managed for profit. What, for example, happens during the conifer cycle,

A dunnock feeding her young. These birds may be found in many different habitats such as hedgerows and gardens, as well as woodlands.

when a spruce woodland is prepared, planted, establishes itself, matures and is then felled?

High up on the fells the spring sunshine breaks through the watery cloud and mist rises from the rough grasses. Thousands of years ago most of this area would have been dominated by a forest of birch but this has long since been cleared. The soaring flight song of the skylark (*Alauda arvensis*) fills the air but there is often room for the less impressive notes of the meadow pipit (*Anthus pratensis*) and the onomatopaeic call of the cuckoo to join in the chorus. From the heather the red grouse (*Lagopus lagopus*) shouts its warning call which sounds very like *Go-back, go-back*. That tiny killer, the merlin (*Falco columbarius*) swoops low over the moor in search of any unwary bird.

The whole population is under threat, however, as bulldozers move in to lay drainage channels and build roads, which will come into use many years later, to remove the mature timber. Trees have been planted and they begin to grow.

Although the habitat is changing, the moorland species survive for a while and may even find the new saplings beneficial. The increased cover, however, provides nest sites and roosts thereby encouraging such species as the linnet, tree pipit (*Anthus trivialis*), whitethroat (*Sylvia communis*), willow warbler, whinchat (*Saxicola rubetra*) and the robin (*Erithacus rubecula*). These early stages are also attractive to the short-eared owl (*Asio flammeus*) which, although predominantly a moorland species, welcomes some cover for its nest. The increased protection also allows the population of short tailed, field voles (*Microtus agrestis*) – occasionally reaching epidemic proportions. The short-eared owls can be surprisingly efficient in controlling rodents and in times of a vole plague they may hunt in parties of up to a dozen birds. This in turn helps feed the young, and the short-eared owls may succeed in raising more than six to flying stage during such plagues, whereas they can normally raise only two.

Gradually, however, the trees grow, shut out the light and open spaces are at a premium. The willow warbler and the robin both manage to remain and perhaps increase a little in quantity but the goldcrest soon moves in and assumes a dominant position. Other species appear, too, including the song thrush, blackbird and more especially, the coal tit (*Parus ater*) and the wood pigeon.

While there is the sad loss of the short-eared owl when the conifers mature, it is replaced by the long-eared owl (*Asio otus*) which has undergone an increase in both range and population as the new coniferous woodlands of Britain approach maturity. There may be as many as 7,000 pairs now breeding in Britain – almost twice as many as in the 1950s. The species is quite difficult to number since it is much less vocal than the tawny owl (*Strix aluco*) and is also almost completely nocturnal and unlikely to venture into the open countryside to hunt unless it is dark.

The two features that separate the long-eared owl from the tawny are its smaller size – 35cm (14in), compared to 38cm (15in) – and greyer appearance, both of which are difficult to detect in the field. The two reliable features are the orange rings around the eyes and the prominent ear tufts which the owl can erect at will. Both these features are lacking in the tawny owl, which has a typically round-headed appearance and black eyes. A few nests are sited on the ground, but most pairs take over an old crow's nest in which the female incubates the clutch of around five eggs for almost 30 days. The young, though still dependent upon their parents for food, leave the nest when they are between three and four weeks old. In a few years, when the conifer forests of Britain mature, there will doubtless be an outcry at the threat to the habitat of the long-eared owl. The foresters' reply is that this should be good news for the short-eared owl when the tree cycle begins all over again.

Researches have established that the chaffinch was the most numerous breeding bird in both pedunculate and sessile oak woods as well as those dominated by birch and beech. In the native pine woods of Speyside the chaffinch maintained its dominance but in mature spruce forests it was replaced by the goldcrest and had to settle for second place.

Many species including the blackbird, song thrush, robin and dunnock (*Prunella modularis*) are found not only in woodlands but are so adaptable that they find other habitats such as hedgerows and gardens. Other families of birds, however, are real tree specialists including the woodpeckers and the diurnal birds of prey, whilst the titmice, finches, flycatchers and crows are also more at home in woodlands than anywhere else.

The order of birds called the *Piciformes* includes the **woodpeckers** and the toucans all of which are tree-dwellers. The woodpecker family are divided into three sub-families. There are 143 species of piculets, none of which occur in Britain, 179 species of true woodpecker, of which only three occur in Britain, and there are also two species of wrynecks of which one is found occasionally in Britain.

The true woodpeckers are typified by having two toes pointing forwards and two behind which is a condition known as zygodactylic and is an ideal adaptation for climbing trees. There are also several other adaptations including 12 specially stiffened wedge-shaped tail feathers acting as props and are moulted in such a way that the central pair are not shed until those surrounding them have been replaced and can take on the supportive function. The wedge-shaped bill is perfectly adapted to chisel away at wood and the nostrils are protected by bristle-like feathers preventing saw-dust from entering the breathing tubes.

The birds also have very long mobile tongues for seeking out insects. The bones supporting the tongue are long and secured to the back of the skull while the end of the organ is either bristled or covered with barbs. Glands secrete a sticky mucus covering the surface of the tongue and adds to the efficiency of the tongue as an insect trap. The three British woodpeckers avoid competition by each feeding in a different niche.

The green woodpecker is, at 32cm ($12\frac{3}{4}$in), our largest species, easily recognized by its green upper parts with prominent areas of bright yellow on the back and the

A wood warbler. Warblers are not easy to distinguish from their physical appearance alone which is why they have such distinctive calls.

rump. The crown of both sexes is red but the male also has a red moustachial stripe, whilst that of his mate is black. Their food consists mainly of ants and their pupae, meaning that they spend a great deal of time stabbing into the nest of the wood ant. The new coniferous plantations are a good habitat for the wood ants which in turn feed the green woodpecker. In the depths of winter, however, when the ants' nest is covered with a thick layer of icy snow, the green woodpecker may hack into the bark of a tree and push its tongue deep into the rotting timber in search of hibernating insects.

It seldom drums, but its characteristic laughing call is a feature of many woodlands especially in recent years during which it has extended its range. There may well be as many as 25,000 breeding pairs and although they suffer badly in cold winters their range now extends into central Scotland, although like the other two species of woodpecker, it does not breed in Ireland.

The great spotted woodpecker (*Dendrocopus major*) is more widespread than the green and there are probably more than 40,000 beeeding pairs in Britain. The species obtains most of its food by chipping away at tree trunks – a practice not effected by the weather and bad winters usually have little, if any, effect on the population. It is also more of a true woodland bird being found in both coniferous and deciduous areas.

The great spotted woodpecker is around 23cm (9in) long, very obviously black and white and has a red patch under the tail. The male can be distinguished by a red spot on his nape.

In addition to the native population of woodpeckers, large numbers flock into Britain from Scandinavia, including a few lesser spotted woodpeckers (*Dendrocopus minor*). It is a much more retiring species and is only around 14.5cm (5¾in). It may be recognized by the prominent black and white barring across the back and the lack of any red on the rump. The male, however, does have a red crown, a feature lacking in the female. Although it is a difficult species to number because of its secretive habits, there are probably only around 10,000 breeding pairs in Britain, almost totally confined to England and Wales. There have been a few breeding attempts in Scotland in recent years thought to be by immigrants from Scandinavia rather than by English birds expanding their range. This is also thought to be the case with a few pairs of wrynecks (*Jynx torquilla*) which is now all but extinct as a British breeding species.

Like the great spotted woodpecker the lesser spotted drums to advertize its territory. The great spotted, however, delivers only eight to ten blows compared with the lesser spotted's strike rate of ten to 30. The two being of different size there is little competition for food and, unlike the larger species, the lesser spotted woodpecker does not kill and eat the nestlings of small birds such as the tits – great spotted woodpeckers often chip their way into nest boxes to get at eggs and young. They will also eat young red squirrels which is interesting since squirrels may also eat young woodpeckers if they get the chance.

The chiff-chaff repeats its own name continually, but when it is not singing it takes some skill to separate it from the wood warbler. At 12.5cm (5in) the wood warbler is a larger species than the chiff-chaff which is just over 10cm (4in). This does not help, however, unless the two species are seen side by side. The comparatively longer wings of the wood warbler are not likely to be obvious either, but its yellow-green back and much more yellow throat and breast contrasting to the lighter belly are more reliable features, as is the broad yellow stripe above the eye. The chiff-chaff also has a habit of flicking its wings during display which is not part of the wood warbler's breeding behaviour.

No order of birds has excited the human mind or been more persecuted by us than the *Falconiformes* – the diurnal **birds of prey**. The hawks and eagles make up the accipitridae family whilst the falcons belong to the falconidae family – generally more active flyers and killers rather than seekers of carrion. There is a somewhat bizarre method of distinguishing between hawks and falcons by the way they defecate whilst at the nest. The hawks squirt out their waste several feet from the nest whereas falcons defecate directly under the perch and many a peregrine's eyrie has been discovered by the tell-tale 'whitewash' directly beneath it.

The role of the birds of prey in the woodland web is to control populations of

Wrynecks have declined because of weather changes in Britain.

rodents and, more particularly, small birds. In the days when fresh meat was not readily available falconers learned to train birds of prey to catch birds and return to a lure. The small birds were sold or eaten by the falconer and the predator rewarded by a tit-bit. This was a legitimate method for a hunter to feed his family, but after the invention of efficient guns the falcon was no longer needed. The sport, however, continues and the true falconer stays within the law. The illegal taking of wild falcon from their nests can seriously reduce the populations of birds of prey, some species of which have already been decimated by the persecution of Victorian gamekeepers and agricultural chemicals.

The rearing of pheasants and partridges for the sporting man to shoot, led to the gamekeepers' efficiency because his job was based upon the size of the bag. It was inevitable that anything with a hooked bill and powerful talons would be trapped, shot or poisoned. Many woodland birds of prey disappeared during this period but from the 1940s onwards a more realistic attitude began to prevail.

In the aftermath of the Second World War, however, there was an effort to improve agricultural efficiency and hydrocarbon based poisons began to be spread on the land. These were picked up by small mammals and seed-eating birds, which in turn were eaten by birds of prey roosting in the woods and hunting over the fields. The strong predators were not killed quickly, but the female's reproductive efficiency was affected, causing her to produce egg shells which were so thin that they were crushed during incubation. The poisons, particularly aldrin and dieldrin, find their way into the body fat and as long as the bird is well fed are not released. Just as the bird comes under real stress and needs to draw on these reserves the poisons are released and the bird dies. The resulting combination of breeding inefficiency and sudden death of adults in winter led to the decline of many birds of prey particularly the peregrine (*Falco peregrinus*) and the sparrowhawk (*Accipiter nisus*).

The sparrowhawk has recovered some of its losses since the use of really dangerous chemicals was discontinued, but it is still very rare in the south eastern

The green woodpecker feeds on the ground more often than other members of the family. The arrangement of two toes set forward and two behind still makes the bird an excellent climber.

Birds killed by poisonous agricultural chemicals.

counties. There may, however, be as many as 30,000 pairs now breeding in Britain. Sparrowhawks prefer to nest in conifers and it may well be that the maturing forests have helped in its recovery, together with a reduction in the use of harmful pesticides and keepering pressure.

The goshawk (*Accipiter gentilis*) has also shown some signs of increase due to the spread of coniferous forests, although it is doubtful if the population is yet more than 30 pairs. The goshawk looks like a huge female sparrowhawk the size varying from 48cm to 60cm (19in to 24in), the females being larger than the males. The size of the sparrowhawk varies from 28cm to 38cm (11in to 15in) and the female is, similarly, much the larger bird. Some workers are of the opinion that the two sexes can tackle different food items and avoid direct competition with each other. The female sparrowhawk is brown above with a pale undersurface barred with brown, and the male is blue-grey and his underparts are barred with red.

The buzzard (*Buteo buteo*) has been much slower to recover than the sparrowhawk, although the British breeding population may now exceed 10,000 pairs. There is no doubt that is size, varying from 50cm to 59cm (20in to 23in), led to the belief that it was much more of a danger to the farmer and gamekeeper than it actually is. Its favourite prey is small mammals which it catches by flying slowly over open country or woodland glades, but more usually by selecting a post or tree and watching the area below waiting the chance to pounce. Areas most favoured by buzzards are the woodlands clothing the steep valleys of Wales, the English Lakes and Scotland which provide food, cover and ideal nest sites. The nest is a huge, untidy bundle of sticks in which two or three bluish white eggs heavily blotched with red-brown are laid. After an incubation period of around five weeks the young hatch and are fledged at seven weeks.

While watching a pair of buzzards feeding their young in an old oak wood in Wales I quickly learned to recognize both birds by their appearance and I could also easily distinguish any visiting buzzards occasionally soaring above the wood. Buzzards do vary a great deal in colour although they are brown above with lighter areas on the undersurface. Dark marks on the carpal area of the wings (equivalent to the wrist) can be seen when viewed from beneath. I am sure that individual differences will be present in every species of bird if only we had the time to look. This should hardly be surprising since no two people look exactly alike, and we can identify our own pet cat or dog from any other animal.

It was while watching my Welsh buzzards that I noticed a red kite (*Milvus milvus*) easily identified by its colour and forked tail. Although it was once widespread in Britain the population has been reduced to less than 30 pairs. They are concentrated, and therefore highly vulnerable, in the sessile oak woodlands overhanging the upland valleys of Wales, areas which have long been coveted by commercial foresters. The farmers of the area have also taken some convincing that the red kite prefers to eat carrion than kill for itself and are still occasionally inclined to put down poison bait for the bird.

The Scottish fishermen, however, were much more effective in removing the osprey (*Pandion haliaetus*) and by 1916 the upland lochs surrounded by pine woods were 'free of the nuisance'. Ospreys, fortunately, are migrants and during the 1950s African birds began to explore the forests of Scotland once more and there are now more than 30 breeding pairs and the range is expanding. It may not be too long before the forests of England welcome their first breeding ospreys for more than a century.

The size of the bird varies from 50cm to 60cm (20in to 24in) and no British bird of prey has a dark upper surface contrasting so sharply with the very light colour of the chest and belly. It also has no competitors in its chosen niche for feeding which involves hovering over water and plunge diving for fish. The light coloured underparts blend perfectly into the skyline making it difficult for the fish to detect the plunging bird.

When the osprey roosts in the surrounding conifers with its wings closed, the dark surface of the back is difficult to see against the coniferous foliage. Further adaptations to its fishing life style include very rough areas on the feet working like tiny fish hooks to hold the struggling fish firmly in the talons whilst being carried to the nest or killing perch.

Two even rarer birds of prey are only just surviving in the deciduous woodlands of southern England are the honey buzzard (*Pernis apivorus*) and the delicate little hobby (*Falco subbuteo*). The former is so dependent upon the insects on which it feeds, especially bees, that it only arrives and breeds when the population of bees and wasps are at their highest. The number of pairs breeding in any one year is therefore impossible to estimate but it is certainly a species to excite those who bird-watch in southern woodlands. The New Forest is an especially favoured habitat there being areas of trees with extensive clearings. Although about the same size as the common buzzard, the honey buzzard has a much smaller head and narrower neck and the wings and tail are longer and similarly narrower. Obviously because of its diet it spends more time scratching around on the ground than *Buteo buteo*.

These young little owls are very much at home in a hollow tree on a Pennine hillside. Their parents are found hunting both by day and night, the diet consisting mainly of insects.

In complete contrast the tiny hobby, only measuring around 35cm (14in) sweeps among the trees and open glades with its powerful wings swept back like those of a swift. It will take small birds and is even fast enough to catch swallows and martins but it really specializes in taking insects on the wing and is therefore often seen feeding at dawn and dusk. When at rest chestnut patches on thighs and under the tail may be seen in addition to the thin moustachial stripes giving the bird the appearance of a tiny Chinese mandarin. Like all birds of prey, hobbies were persecuted by gamekeepers and there are seldom more than 100 pairs visiting Britain each summer to breed.

The woodlands have been a human larder for centuries, but only in the last 150 years have they been the domain of the sportsman shooting for fun rather than for the pot. **Game species** such as the native woodcock, wood pigeon and even the heron have been netted, hawked, limed, trapped and shot while gamebirds such as capercaillie, grey partridge and pheasant have all been protected from their natural predators in order to provide high populations and good sport.

The woodcock is the only member of the wader family habitually found both feeding and nesting in woodlands and therefore avoids competiton with other similar species. Its bill is long, almost enough to make the 34cm (13in) long body appear top heavy. Another obvious feature is the woodcock's large, laterally situated pair of eyes. They enable the woodcock to see enemies approaching both from the side and from the rear while it is plunging its bill into the soft woodland earth in search of insect larvae, which form the bulk of its food. It will also take some vegetable matter and the only time it really suffers is when the cold winter frosts solidify the ground. The British climate, however, is not nearly as severe as

The partridge is still common along the edges of woodlands which provide it with cover. It then emerges to feed in the fields.

that of northern Europe and it is no surprise to find that the British breeding population of around 50,000 pairs is swelled by large numbers of immigrants.

The sight of the reddish brown, thick set woodcock twisting its way in and out of trees when flushed has long delighted the hunter and being good to eat they are shot in large numbers. In the days before efficient guns they were caught in nets called cockshots which provided many a peasant family with a good dinner and the bird catchers with a profitable living. They have, however, never been bred specially for sport and neither have wood pigeons, which is also a favourite quarry of the rough shooter.

Originally a woodland bird, the wood pigeon has quickly adapted to feeding around farmland and is the largest member of its family measuring around 40cm (16in). The bird has a white wing patch, a long tail and a white patch on the neck which is a delightful combination of shining green and red – easily recognized features. The wing-clapping display echoes like a rifle shot through the woodlands, and its much more soothing *coo-coo-coo* call is typical of the breeding season lasting from February to November when three broods of two can be raised.

Conifers are favourite nest sites and the very flimsy nest is usually close to the junction of the branch and trunk and the eggs can often be seen through the floor of the nest. The value of this loose arrangement may be appreciated when it rains for instead of flooding the nest, the water drips straight through. Both parents incubate the eggs which hatch after 17 days with the squabs, as the young are called, fed by both parents until they fledge after a further three or four weeks.

Pigeons are the only birds to feed their young directly from the throat of both parents on a liquid almost identical to the milk of mammals in its chemical make up. The flesh of the pigeon is good to eat accounting for the dovecots, so much a part of medieval manor houses which were in constant need of fresh protein.

The true gamebirds found in woodlands include the partridge, pheasant, capercaillie and black grouse. The native grey partridge (*Perdix perdix*) breeds occasionally on woodland edges, but has become much more of a hedgerow bird in recent years unlike the pheasant which was almost certainly introduced by the Romans, with the Normans also bringing in fresh blood. The original stock had black necks, but other types with white rings around the neck were introduced as shooting stock and the interbreeding of these races has led to a fascinating array of colour patterns in the stock found living wild in the woodlands of Britain.

The capercaillie breeds in the belt of coniferous forests from Norway to Scandinavia and a few populations remain as relics in other highland areas with a climate similar to that which existed soon after the Ice Ages. The Scottish populations seem to have been exterminated by 1800, but birds from Sweden were introduced to Tayside in Scotland in the late 1830s, and apart from some setbacks in the periods of the two wars when many trees were felled, they have spread steadily.

Doubtless, new plantations have benefited the species allowing the black grouse (*Lynurus tetrix*) to colonize new areas. It seems that the capercaillie dominates the deep confines of the woodlands and the black grouse takes over on the fringes of the forests and the wet acid moorlands surrounding them. The blackcock is 53cm (21in) long and may be distinguished by his blue-black plumage contrasting with the white wing bar and undertail coverts. The tail itself is shaped like a lyre especially during the communal breeding ceremonies called leks. The greyhen, like her mate, has red wattles over the eye, but she is much smaller being around only 40cm (16in) and has a mainly grey plumage.

Fortunately,not all birds have suffered as a result of human activities and the **titmice** in particular have been able to thrive in areas from which almost all their predators have been removed. The only brakes on rising population levels is the availability of food.

A study of the anatomy of birds, particularly their feet and bills, will show how each is adapted to a particular diet. The tree-creeper (*Certhia familiaris*) with its thin curved bill and stiffened tail feathers reminiscent of the woodpecker, for instance, is able to hang on to tree trunks and probe deeply into the bark to take spiders, insects and the larvae from the crevices. These niches, however, cannot be reached by the blue tits (*Parus caeruleus*) or great tits, which although inquisitive and resourceful have bills which are far too short to compete with the treecreeper in this niche. Like the great tit, the nuthatch feeds upon beech nuts but the latter is also able to tackle hazel nuts because its bill is much more powerful. To avoid direct competition with the great tit the blue tit, smaller and more agile, feeds higher in the canopy and less often on the woodland floor where it is likely to be bullied by the more aggressive species.

The long tailed tit is even more agile than the blue tit, its 8cm (3½in) body beautifully balanced by a 7.5cm (3in) tail allowing the bird to feed on seeds carried on the side branches of trees such as birch and alder. The long tailed tit is frequently seen in flocks of titmice but it does not actually belong to the titmouse family (the paridae) but is the only British example of the aegithalidae family.

The coal tit is even smaller and less aggressive than the blue tit being only 11cm (4½in) long and recognized by its black crown and a bold white patch on the back of the neck. Whether it chooses to live in conifers to avoid being bullied by other species or because its bill is perfectly adapted for feeding in these areas it is difficult to say, but the maturing plantations have allowed some recent increases in population. More than 1,000,000 pairs nest in Britain compared with 5,000,000 pairs of blue tits and over 3,000,000 pairs of great tits. While the coal tit may be regarded as common in all coniferous areas the crested tit (*Parus cristatus*) is confined to the old pine wood areas of Scotland and is the rarest and most specialized of the British tits there being only 1–2,000 breeding pairs. As its name implies, the crest makes the species easily identified, as does the white face, narrow black collar and bib, and low pitched *choo-rr* call. This can sound very like that of a long tailed tit but there is also a high pitched *tzee-tzee tzee* call, quite diagnostic of the crested tit. It is more often heard than seen since it is much less gregarious than the other titmice and it often occurs singly or in small family groups. The nest is situated close to the ground, preferably in a hole in a tree or boundary fence.

There is no doubt that the black grouse is struggling to survive in some areas, and many naturalists feel that until these populations recover the shooting of the species at any time of the year should be suspended.

The capercaillie is a huge member of the grouse family, the dark coloured males measuring as much as 85cm (34in) with his browner mate much smaller but still formidable at 60cm (24in).

A spotted flycatcher. Truly a fly-eater, this bird catches flies in a unique manner by remaining still on a perch and then darting out on fluttering wings before returning to its perch to swallow its prey.

A greenfinch is a colourful bird well camouflaged against the spring greenery.

The redstart, the male especially, is among the most attractive of our woodland birds, looking robin-like, in shape and in size which is around 14cm ($5\frac{1}{2}$in). The male has a white forehead which contrasts sharply with the bluish-grey upper surface, black face and throat and both the breast and tail are orange – the word start is the Old English for tail. The female also has a red tail but she is otherwise much duller, although the light brown upper surface does blend attractively with the buff underparts. Redstarts have learned to adapt their feeding behaviour from total dependence on woodland invertebrates and seeds and are occasionally found breeding in stone walls with just a few gnarled trees such as hawthorn, ash and rowan in evidence.

RIGHT: **The breeding behaviour of the titmouse and long tailed tit families is different. The titmouse prefer to site their nests in holes while the long tailed tit creates one of the most intricate and beautifully woven of all nests. It is composed of lichens and mosses stitched together with spiders' webs and lined with hundreds of feathers. The holed entrance of the domed nest often presents a most confusing picture as the long tail of the incubating bird is folded over the body and pokes out just above the bill!**

BELOW: **The wren is a common, but charming woodland resident.**

The flycatchers are **summer visitors** which also specialize by living in trees but have a unique method of feeding in order to avoid competition with other families. Two species visit Britain during the summer, the spotted flycatcher (*Muscicapa striata*) is the more numerous and has a wider distribution and the pied flycatcher (*Ficedula hypoleuca*). Almost 200,000 pairs of the spotted flycatcher may breed in Britain compared to only 20,000 pied flycatchers, which tend to be restricted to valleys with deciduous trees, especially oak growing up the sides. The spotted flycatcher, on the other hand, is quite happy in all types of woodlands and even in the parks and large gardens of towns especially those close to water.

Male and female spotted flycatchers are alike being 14cm ($5\frac{1}{2}$in) long with a grey-brown back, dark streaks on head and breast and paler underparts. The pied flycatchers are slightly smaller being 13cm (5in) long. The male is a very attractive bird with black upper parts except for the white on his forehead and wingbars. The undersurface is white. The female is also white below but the upper surface is brownish grey and she also has a whiteish and quite obvious wing bar.

Increased levels of forestry planting, including a few broad-leaved trees, the reduced levels of egg collecting and, most of all, the provision of nest boxes have allowed some extensions of range in recent years. These gains have, unfortunately been offset by losses in south eastern England where insecticides in arable areas have reduced the amount of prey available. Birds, therefore, have no incentive to stop to breed in the few small areas of woodland which remain.

Two other summer birds, the whitethroat (*Sylvia communis*) which nests in woodland shrub and the lovely redstart (*Phoenicurus phoenicurus*) are visitors whose populations similarly declined quite suddenly in the 1970s. This has been found to be due to a drought in the Sahel region of Africa where migrants normally stock up with water prior to crossing the Sahara to the wintering areas. In the case of the redstart there was a simultaneous loss of habitat, particularly in oak dominated woodlands, and this added to the problem already faced by the species. In recent years, however, there has been an improvement both in water supply and habitat availability. Its ready acceptance of nest boxes has helped the population to increase to around 100,000 pairs.

The nightjar (*Caprimulgus europaeus*) is normally found breeding on dry heaths but these have been gradually encroached upon for building, farming or forestry. The 27cm (11in) owl-like summer visitor has, therefore, adapted by siting its nest on the wide firebreaks of forestry plantations or the drier areas of old deciduous woods. At one time it was called the fern-owl because of its slow evening flight in search of insects, especially large moths caught in its huge mouth full of sticky mucus. There are probably less than 5,000 breeding pairs in Britain these days, but this may well be due to climatic changes as much as to loss of habitat and the effect of pesticides. The same factors may be responsible for similar declines in the populations of the wryneck and the red-backed shrike (*Lanius collurio*). It is essential that research provides us with an answer soon or we may well lose the evocative rusty mechanical sound of the churring nightjar.

Not all woodland birds have declined in recent years and some have been so successful in dealing with man that their populations have soared. Species such as the house sparrow (*Passer domesticus*), greenfinch (*Carduelis chloris*), bullfinch, starling (*Sturnus vulgaris*), wren (*Troglodytes troglodytes*) and the thrushes have all made the transition from woodland to town park and garden very easily. The crow family have also proved equal to the task, of which the magpie has risen from a relatively uncommon woodland bird to become the scourge of hedgerow wildlife over a period of around 50 years. The breeding population is now approaching 300,000 pairs which is probably too high when one considers how it affects the other wildlife. Not all the crows have found survival during a period of woodland erosion so easy and this certainly applies to the jay.

The new conifer plantations are used by jays for cover and food – they really are quite happy in the new woodlands.

Although it is found in parklands the jay is still shy enough, especially when breeding, to prefer woodland. Large numbers were, and still are in some unenlightened areas, shot to protect game eggs and young. In Victorian times there was a continual demand for the feathers especially those making up the lovely blue and white patterning on the wings. The millinery trade also had use for the pinkish feathers of head and back, and those combining to produce the distinctive white rump. Fortunately a more realistic knowledge of the diet, consisting of worms, small insects and a great deal of vegetable matter including acorns in addition to the odd egg and small bird, has cut down the shooting.

Jays have always played their part in spreading trees since they carry acorns quite long distances before burying them, squirrel-like, in case of a bad winter. Any unclaimed caches will germinate and many a mighty oak has been spread in this manner. One of the wonders of woodland study is the understanding of the way every organism depends upon another, and not even the dominant tree of the forest is an exception to this rule.

Woodland mammals

MOST of our mammals had their origins in the wildwoods and out of the 17 orders of mammals in the world, six occur in Britain. It seems a shame that the name of the primitive order *Insectivors* suggests that these mammals only eat insects when in fact their diet is much more catholic. Three of the eight families in this order occur in Britain and they may be represented by the hedgehog (*Erinaceids*), the mole (*Talpids*) and the shrews (*Soricids*) all of which are seen in woodlands.

The **hedgehog** (*Erinaceus europaeus*) is one of Britain's most ancient mammals and there is no doubt that it once snuffled about in the wildwoods. It used to be called the herichun in Norman French from which the English word urchin derived. Only after Enclosure Acts made hedges common did the word hedgehog become part of our language although the beast does look surprisingly pig-like. Those still living in woods seem to show a preference for clearings and edges rather than for the dark recesses of the wood accounting for their ready acceptance of hedgerows and large gardens.

Each autumn hedgehogs go into hibernation, which must not be regarded as normal sleep. First the animal builds up large reserves of energy and hedgehogs have two types of fat tissue. The normal fat is white and stored in adipose tissue under the skin and in the mesenteries, lining the abdominal cavity. Brown fat, usually called the hibernating gland, gathers around the shoulders just prior to hibernation, and is both richer in energy and allows its release at a faster rate. This will be essential when the hedgehog wakes up from hibernation and is required to raise the metabolism to the normal rate as soon as possible. During hibernation the hedgehog's pulse and respiration rate slows down to less than ten per cent of its normal rate, an anti-coagulent is produced to prevent the blood clotting and white blood cells gather around the gut to destroy any bacteria which build up around undigested food.

Once hibernation is over the hedgehogs must prepare for breeding and the boar can always be distinguished from the sow by his very large penis which is situated towards the centre of the abdomen, essential if he is to enter the vagina of the female without being prickled to death during the act. The gestation period of the four or five young is about 35 days during which time the female builds a large grass or moss nest to accommodate them. Female hedgehogs disturbed at this stage have been known to eat their own young but normally they are good mothers who return to feed their offspring after an evening out foraging.

The young are blind for a fortnight and toothless for a further week but at eight weeks they are weaned and although still tiny and weighing only 200 grams (about 4 ounces) they are expected to manage on their own. It is then a battle to find

OPPOSITE: **Long eared bats do not usually emerge from their roosts until the sun has set and the best time to watch them is during a moonlit night in August, a time when the woodlands look at their glorious best and the smell of late flowering honeysuckle fills the air.**

British woodland mammals

- **Insectivors**
  - **Erinaceids** (*hedgehogs*)
  - **Talpids** (*moles*)
  - **Soricids** (*shrews*)
- **Chiroptera** (*bats*)
- **Lagomorphs** (*rabbits, hares*)
- **Rodents**
  - **Hystricomorphs** (*porcupines, guinea pigs*)
  - **Mycomorphs** (*rats, mice, voles*)
  - **Sciurmorphs** (*squirrels*)
- **Carnivores**
- **Artiodactyls** (*deer*)

enough food to build up size and body fat sufficient to carry them through the harsh winter. Hibernators are very much in a minority in British mammals even in such a primitive order as the *Insectivors* and both the mole and the shrews are active throughout the winter.

The **mole** (*Talpa europaea*) is another mammal of the wildwoods of Britain which took advantage of human changes to move out into the fertile fields where the living is easy. For a burrowing animal it is easier to follow the harrow and the plough than it is to dig through the thick soil and tangled roots of trees in woodlands. Despite this, there are still large numbers of moles living underground in woodlands. Their presence is often not detected because the soil displaced as they dig their burrows is deposited in spaces between tree roots rather than on top of the ground in the form of a mole hill. Some of these woodland mole runs can be almost permanent, and are not just the home of the mole but also the area where it hunts for food and at times stores the surplus.

The main creature in the diet is earthworms which in the course of their own

Moles spend more time on the surface than is imagined and I have often seen them wandering about in the woods at night scavenging for carrion and slugs.

burrowing may fall into the mole's tunnel – nature's own variation of the pit-fall trap. On a good day the mole may catch more worms than it needs but it has the knack of biting the worm at the front end and severing the ring of nerve cells, preventing the creature from moving, but without killing it. The mole now has its own apparently cruel but highly efficient 'deep freeze'. Some workers have even suggested that its saliva may contain a narcotic which slows worms down to prevent them using up food in a fruitless effort to escape.

Their main sense is one of smell – the eyes of the mole are so tiny that they only record the difference between night and day – with the snout playing a vital role. The tip of the snout can be extended by being dilated with blood and is covered with tiny raised pimples called Eimer's organs after the scientist who discovered them. These may well record temperature, pain and vibrations so important to animals living in tunnels. The mole may be able to detect the air pushed in front of an intruder in its burrow in the same way that travellers on London's underground are warned of the arrival of a train by the air pushed along before it.

Vibrations are also thought to play an important role in the life of **shrews**. Three species of shrew occur in our woodlands including the water shrew (*Neomys fodiens*) which occurs in damp areas dominated by willow and especially in alder carr. Much more regular members of the community, however, are the common shrew (*Sorex araneus*), and Britain's smallest mammal the pygmy shrew (*Sorex minutus*) which is only 5cm (2in) long. The common shrew is around 7.5cm (3in) and is typified by a pointed snout, a short naked tail of less than 4cm ($1\frac{2}{3}$in) and a pelt of red-brown on the upper surface with pale grey below.

Shrews form an important link in the woodland food chain for they feed upon invertebrates such as woodlice and earthworms. They, themselves, are eaten by birds of prey particularly owls which swallow them whole and have little sense of taste. Apparently shrew flesh is not pleasant and although mammals such as cats will kill the animals they seldom eat them. The teeth of the shrew can be examined by dissecting an owl pellet and may be seen to have red around the edges. This marks the position of poison glands which produce a narcotic to slow down the prey and also prevents the earthworm's blood from clotting.

Shrews have long had a reputation for being quarrelsome but it may well be that the high-pitched squeals they produce may not be a sign of anger but the animal's method of echolocation – a technique which has been perfected by bats.

The **bats** (*Chiroptera*) are the only group of mammals to have perfected powered flight. They have, however, had to sacrifice the multi-purpose function of limbs which now serve only for locomotion and hanging up to roost – chiroptera means hand-wing.

All British bats feed on insects caught during flight and there are no blood suckers or fruit eating bats. Their biology is fascinating, and watching the common pipistrelle (*Pipistrellus pipistrellus*) hunting moths and weaving in and out of trees as darkness falls on the woodland is one of the most exciting things that a naturalist can do. Since the bats were protected by law in 1983 more effort has gone into studying them and relatively inexpensive 'bat detectors', working on the same principle as metal detectors, are now on the market. Bats produce high-pitched sounds whilst hunting which rebound if they strike an object and are picked up by the animals' very efficient ears. They can obviously distinguish between solid objects which are potentially damaging and mobile food such as a nice juicy moth. Imagine their surprise when scientists using their bat detectors found that the moths also produced sounds which were often successful in jamming the bats' radar – once more our inventions have been anticipated by nature.

The shrew is a tiny animal with a prodigious appetite.

Since the increased interest in bats, distribution is being mapped accurately, perhaps for the first time. It has always been known that the pipistrelle was ubiquitous but the long eared bat seems to be more widely distributed than was once thought and it is these which will be among the first species to be encountered by the woodlander. Most species find the British climate unsuitable and although the noctule (*Nyctalus noctula*), barbastelle (*Barbastella barbastellus*) and natterer's (*Myotis nattereri*) bats are fairly widespread other species are of restricted range.

It would not be true to say that the pipistrelle, which measures only around 4cm (1⅔in), is only a woodland species since it is found in city centres and in caves on hillsides. It is, however, at home in woods using its 25cm (10in) wing span and efficient radar to weave in and out of trees. The reason for their success would seem to be the very short period of hibernation and they have been recorded hunting on mild January evenings. The roosts can be quite heavily populated and some nursery colonies have been estimated to contain up to 1,000 females and young. In woodlands there are usually less than 100 in a colony.

Bats have a most unusual breeding cycle. The female is mated before going into hibernation and the sperm is stored without being brought in contact with the egg. Fertilization occurs when the female has had time to feed and recover her strength. After a gestation period of just over six weeks the young are born towards the end of June or early in July. Compared to mice, which are about the same size, bats live a long time and the pipistrelle is quite likely to survive for ten years. Thus, despite only producing one young (occasionally twins) each year, quite large populations can build up. They do not have many enemies, but I have seen a grey squirrel eating a pipistrelle found hibernating in a hollow tree.

Watching the hovering, fluttering flight of the delicate long eared bat (*Plecotuus auritus*) as it picked off moths and their larvae from the leaves of an oak, all I could see was the huge pair of ears.

The diet of the hedgehog is varied and it can often be seen tearing at carrion although it will take live food especially slugs, earthworms and even adders. On one memorable occasion I was awoken from an afternoon siesta under my favourite ash tree by a loud crunching sound punctuated by snuffles and grunts. This turned out to be a hedgehog, which is normally nocturnal, taking an early supper of fat juicy snails found in a damp hollow. The following autumn a hedgehog, probably the same one, chose the same hollow which was overgrown by sheltering brambles, to hibernate.

The body and head of the long eared bat measures almost 5cm (2in) and it has a wingspan approaching 30cm (1ft). Hollow trees are favourite roosting and hibernating areas, and they take easily to bat-boxes which are now becoming a feature of many woodlands managed by conservation bodies.

The **rabbit** (*Oryctolagus coniculus*) – belonging to the *Lagomorphs* order – originated in Iberia and north west Africa but was introduced to Britain, probably in the twelfth century, by the Normans as a luxury food item. They were carefully farmed in secure enclosures until the time of the black death in the late fourteenth century when the reduced peasant population could not fulfill all their tasks with efficiency. Since that time rabbits have been running wild.

Although the population was drastically reduced by the myxomatosis virus introduced in the 1950s and 60s, rabbits are now recovering. Those living deep in woodlands and spending more time under bramble bushes than in the underground burrows suffered less from the disease which is spread by the rabbit flea (*Silopsyllus cuniculi*). This obviously depends upon close contact so that it may jump from one animal to another. Fortunately, the swollen eyed suffering heap of festering flesh which typifies an infected rabbit is less common than it used to be, and, fortunately, the disease does not affect the brown hare (*Lepus capensis*).

Hares are much larger animals with even longer ears obviously tipped with black. A good sized animal can measure 60cm (2ft) with females slightly larger than the males. The breeding behaviour is different to that of the doe rabbit which gives birth deep underground to blind, naked and helpless 'bunnies'. Young hares, called leverets, are born furred and with their eyes open. The female flattens vegetation and deposits one or two young in these forms. She may give birth to six young and visits each form in turn to suckle her offspring. This seems to be a sensible idea as the young are separated and wandering predators such as the fox,

The acrobatic ability of the wood mouse is seen at its best in autumn and winter when it uses its long tail as a balancing organ as it goes in search of berries in the tree.

weasel and stoat are not likely to wipe out the complete litter.

Rodents are the most successful mammal order and are divided into three sub-orders. The *Hystricomorphs* includes the porcupine and the guinea pig, but do not occur in the wild. The *Mycomorphs* includes the rats, mice and voles. Those naturally occurring in woodlands are the bank vole, short tailed vole, dormouse, long tailed field mouse and harvest mouse whilst the accidentally introduced house mouse (*Mus musculus*) may also occasionally wander away from our buildings. The third sub-order are the *Sciuromorphs* or squirrels. Although there are around 1,400 species in the world only the red squirrel is native to Britain while the grey was deliberately introduced in the late nineteenth century.

Voles are much more sturdy animals than mice and can be distinguished by shorter and stouter tails, smaller ears and much rounder muzzles which gives them a friendlier appearance.

The bank vole (*Clethrionomys glareolus*) is often called the wood vole, red vole or, more accurately, the red backed vole which is a good description of the rusty coloured dorsal surface. The head and body measures 10cm (4in) and the tail adds a further 4cm ($1\frac{2}{3}$in) to this. The teeth of the bank vole are not as powerful as those of the short tailed field vole (*Microtus agrestis*) which is slightly larger in the body at 11cm ($4\frac{1}{2}$in) whilst the tail is also 4cm ($1\frac{2}{3}$in) and looks shorter by comparison. Because of its weaker teeth the bank vole is restricted to the lush vegetation found in woodlands whilst the short tailed vole is able to venture out into the fields and moorlands. Here the tough grass roots are eaten by the rodent.

Bank voles are mainly nocturnal, but in quiet areas they move around during the day. The territories are marked and there are usually large numbers in suitable areas where the burrows can be quite extensive. There are also well used runs through leaf litter to be found. Males in search of females on heat can occasionally travel quite long distances.

Careful live trapping or a scientific investigation of owl pellets will soon reveal that the most common members of the **mouse** (muridae) family is the well named long tailed or wood mouse (*Apodemus sylvaticus*) measuring 10cm (4in) from head to tail and the tail doubling the length. They tend to live in small family units

Neither the native brown hare nor the introduced rabbit are thought of as true woodland animals, but clearings in deciduous areas and fire rides in coniferous forests are every bit as popular with both animals as the open fields.

Voles

On one occasion I watched a bank vole (left) sitting rather like a hamster but high up in a tree on the rim of an old blackbird's nest eating a snail. I could hear its teeth cracking the shell – pure proof that voles are not totally vegetarian.

Occasionally the water vole (right) turns up in wet woodlands dominated by alder and willow, or those through which a stream passes.

The short tailed field vole (top) occurs in woodland clearings and is a vital part of the diet of many predators – especially owls, foxes, weasels and stoats.

Much larger than the other two species, water voles can measure up to 20cm (8in) and they have a tail adding a further 12cm (4$\frac{3}{4}$in). They are also active during the day and the diet includes plants and animals such as amphibians, reptiles and young birds as well as invertebrates. Voles are an all important addition to the diet of woodland owls and carnivorous mammals.

although males in search of a mate may wander quite widely and territories also show some degree of overlap. There are peaks of activity at dawn and dusk during the winter and there is no period of hibernation. In summer they are most active at night and during the breeding season the complicated series of underground burrows and runs through the leaf litter can be very busy. Apart from the occasional high-pitched squeak wood mice are silent animals.

The breeding season lasts from March to October although in mild weather this can continue into December. During this time a number of litters of up to nine young are produced in underground nests made of dried grass. With these reproductive statistics it is not surprising to see how quickly populations can build up.

Even more efficient in its acrobatics is Britain's smallest rodent the delightful little harvest mouse (*Micromys minutus*), only around 8cm ($3\frac{1}{3}$in) plus a tail of about the same length which is prehensile and used effectively as a fifth limb. It is often stated that the harvest mouse has a specialized habitat and is quite rare in parts of England and absent from most of Scotland and Ireland. It does not occur in Ireland, but recent interest in the species has revealed a wider distribution and higher populations than previously realized.

Grey squirrels (above) prefer deciduous woodland and in times of hunger they can chew the bark of trees to such an extent that valuable timber is lost. They have very light coloured tails and the prominent tufts of fur on the ears are also white. These tufts are a point of distinction between the red (below) and grey squirrel for the latter have naked ears.

The dormouse is mainly restricted to the south of England and Wales and is absent from Scotland, the Isle of Man and Ireland. They show a distinct preference for woodlands containing hazel and if the trees are entwined with honeysuckle suitable for building their nests, they are even more likely to have the common dormice in residence. The upper surface of the body is bright chestnut while the chest and belly are almost white. The body measures 14cm ($5\frac{1}{2}$in) and the thick, bushy tails add a further 7.5cm (3in). Almost totally nocturnal, the dormouse spends the day sleeping in its nest – a favourite site is in the base of a coppiced tree, although the tangled roots of wind-blown trees are also popular. The female produces two litters per year each containing two to four young which

are independent after 40 days and can breed the following year. It appears that the species has declined since Victorian times, when it was trapped and was very popular as a pet. Of even greater rarity is the introduced edible dormouse (*Glis glis*) around 30cm (1ft) long and occasionally confused with the grey squirrel of the *Sciurmorphs* order.

I remember as a child in the Lake District not far from the home of Beatrix Potter looking at a picture book. As the wind whistled through the trees I read of the **squirrels** hibernating in their dreys with their bushy tails wrapped round them to keep out the bone chilling cold. In fact, neither of Britain's two squirrels hibernate and both begin their breeding cycle in February.

The red squirrel has had its ups and downs over the centuries and is now only abundant in the coniferous areas of Scotland. It also occurs in a few isolated spots including Wales and parts of the Lake District. During the late eighteenth and early nineteenth centuries the species almost became extinct in Scotland but re-introductions proved very successful. In England and Wales there were further problems as destruction of habitat, disease and the introduction of the grey squirrel caused a decimation of the red squirrel from their native woodlands. It is quite capable of thriving in deciduous woodlands, and Britain has its own sub-species called *Sciurus vulgaris leucourus* – once we have lost this it cannot be replaced by topping up the population from the forests of Europe.

Red squirrels have an average body length of 21cm ($8\frac{1}{4}$in), the tail adding a further 18cm ($2\frac{1}{8}$in) and the weight is around 300 grams ($8\frac{1}{4}$ ounces). It is thus a smaller and much less bulky animal than the grey squirrel weighing more than 520 grams (18 ounces), has a body length of 26cm (10in) and a tail of 21cm ($8\frac{1}{4}$in).

Normally the red squirrel has two breeding periods the first beginning as early as January when chattering males chase the females through the branches. After a gestation period of around 40 days the litter of two to four kittens are born in March with the second littler appearing in late July or August, after the first family has been weaned – the dependence upon the mother is normally two months. Once weaned the red squirrel is vegetarian although some insects and birds eggs are eaten during the appropriate season. They do not have very many predators except for some agile weasels and stoats reaching the occasional drey.

The grey squirrel was introduced from north America in the period between 1876 and 1930 before it was realized just what a pest they can be. Their breeding cycle is rather similar to the red squirrel but the litter size is larger and often six kittens are raised. As they live for six or seven years and occasionally longer, large populations can build up.

Many people, who ought to know better, continue to destroy stoats, weasels and other carnivores which are grouped under the title of vermin. However, these are the very animals which could control the population of the tree rat – a derogatory term applied to the American squirrel.

In British woodlands there is a shortage of *Carnivores* – hardly surprising considering the way we have treated them over the last 2,000 years. We still have one wild cat, a dog in the form of the fox and five members of the mustelid family. These are the badger, stoat, weasel, polecat and the pine marten.

The **wild cat** (*Felis sylvestris*) is mostly confined to Scotland, but, due to a relaxation in persecution, it is beginning to extend its range. It is not, as often suggested, a northern species but has merely been hunted to extinction in many areas. A look at a map will reveal areas where wild cats once had a lair. Catbells near Keswick indicates the presence of felis, and there are many references to Catfords, Catbanks and Cathills throughout the country.

The harvest mouse is often found in damp woodlands where it constructs its domed nest among the tall reeds which it climbs. The winter nests are sited at lower levels.

Stories of their ferocity are much exaggerated and they could exist in large woodlands without their presence being suspected. They tend to be mainly nocturnal spending the day holed up in a hollow tree, in a hole beneath the roots or among rocks. Care must be taken to distinguish between a true wild cat and a domestic pussy cat, but the sheer size of *Felis sylvestris* should remove all doubt. A wild tom can be 60cm (2ft) long with a blunt and bushy striped tail adding another 30cm (1ft). The females are just a little smaller. The weight can be as much as 5kg (11 pounds), almost twice the size of a domestic cat. The brown grey coat also tends to be very heavily striped.

They are fiercely territorial and solitary animals but their diet can do much to control the population of small mammals. They also take rabbits, squirrels and even hares as well as small birds which they hunt by stealth rather than speed. The tendency of gamekeepers to overestimate their effect upon pheasants is unfortunate since a wild cat in a woodland does more good than harm.

This is almost certainly true of the **fox** (*Vulpes vulpes*), another **Carnivore** which has earned its evil reputation because of the behaviour of a small minority of the population which wander into adjacent farmyards. Foxes are naturally woodland mammals feeding upon other, small mammals, birds, carrion and even fruit and plant roots. On one memorable occasion I was gathering hazel nuts on an October evening and sat down quietly to eat my picnic supper and drink a flask of coffee. Almost silently, a dog fox appeared and stood delicately on his hind legs to reach first a juicy spray of blackberries. He then noticed a heavy bunch of elderberries and with a muscular bound grabbed them in his teeth and I could see the purple juice run from his mouth and stain his pale chest. A breeze disturbed an empty crisp packet left by an untidy picknicker and blew it across the fox's line of vision. His brush swept from side to side like an angry cat, and he then crept

Fox cubs emerging from their earth for the first time.

forward and pounced on the packet rolling over with it in his jaws like a playful puppy. Sightings such as this make all the hours spent in woodlands when nothing happens more than worthwhile.

Most larger woodlands have a fox earth and on the cold moonlit nights in January and February the vixen screams to attract a mate. Apart from when breeding, foxes live a solitary life. After a gestation period of around 53 days, four to seven cubs are born in the underground earth. The dog fox provides the vixen with food during this period and it is at this time that rabbits, voles and mice, as well as small birds, are most important in the diet. A fully grown fox can weigh from 6kg to 10kg ($13\frac{1}{4}$lb to 22lb), the vixen being slightly lighter on average. The body length is from 58cm to 77cm (23in to 30in) and the tail 30cm to 50cm (12in to 20in).

Foxes and **badgers** often share the same site, but the pungent smell associated with a fox's earth is not typical of a normal badger's sett. Brock's home is a much more permanent base and many individuals may live within it, some setts having been in permanent use for centuries.

The wild cat is not as fierce as is often thought and it is now increasing its range.

Badgers have suffered from persecution by badger diggers who still get enjoyment from badger baiting despite the fact that the animal is protected by law. If this law was to be rigorously applied then the badger would once more become a resident in most woodlands. There would, however, remain one black spot which most naturalists and many vets find grossly unfair. In south eastern England badgers are still being destroyed because they are said to be carriers of Bovine TB. The evidence for this does not stand up to statistical tests and much more research is required before badgers are found to be carrying such a disease and only then should they be destroyed.

Like wild cats the presence of badgers in times past can be deduced from an examination of old maps when Brockholes, Brocklehurst, Brocklebank and Brockwood indicate the presence of old setts. The traditional habitat was deciduous woodland and evidence of an occupied sett can be seen in the form of old bedding which badgers remove periodically and replace with dry bracken and leaves. There is also an outside latrine littered with the slimy droppings having the musty smell typical of the mustelid family to which the badger belongs. The favourite site is on a sloping bank which ensures good drainage and there are several entrances.

Mating takes place during the spring and summer, but the implantation of the fertilized eggs is delayed until December. The litter of one to five cubs are born in late winter or early spring and by the time they are two months old they appear above ground and, like most *Carnivores*, are very playful. Play is a rehearsal for the serious business of life such as catching and killing food and defending territory. A fully grown badger is a formidable beast, a good boar measuring 75cm (30in) plus his short tail of 15cm (6in) and in the autumn can weigh up to 20kg (44lb).

The **Polecat** (*Mustela putorius*) is another mustelid which has suffered from human persecution. Once common throughout Britain, the activities of gamekeepers reduced it to a few isolated spots in Wales and surrounding counties such as Shropshire. Despite the smell generated by the anal glands polecat pelts were popular in the fur trade which also contributed to its disappearance from most British woodlands. Some significant recovery has been evident in recent years, but sightings are often confused due to the presence of the American mink (*Mustela vison*) and the domesticated ferret (*Mustela furo*) which has been bred to hunt rabbits. Many escape and live wild in the woodlands. The true polecat can be identified by a distinctive white pattern on its face, a long body measuring 45cm (18in) and tail 18cm (7in), plus its dark brown, long haired pelt.

The antlers of the native roe deer are simple in form and only around 30cm (12in) long. Antlers are grown annually from the pedicle bone and are initially covered by a protective skin called velvet, beneath which is the blood and nerve supply. At the time of mating the antlers become important as the males posture and compete for females. Prior to the rut the blood supply is cut off and the velvet begins to peel, a process under the control of male reproductive hormones. In order to rid themselves of the itching covering of velvet the deer thrash their antlers against young trees causing a great deal of damage.

Much more common are the **weasel** (*Mustela nivalis*) and the **stoat** (*Mustela erminea*), the latter distinguished by its larger size and black tip to the tail. The weasel is the smallest of *Carnivores* having a head and body length of almost 23cm (9in) plus a tail of 7.5cm (3in), but the females, called jills, are significantly smaller than their mates which are called hobs. At one time it was thought that the jill and hob were separate species and one can understand this because apart from coming together to breed they lead solitary existences being active by day and by night. Their little sinuous, shiny brown bodies move snake-like among the undergrowth and down burrows in search of rodents. Their own enemies include owls but the human desire to shoot pheasant and partridges has resulted in weasels and stoats being frequently seen hanging on the gamekeepers gibbet.

The male stoat is also larger than his mate and can reach a length of 30cm (1ft) plus a 10cm (4in) tail. It is also a much more bulky animal and its pelage is much greyer than that of the weasel. In the northern areas the stoat often turns white and in this condition it is known as an ermine. British weasels never turn white but in some parts of Europe they moult into ermine. The stoat is common in Ireland but the weasel does not occur there at all.

Adult stoats, like weasels, are solitary apart from the mating season and the period immediately following, when the jill is accompanied by her kittens. Mating occurs in late spring but there is a delayed implantation of the fertilized egg until the following spring when a litter of six to nine are born. They are weaned when around five weeks old, but remain with the female for several weeks during which time they hunt as a pack. Such a group can be terrifying if disturbed in their lair, but I do not believe they would attack humans unless their escape route was blocked. Like many such stories the tale of rampant stoats derives more from

A red deer stag. The ability of red deer to jump fences is legendary and having seen this for myself I can see why barriers need to be ten feet high.

superstition than from careful observation of woodland wildlife as it really is.

Pine martens (*Martes martes*) were once a threat to the red squirrel but centuries of persecution by human hunters in search of sport reduced the sweet mart almost to extinction. Pine martens are creatures of mature woodland and can hunt efficiently both in trees and on the ground. They often raid a squirrel's drey, consume the inhabitants and use the cosy nest to sleep in themselves. Male martens are larger than the females and average some 50cm (20in) in length with the tail, which they use as a balancing organ, averaging around 20cm (8in). In Scotland and the Lake District the pine marten is showing signs of a comeback as I discovered during the wet summer of 1985. I watched the lithe brown body of this lovely member of the weasel family chase a squirrel through the dripping branches of a larch. On this occasion it failed to catch its breakfast and stood delicately on a branch, its flanks heaving with the effort and steam rising from its body as water evaporated from its coat warmed by a shaft of sunlight peeping through a bank of cloud.

Deer belong to the *Artiodactyla* order of mammals and are grouped in the family Cervidae. Six species of deer occur in Britain but only two are truly natives. The Chinese water deer (*Hydropotes inermis*), Reeve's muntjac (*Muntiacus reevesi*) and the sika deer (*Cervus nippon*) were all introduced during the nineteenth century but are not yet common in British woodlands. The sikas could become a problem because they can interbreed with the native red deer which has had enough problems with persecution and loss of habitat without having its genes diluted by those of a smaller, less hardy species.

The fallow deer (*Dama dama*) is often thought of as native, but it seems to have become extinct and then re-introduced either by the Phoenicians or by the Romans. The population was certainly topped up by the Normans who were very fond of hunting. They mainly feed by grazing grass, but should the winter weather become severe they wander into woodlands to feed upon holly, ivy, rowan, blackberries acorns and beech nuts. Fallow deer measure about 100cm (40in) to the shoulder and the antlers of the males can add a further 70cm (28in) to this. Bucks weigh 70kg (154lb) and does 45kg (99lb).

The native roe deer (*Capreolus capreolus*) is small by comparison and males seldom weigh more than 26kg (57lb) and measure around 75cm (30in).

The reproductive cycle of the roe is in complete contrast to the other British native, the huge red deer. Roes are solitary animals, mostly nocturnal and breeding in July. The bucks rub their heads against saplings and trees to scrape off a scent from glands on the forehead. They also mark territory by scraping the ground and urinating into it. When I first began my deer watching I failed to find roe deer because I mistook their barking alarm call for that of a terrier on an illicit night prowl.

After a courtship chase mating occurs, but there is a delayed implantation until the following spring and the young, usually twins, are born in May or June. It is possible to come across herds of up to 20 roe deer, especially in winter, but it is more usual to find a family group consisting of a buck, doe, and the pair of young.

On balance recent human activity in Britain has been beneficial to the roe for predators such as the lynx (*Felis lynx*) and the wolf (*Canis lupus*) have been hunted to extinction. Recent plantings by the forestry commission have also given them more cover. It is to be hoped that woodland planting of both conifer and broad leaved species continues and that conservationists manage to resist attempts to cull

Badgers are almost totally nocturnal, which is probably due to the fact that they prefer to eat animals such as slugs and earthworms active at night when the humidity is high. They also take a surprising amount of fruit and seeds, especially during autumn when they become very fat. This suggests that they hibernate which is not, in fact, the case although spells of really bad weather may keep them in the warmth and comfort of the sett when they can draw upon the body fat.

deer in areas where damage is minimal. As the demand for venison increases so is deer poaching but this is more likely to affect the red deer which has much more palatable flesh.

Red deer (*Cervus elaphus*) is easily recognized as it is our largest land mammal, a stag averaging 120cm (48in) at the shoulder with antlers of 80cm (32in) and weighs around 100kg (220lb). The hinds, like the roe and fallow deer, lack antlers and are much more lightly built, averaging 70kg (154lb). The red deer was once not only the monarch of the highland glens, but lord of the lowland forest. Centuries of hunting and tree felling has reduced the species to a few remnant populations in Cumbria, Devon and Somerset, especially on Exmoor and in the Scottish Highlands. In parts of Scotland and the Lake District more controlled hunting, as well as tree planting, has allowed populations to build up so quickly that there is now not sufficient food in an area to prevent some animals starving during the winter. Any sensible naturalist would not in these circumstances object to humane culling of the weaklings in the population.

During the winter, when food is scarce, the red deer will desert their woodland mosses and fungi and descend with a bravery generated by hunger into the lowland fields and ravage crops of vegetables or seedling trees being raised by the forester.

The elegant reds, however, are seen at their best from September to November when the rutting sounds echo to the bellowing of the stags and the clashing sound of antlers as they wrestle for supremacy and the right to mate with a harem of hinds. Until the start of the rut the stags and hinds are found in separate herds. These days the rutting grounds are mainly on open moorland but wet woodland clearings were without doubt the original sites and these are still the most exciting places to watch the proceedings, preferably in a tree downwind of the combatants.

I had always thought that the strongest stag was selected to perform the mating but a recent observation leads me to believe that cunning also has something to do with it. Dawn had just broken on a bright autumn morning in the Lake District and I was watching a group of 12 hinds waiting for the result of a fierce encounter between two fine stags. From my position in a specially built observation tower I noticed a huge stag with no antlers which both the fighting males had noticed but ignored. Suddenly he crept in among the hinds mating with first one and then a second before trotting away into the concealing scrub. These males without antlers are called hummels and their lack of adornment is not apparently passed on to their offspring. No doubt the fact that they do not have to fight keeps them in good breeding condition but they must be quite rare or antlers would long since have become unnecessary in the world of the deer. It is yet another example that things are seldom what they seem to be in the natural world, and there is much remaining to be discovered by amateur enthusiasts.

A weasel (top) and stoat (bottom). Both species feed upon rabbits, as well as rodents, and populations declined dramatically immediately following the myxomatosis outbreak. They are active both by day and by night and are so inquisitive that they are often seen in woodlands especially those with sloping, well drained banks which have high populations of rodents and rabbits.

Ecology of woodlands

THERE are two schools of thought regarding when the ecology of woodlands should be considered. One suggests that it ought to be tackled first. This may well be the correct way for biology students wishing to understand woodlands as a whole. For the naturalist, however, it would be wrong to inflict the rigours of a scientific discipline on top of learning the names of trees, flowers, mosses, liverworts, ferns, lichens, fungi as well as invertebrate and vertebrate animals. Only when some of these names and behaviour have been mastered as a result of many happy hours spent in woodlands in all weathers and seasons should the naturalist embark upon a serious study of ecology.

Ecology derives from the Greek word oikos and deals with the inter-relationships between living organisms and the environment in which they live. The idea is simple enough – the problems only arise when attempting to study these inter-relationships and define precisely what we mean by environment.

The whole of the earth's surface is termed the biosphere. It is made up of a number of definable zones such as oceans, temperate woodlands, grasslands and tropical rain forests called biomes, each covering a huge area. Where a group of organisms are living together in the same place they are defined as a community and within this there will be competition for both food and living spaces. In woodlands there may be several levels in which communities live – the tree canopy, shrub layer, field layer, ground layer and the soil itself – each called an ecosystem.

There is one final term to define and this is a habitat. Think of the high canopy of an oak woodland in summer. The blackcap (*Sylvia atricapilla*) sings from his perch breaking off periodically to carry the larvae of the oak eggar moth to his family. He gathers them from the surface of the oak leaf on which they are feeding and while doing this he must keep an eye open for the sparrowhawk which has its own nestlings to feed. In the habitat of the high canopy here is an example of what is termed a food chain:

oak leaf → oak eggar larvae → blackcap → sparrowhawk

Lower down in the same ecosystem are other habitats, one being the field layer. Here we have a woodland clearing dominated by rosebay willow herb being fed upon by the 10cm (4in) long caterpillar of the large elephant hawk moth. This juicy morsel is eagerly hunted by the blackbird and if it goes home late it will become part of the pellet of the tawny owl. Here then is another food chain showing the constant struggle for energy:

rosebay → elephant hawk moth → blackbird → tawny owl

The plant – in the two examples oak and rosebay – is clearly the producer of the food. This is the result of the process of photosynthesis during which sugar is made from atmospheric carbon dioxide and water is derived from the soil. Under the

OPPOSITE: **Many foxes live quietly in woodlands and give the local farmer no cause for complaint.**

influence of the energy of sunlight this reaction proceeds very slowly but is accelerated by the presence of the green catalyst, chlorophyll. The reaction is summarized as follows:

$$\text{carbon dioxide} + \text{water} \xrightarrow[\text{chlorophyll}]{\text{sunlight}} \frac{\text{glucose}}{\text{sugar}} + \text{oxygen}$$

During respiration this process is reversed, living organisms use the sugar to obtain energy while the water and the carbon dioxide is recycled. Only the energy originally powering the process of photosynthesis is lost, and the sun shows no sign of losing its strength! Plants, as we have seen, are the producers of the food while the animals eating these plants – such as the oak eggar and elephant hawk caterpillars in the examples – are called herbivores or primary producers. The carnivorous birds feeding on the caterpillars are secondary consumers and the top predators, like the hawks and owls, are tertiary consumers.

The description tells only part of the story for it must not be assumed that each consumer feeds upon only one item. This error can be rectified by drawing one complex web rather than several chains as shown in the diagram. Furthermore, food chains and webs leave us with two problems.

Neither give any indication of the relative abundance of the various organisms although it seems fairly obvious that predators must be far less numerous than their prey. The term biomass helps since the total weight of prey must always be greater than that of the predator which hunts it. If this was not the case then both organisms would become extinct. The production of a food pyramid presents this data in an acceptable form, but we are still left to explain what happens when an animal dies. How is the food material re-cycled? To understand the work of the tiny organisms which act as decomposers it is necessary to describe the soil, a most vital habitat in the woodland ecosystem.

The production of **soil** depends upon four factors. The most important is the rock beneath from which it is formed, although some soils called alluvial may have been swept into position by water or ice. The second factor is the climate when sun, frost, ice and rain combine to break down the parent rock, although a third factor –

The blackcap is a warbler which breeds in deciduous woodlands with a rich tangle of shrubs, especially brambles.

A food pyramid featuring the tawny owl, blue tit, moth caterpillars and oak leaves.

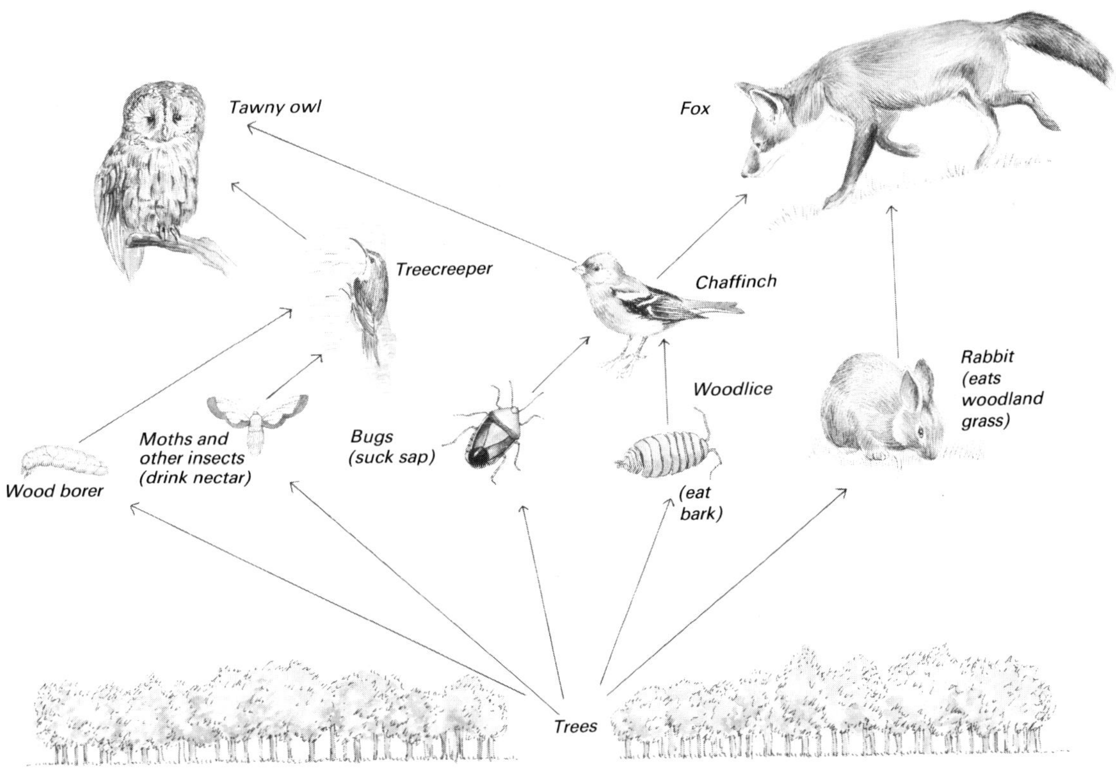

A WOODLAND FOOD WEB

A millipede (right) and centipede (far right) – the smaller species of the two is the millipede. Together with the centipedes, they are to be found in the air spaces in soil.

time – is essential for this to happen. It has been calculated that it can take over 300 years to produce 2.5cm (1in) of soil. The fourth factor is the plants which root into the soil preventing it from blowing away.

When plants, and the animals which feed directly or indirectly upon them, die their remains, called humus become incorporated into the soil – the effect of living organisms on the soil are often referred to as the biotic factor. The combination of soil and humus is referred to as the top soil. In Britain, soil as a general rule is rich and well aerated, even below the top soil where there is less humus and the soil tends to be more compact. Such soils are called mulls and occasionally a distinct zone can be seen between these and the top soil although the burrowing activities of earthworms can ensure thorough mixing.

The activities of earthworms, however, can sometimes be nullified by factors both climatic and chemical. When the soil has been formed from sand and gravel it is very porous and the water passing through leaches out basic compounds of sodium and potassium leaving the soil very acid. Such an acid soil is called a mor and can be created when woodlands are felled and not replanted. The situation may develop still further over a longer period of time as the rain continues to fall, flushing compounds of iron and aluminium into an impervious layer known as a pan where all the compounds become concentrated.

Such concentrated soils are known as podsols and their formation has been rapidly accelerated these days by the production of acid rain in industrialized countries. This issue is highly controversial since pollution produced in one county, or even country, can have its maximum destructive effect many miles away depending upon the strength and direction of the wind. Sulphur dioxide and oxides of nitrogen are discharged from oil and coal burning systems out of tall chimneys into the atmosphere. These gasses dissolve in rain to produce sulphuric and nitric acids destroying huge areas of forest.

Some ecologists, however, feel that the foresters may have brought about some of their own problems with too acidic soil. In the past many leaves and twigs from felled trees were burned to clear paths for removing valuable timber producing potash which is strongly alkaline, neutralizing the acids in the soil. Modern technology has found uses for every scrap of the tree and no burning takes place.

It is also true that many conifer needles are much more acidic than the leaves of deciduous trees. Ecologists have measured the acidity of rain water striking the crown of conifers and report a considerable increase in acidity as the water runs down towards the base of the tree. Many woodlands are now being destroyed as a result of the increases in acid levels and more research will be necessary to find the essential solution.

In podsolized soils at least the water percolates, but in low lying areas – some in the middle of woodlands – the water gathers above the pan and becomes stagnant producing a bog. Here the absence of air prevents the breakdown of dead plant material resulting in the formation of peat. Such areas are not suitable for living organisms but it is surprising how life has adapted to take advantage of even the smallest spaces within the soil and may be divided into four groups – leaf litter organisms; burrowers; those living in the air spaces of the soil and those existing in the soil water.

Of all the zones making up the soil, the leaf litter layer is most typical of woodlands and in rich areas can be up to 5cm (2in) deep. It is very important to the soil below since it provides a continual supply of humus as well as holding water and maintaining the humidity required by many organisms.

Three major animal groups find their ideal ecological niche by burrowing into the soil – *Annelids*, *Arthropods*, such as beetles, centipedes and millipedes and *mammals* such as rabbits, long tailed field mice, foxes, badgers and more especially moles. All can be of great benefit to woodlands through their burrowing activities providing aeration and drainage of the soil.

Soil is not the solid material often imagined and each particle is separated from its neighbour by an air space. Where large lumps of soil occur air spaces are correspondingly larger. In a good rich soil there can be as much as 25 per cent air and its presence can easily be demonstrated. Take a tin with a detachable press-on lid, and make some holes in it with a nail. Fill it with soil before pressing on the lid and then drop it into water and watch the air bubbling out as it is displaced by water.

These air spaces are ideal niches for many small animals living there safe from dessication, although some of them may venture to emerge at night to hunt. By far

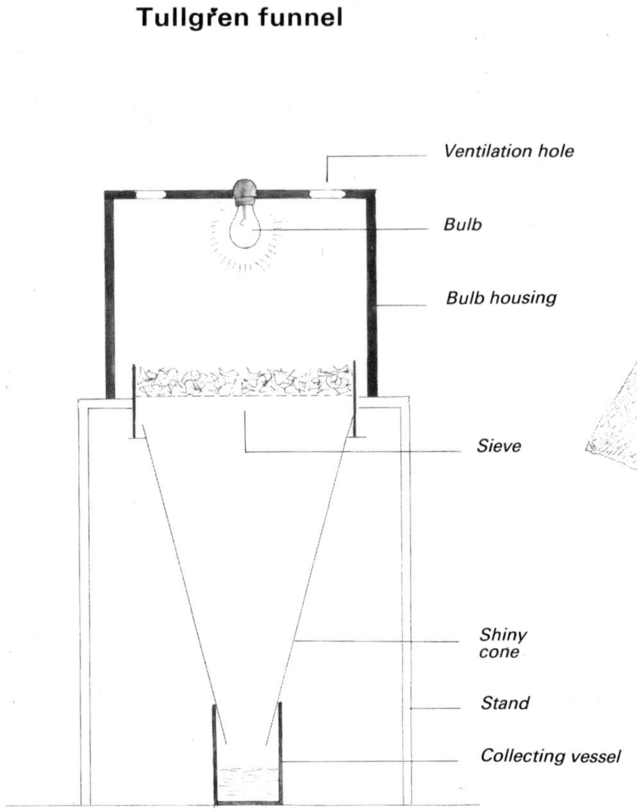

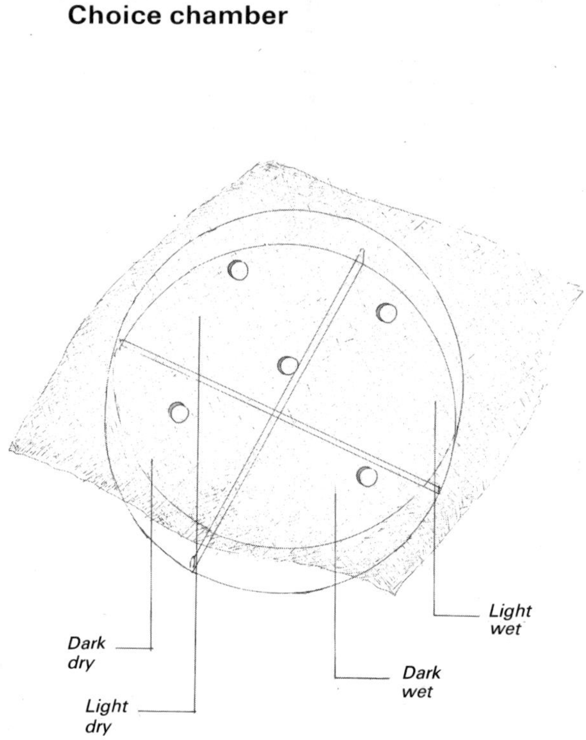

THERE are two methods used to catch invertebrates. One is to use a Tullgren funnel which drives out organisms liking dark, cool, damp conditions by providing conditions which are opposite. A sample of litter (it even works with soil) is placed in a wire mesh and then illuminated from above – the lamp used should never be more than 25 watts. The soil animals move away down the funnel and fall into a smooth walled vessel below. The initial design used to involve filling the collecting vessel with a preservative such as alcohol or formalin. Now, however, there is no need for this and the animals should be identified or perhaps even photographed and then released. Care should be taken not to place the lamp too close to the soil or litter sample or the animals will be killed and if the sample is too thick then the outer layers will bake hard not allowing the creatures to escape. If these rules are obeyed then a simple Tullgren funnel can be made and will prove to be surprisingly efficient.

The other method is by using a choice chamber. None of the litter animals like hot dry conditions and this can be shown using a choice chamber, another piece of equipment easily made by the interested amateur, although commercial models are freely available. Choice experiments work very well with centipedes, millipedes and, more especially, woodlice. The chamber has four inter-connected segments of the same size. Two are dark and two light whilst two are wet and two dry giving the animals the choice of dry–dark, dry–light, wet–light and wet–dark. Equal numbers of animals are placed in each of the segments, but in a short space of time all have gathered in the wet–dark area, exactly the conditions found in the leaf litter and in and under rotten timber. Woodlice are obliged to seek out these conditions because they have only recently evolved from aquatic creatures and they easily lose water through their body surface. *Armadillidium* normally avoid light and seek out moisture but if they are subjected to dry air they immediately move towards light and wander around in the open until they find moisture or die in the attempt.

The combination of Tullgren funnel and choice chamber can provide the naturalist with many hours of informative entertainment and the former is often the only available method of obtaining specimens for identification.

the majority of these organisms are insects belonging to the orders *Diplura*, *Protura* and *Collembola*. Unfortunately it is quite beyond the scope of this book to help in the identification of the several hundreds of species involved.

Water also occupies the spaces between the soil particles. A good mull soil lying over a low water table is well drained leaving plenty of room for pockets of air in addition to essential water. Water also clings to each particle by surface tension and these areas are ideal ecological niches for millions of bacteria, protozoa (including *Amoeba*), flat worms (*Platyhelminthes*), wheel animalcules (*Rotifers*), roundworms (*Nematodes*) and the well named water bears (*Tardigrades*) – despite their small size, they really do look like bears when examined under the microscope.

In order to see these creatures they must first be extracted from the soil and this can be done using a Baerman funnel. The tullgren funnel is useless in these situations because the organisms concerned are so water dependent the slightest reduction in humidity kills them. The soil or litter is placed inside a mesh bag and actually suspended in a funnel of water. The animals move down towards the clip as the water near the lamp warms up and are then flushed into the receiver by opening the clip. Again time, patience and a great deal of skill will be needed to identify these organisms.

Food chains, webs and pyramids depend upon the presence of a huge biomass of producers living in the soil developed, in turn from the parent rock. But how did woodlands arise from bare soil?

Woodlands may be said to have their origins almost as soon as virgin rock begins to crack under the pressures of the weathering process. This area is so deficient in food that only lichens are able to gain a foothold by their remarkable symbiosis. Into this still hostile environment come the liverworts, mosses and then ferns. As the number of species enlarges there will be an increasing degree of competition – interspecific competition. As the populations increase there will be competition between the individuals making up the species – intraspecific competition.

The competition theory is best demonstrated in the period between the appearance of the pioneer annual flowering plants and the establishment of an adolescent broadleaved woodland. Initially the annuals, including shepherd's purse (*Capsella bursa-pastoralis*), form what is termed an open pioneer community. There are only a few flowers dotted about, quite insufficient to provide cover for any animals except those which emerge from the soil at night. Few birds find much food here, apart from the worm eating starling and blackbird. This period is quite short and in often less than three years the herbaceous perennials have moved in denying the annuals the light they need to grow. Rosebay willow herb, purple loosestrife, hogweed and ragwort are among the many species which dominate this period occupying as long as 15 years and constitutes the closed tall herb community. The occasional shrub or small tree such as raspberry (*Rubus idaeus*), blackberry and dog rose may begin to make their appearance at this stage adding to the profusion of fruits and seeds available for birds such as the greenfinch, chaffinch, goldfinch (*Carduelis carduelis*) and yellowhammer (*Emberiza citrinella*).

Over the period of the next 20 years or so scrub vegetation gradually begins to develop, many of the seeds having been carried in by birds and mammals. Bramble and dog rose now become more frequent but are eventually shaded out by blackthorn, crab apple (*Malus sylvestris*) and in damp areas by willow and alder. These will eventually dry up the soil and make way for hazel to become the dominant species. The habitat is now ideal for butterflies, moths and other insects which are vital links in the food chains. The presence of seeds encourages birds such as wood pigeon and jay, while the juicy insects and dense cover for nesting proves irresistible to warblers such as the whitethroat, grasshopper warbler (*Locustella naevia*) and willow warbler.

Once the scrub area is established the time is ripe for pioneer trees to move in and the birches may be among the first. In British deep mull soils, however, there can be only one winner and that is oak, although it may take up to 150 years to become dominant. In a few areas beech may become the dominant species. The broad-leaved woodland dominated by oak is known as the climax and the stages it evolved through are called seres, the whole process known as a succession. If the conditions are not ideal the climax will be deflected which is why we have woodlands in Britain dominated by trees other than oak or beech.

Unless specially planted, with the possible exception of the yew, British native woodlands can be dominated by one of six species – birch, alder, ash, pine, beech and oak.

Birch is a pioneer tree showing great resistance to adverse weather. It makes the soil more fertile and then makes way for other species, especially oak. This does not happen in the Scottish Highlands where conditions are too harsh and birch is left in splendid isolation to become the climax vegetation. The National Nature Reserve of Craigellachie, close to Aviemore, consists of a loch ringed by birches and the Birks of Aberfeldy waterfalls cascade through rocky gorges overhung with gnarled dripping birches.

Birchwoods are not renowned for their flowers, especially in highland areas, but bilberry (*Vaccinium myrtillus*) is often the dominant plant of the field layer whilst petty whin (*Ulex minor*) and chickwood wintergreen (*Trientalis europaea*) also occur. Mosses are also common but it is the fungi which bring the real joy to the birchwoods. *Russula euruginea* is recognized by its pale stipe and green cap. *Lactarius turpis* has a slimy yellow-brown cap and if damaged often oozes a creamy fluid accounting for its scientific name and also its occasional vernacular name of milk mushroom. *Lactarius glyciosmus*, however, also has this property and is often given the same name – scientific names are vital. This species can be identified by its small size and pale, lilac stipe and cap. As a general rule the fungi growing on the floor of birchwoods are beneficial or at least neutral to the tree but this certainly cannot be said for the birch bracket fungus (*Polyporus betulinus*) which are long lived and often kill the tree.

A brimstone. Vast insect populations thrive in the shrub layer, especially bees and butterflies – including this lovely species which hibernates as an adult usually among the leaves of ivy.

Being a very common native tree it is not surprising to find many insects feeding upon it and over 100 species of moth caterpillars have been identified on birch. Among the species found are the large emerald (*Hipparchus papilionaria*). The adult's green colour gives it perfect camouflage amongst the birch leaves where it spends the day. The caterpillar hibernating on birch twigs is a matching brown, but when it wakes up in the spring and starts to feed its colour changes to green, maintaining its camouflage.

The peppered moth (*Biston betularis*), another birchwood species, has proved to biologists that evolution is not always a slow process. Peppered moths occur in different colour phases, the most usual being white with black speckling from which the vernacular name derives. When the insect is resting during the day on the trunk of birches the camouflage is sufficient to protect it from birds, and other predators. Occasionally a darker variety, often called *Biston betularia var. carbonaria*, occurs and is so easily seen that it is soon snapped up. In Manchester in about 1850 it was noticed that carbonaria was more common than the normal type. Obviously the sooty industrial atmosphere had made the light form more easily seen against the trees, while the black form now had the evolutionary advances.

Since the Clean Air Acts came into operation the pale form is making a comeback. This phenomenon has been called industrial melanism and has been noticed in other species, but *Biston betularia* is still regarded as the classic case.

The birdlife of a birchwood includes many tits feeding on caterpillars in the summer and seeds in the winter. A species I consider to be a birchwood specialist is the tree pipit which is a summer visitor. In winter birch seeds provide vital energy for the redpoll (*Acanthis flammea*) and the siskin (*Carduelis spinus*).

Like birch, **alder** is one of our ancient trees, and a large number of insects have adpated to feed upon them. Trees, however, do not remain passive for they are able to produce sufficient foliage to make enough food despite the attention of predators. Alder can produce nitrates from atmospheric nitrogen dominating damp areas until it dries the soil sufficiently to make it attractive to trees such as oak which succeed it – alder often survives close to rivers subject to flooding.

Strangely enough the alder fly (*Sialis lutaria*) is not restricted to alder although it is often seen on the branches and leaves, especially those overhanging water. The larvae mature in the mud of sluggish and stagnant water and the adults are on the wing from May to July.

Other moth species found in alder woods include the white-barred clearwing (*Aegeria spheciformis*), May high-flier (*Hydriomena coerulata*) and the alder kitten (*Cerura bicuspis*) – a species found mainly in the north and south, but seldom in the Midlands, of England in alder and birch woods.

The bird life of alder woods is interesting because the damp area attracts wetland birds including wildfowl. The nightingale and turtle dove (*Streptopelia turtur*) are found in southern areas while in parts of Scotland the redwing now breeds in alder and birchwoods. Woodcocks, sedge warblers (*Acrocphalus schoenobaenus*) and marsh tits (*Parus palustris*) breed here too. In winter, especially after rain or following the melting of snow, mallard (*Anas platyrhynchos*) and teal (*Anas crecca*) feed on the fallen seeds while above them the siskin and the redpoll snatch at the cones. Many seeds fall down into the water below where the ducks are feeding.

Emperor moth larvae can often be found feeding on the heather in upland woodlands.

Three mammals, of which only two are welcome, are found in the streams, pools and marshes in alder woods. These are the native water vole which has the most ridiculous scientific name of *Arvicola terrestris* – surely aquaticus would have been better – and the sadly declining otter (*Lutra lutra*). The third mammal to find shelter, food and a breeding niche is the north American mink (*Mustela vison*) which wreaks havoc with the bird population.

Although **ash** is often regarded as a co-dominant with oak it can form woodlands of its own especially in the Mendips, Pennines and the Dales. Limestone areas such as Colt Park wood, a National Nature Reserve on the slopes of Ingleborough near the rising of the lovely River Ribble, and the Arnside area of Cumbria are fine examples. Botanical treasures may be found here such as moonwort (*Botrychium lunaria*) and another rare fern, the green spleenwort (*Asplenium viride*).

Many of these plants are rarities but any ashwood will reveal an exciting and often bewildering variety of common species including dog's mercury, early purple orchid (*Orchis mascula*) and, especially in the north, giant bellflower (*Campanula latifolia*). Southern ashwoods tend to have impressive growths of wayfaring tree and traveller's joy often known as old man's beard (*Clematis vitalba*) while green hellebore (*Heleborus viridis*), angular Solomon's seal and Jacob's ladder (*Polemunium caeruleum*) also occur.

Ash does not seem to be as popular with insects as birch, alder or, most especially, oak but there are some species of moth whose caterpillars are found almost exclusively on ash. Two such are the drab coronet (*Craniophora lingustri*) widely distributed over most of Britain with only a few Irish records notable in Galway, and the beautiful centre-barred sallow (*Atethmia xerampelina*). This is also widely distributed – as long as there are ash trees, the nocturnal caterpillar feeding on the bursting buds during the late spring. The adults are splendid creatures having orange wings and earning their name from a central purple band running across them. Ash, is, in fact, related to the privet and lilac and it is quite usual to find the caterpillars of the privet hawk moth feeding upon the leaves during July and August. A full grown larva can measure 7.5cm (3in) and is of a delicate green colour marked with seven oblique white stripes edged in front with streaks of lilac.

Not all the larvae found on ash are there for the purpose of eating the leaves and one of these, the goat moth (*Cossus cossus*) plays its part in a most fascinating food chain. The caterpillar can reach 10cm (4in) in length and it bores into and feeds upon the solid wood of the ash tree, although it is also found eating elm and willow. It can take up to four years before leaving its burrow to seek out a suitable spot, often in the soil, to pupate. Being buried deep in the trunk of a tree affords some protection but there is an ichneumon fly which is able to locate the moth larva. It bores into the bark and lays its eggs in the insect's body. Obviously it is the smell of the larva giving away its presence to the parasite and many butterflies, especially red admirals, gather around the entrance to the holes bored by the moth. Ecologists have yet to find an answer for why this should happen.

There are no birds specifically associated with ash woods although I have watched wood pigeon feeding on the purple flowers and yellowhammers often find the combination of tall trees ideal as singing posts and a thick undergrowth suitable as nest sites to be irresistible. Other important species in ash woods include redstart, tree pipit, most of the titmice, chaffinch and blackcap, especially in some northern areas.

There are few mammals associated with pure ashwoods, but I have found the hedgehog, pipistrelle bat and the stoat to be common in those I have investigated, including Colt Park and in parts of the Mendips.

An alder moth caterpillar. Occasionally this moth can be found in alder woods which, despite its name, feeds on other trees including birch and hazel. The full grown caterpillar is basically black with a large yellow patch on each ring. The head is black and shining and is almost always turned towards the tail. The most unusual features, however, are the long black glossy and club-shaped hairs spaced along the sides.

Almost all Britain's native **pinewoods** are found in Scotland and these are among the most fascinating of all our woodlands and should be preserved at all costs. At Loch-an-Eilein in the Highlands of Scotland native pines often over 30m (90ft) high surround the loch and at Glenmore the canopy is so close that apart from a ground carpet of moss only two or three plants occur. These are heather, cowberry also called whortleberry and bilberry (*Vaccinium myrtilus*) also called huckleberry, blaeberry and whortleberry. *Vaccinium vitis idaea* is an evergreen shrub growing up to 30cm (12in) whilst *V. myrtillus* is twice this height and also deciduous. The leaves of the former are darker green and more glossy. The ripe fruit of cowberry is red while that of bilberry is black.

It is often worthwhile searching through the potentially monotonous mass of plants since there are rarities to be found. In eastern Scotland, for example, twin-flower (*Linnaea borealis*) and chickweed wintergreen may be found. Both are rare unlike twayblade and creeping ladies' cresses (*Satyrium repens*). In some pinewoods the wood anemone can form quite impressive stands. Understorey shrubs can survive in clearings especially juniper, holly and rowan which never form woodlands in their own right, although birch can sometimes invade to such an extent that it may become co-dominant with the pine.

Fungi are common in pinewoods, many forming mycorrhizar associations with the roots of *Pinus sylvestris* and are therefore beneficial. Others, however, are killers including an untidy looking bracket fungus called *Formes annosus* which is brown on top and white on the lower surface. *Polyporus schweinitzii* is a red-brown fungus with a velvety feel to it found near the base of the trunk It can penetrate the tree tissues so deeply that it causes heart rot – expensive to commercial foresters.

Insects, too, can be economically disastrous including the bordered white moth (*Bupalus piniaria*). The larvae is bright green, has a broad white line along the back and thinner yellow lines along the side giving perfect camouflage as they feed greedily on the pine needles. This is a diet also enjoyed by the larvae of another moth, the well named pine beauty (*Panolis flammea*). It is also green but has three broad white lines along the back in a successful effort to imitate a pine needle. A yellowish red stripe runs along the side, and the head is the same colour – a good match against the reddish bark of the pine tree. Apparently the two species would seem to be sharing the same ecological niche but direct competition is avoided by the pine beauty larvae feeding from May to July and the bordered whites from August to October. The combined defoliating effect on Scots pine can, in some years, be quite devastating.

Three specialist birds are almost totally dependent upon pines and are confined to the Highlands of Scotland. They are the crested tit, capercaillie and the Scottish crossbill (*Loxia scotica*), but also present are a surprisingly large number of other residents including chaffinch, bullfinch, siskin, goldcrest, treecreeper, long tailed tit and coal tit. Predators include the long eared owl, tawny owl, sparrowhawk and in areas where the trees surround lochs there are increasing numbers of breeding ospreys (*Pandion haliaetus*).

The pine forests are also home to some of our most delightful and yet threatened mammals including the pine marten which is quite rare and its main prey, the red squirrel, which struggles to hold on to its traditional niches except in Scotland. Roe and red deer also survive in what must have been their native habitat.

Beeches cast such a dense shade that few things can survive beneath them, although on sloping land where a few trees have toppled the odd oak may creep in and also yew, holly and whitebeam. Violets of several species occur together with bugle and white helleborine which loves limey soil. Ivy is often found creeping along the woodland floor accompanied by dog's mercury, bird's nest orchid, yellow

OVER: **Winter beech woods offer protection and food to the seed eating birds from northern Europe including chaffinches and the observant bird watcher will notice the occasional flock of brambling, easily identified by both their harsher call and white rump. The blackbird, great tit, blue tit and wood pigeon are all common residents.**

archangel (*Galeobdolon luteum*) and wood anemone. Beechwood flora does seem to depend very much on the soil on which it grows and in those lacking lime, bramble may grow well in the clearings and bluebell, cow wheat (*Melampyrum pratense*), wood sage (*Teucrium scorodonia*) and trailing St John's wort thrive among the swinging strands of wavy hair grass (*Deschampsia flexuosa*).

Despite this list the flowering plants of beechwoods are not impressive, but quite the reserve is true of the fungi. The whole surface of the beech tuft fungus is shiny, greyish-white and covered with slimy muscilage from which it derives its specific name. A large ring is on the stalk hanging downwards and the clusters grow high up on beech trunks found at their best – or perhaps worst – during September and October. Another slimy fungus found in beechwoods in late summer is *Cortinarius elatior* which has a pale brown cap prominently marked with radial grooves and standing on a thick white stalk. The gills are pale brown and when young are covered with a structure called a cortina looking very like a cobweb. As the fungus ages the gills darken often to violet producing brown spores. The death cap is also common in, but by no means exclusive to, beechwoods. This is also true to *Ganoderma applanatum* causing serious heart rot to trees which it infests. The grey-brown upper surface of this bracket type fungus has a hard surface and if cut has a shiny resinous appearance taking some time to fade.

The leaves of beech seem attractive to the larvae of as many as 60 species of moth but, surprisingly, no butterflies seem fond of this source of food. The vapourer moth (*Orgyia antigua*) is widely distributed in the British Isles although somewhat rarer in Ireland. The larva is basically grey with a red dotted line running along the dorsal surface and the flanks are also spotted with red, as is a broken yellow line. There are four yellow brush-like structures tipped with brown along the back and longer greyish hairs towards the head.

Look at the surface of the leaves of beech which are sometimes marked with holes and lines mined just beneath the surface. This is the work of the black weevil (*Rhynohaenus fagi*). If some dead leaves are collected and placed in a Tullgren funnel many springtails, spiders and mites come scuttling out to be identified proving that birds and mammals living in a beechwood will not starve.

The red squirrel is Britain's only native mammal associated with beechwoods. The badger often selects a site for its sett beneath the roots and two introduced species, the edible dormouse and the grey squirrel, also find the habitat acceptable.

The **oakwoods** of Britain are widespread and wildlife so prolific that a huge book would be needed to do even one of them justice. A host of moths and

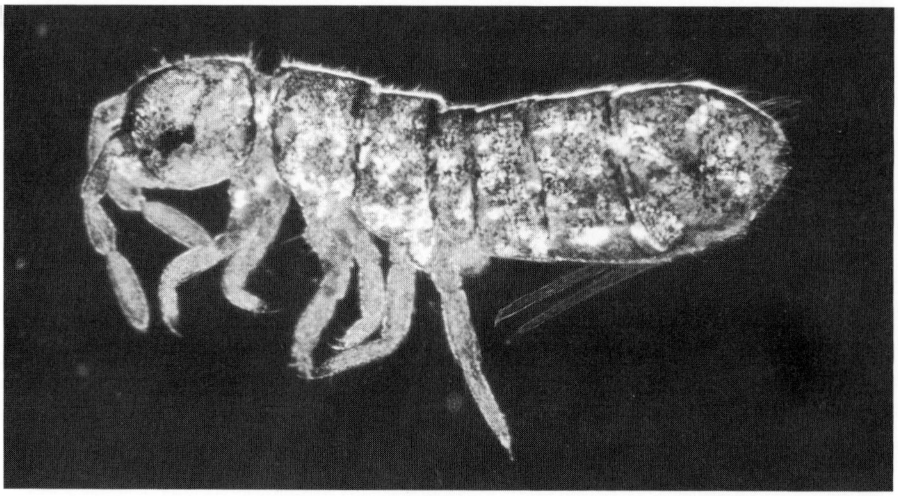

Many species of invertebrates live in the leaf litter. Springtails are particularly common and can be seen if the litter is spread out on a sheet of white paper.

A lobster moth caterpillar. This species may be found feeding on beech together with the grey dagger and the November winter moths.

butterflies feast upon the leaves, including the purple emperor (*Apatura iris*). The acorns are buried by jays, swallowed whole by wood pigeons, nibbled by longtailed field mice and hammered open by nuthatches.

It is in the oakwood that the divisions of vegetation are clearly defined in four zones called the canopy or tree layer, shrub layer, field layer and ground layer.

In the **tree layer** the oak leaves are angled to pick up the maximum amount of sunlight. They grow quickly and are so palatable to a host of insects that the whole canopy becomes a buzz of almost constant activity. The caterpillars of many butterflies and moths are found in this layer, especially the mottled umber (*Erannis defoliaria*) whose specific name indicates the damage it can do to the tree. Fortunately the activity of the tit and warbler families with hungry, fast growing young to feed, does much to control the larvae population. At night many birds come to the safety of the foliage to roost but other species, especially the buzzard, and carrion crow (*Corvus corone*) may have their nests high above the ground.

Beneath the relatively open and late opening canopy of the oak grow a complex of **shrubs** including hazel, hawthorn (*Crataegus monogyna*) and ash is present in varying numbers. Oakwoods, of course, have been so managed over the centuries that, as a result of coppicing to provide poles, a thick shrub layer always sprang up quickly. Now that the demand for such materials has declined, the shrub layer is often so thick that it forms an ideal habitat for nesting birds such as the blackbird, wren, many species of warbler, and, within its range, the nightingale.

Coppicing on a regular timetable allowed sunlight to penetrate the woodland fabric and when this practice was discontinued the field layer was reduced and only retained its former glory in clearings and along the edges.

The **field layer** of oakwoods, especially those with a good sprinkling of ash, is rich in flowers varying a lot from one district to another. On acid soils for example the upright St John's wort will be common. There are other species regularly present whatever the soil. Included is wood anemone, ramsons and lesser celandine dominating wet woods while in dry conditions wood sage (*Teucrium scorodonia*) is found in quantity. Dog's mercury, primrose, bugle, enchanter's nightshade (*Circaea lutetiana*), red campion and wood sorrel (*Oxalis acetosella*) are all to be found and the most common grass is often the slender false-brome (*Brachypodium sylvaticum*).

Butterflies, including small tortoishell and the peacock, feed on the leaves of the stinging nettle. The speckled wood is also found in the field layer its larvae feeding on cock's foot grass.

The field layer is thick enough to provide cover for the nests of the nightjar (*Caprimulgus europaeus*), woodcock and pheasant. Mammals are also common including the long tailed field mouse, bank vole and both the pygmy and common shrew. Although some of the mammalian predators of these creatures have been badly treated, the stoat and fox have both proved very resilient although the polecat has only survived in the hanging oakwoods in the Welsh valleys.

The **ground layer** varies according to the climate. Mosses only survive in damp areas whereas a carpet of dead leaves dotted with fungi is typical of dried areas.

The concept of dividing the oak woodland into four distinct layers should be regarded only as a useful plan and some organisms will be found at all levels. Honeysuckle can twist up from the ground to the canopy of the tree layer, as can ivy while the polypody fern can grow in the field layer or rise from the branches of an old gnarled oak where it is said to live as an epiphyte.

How should a treecreeper be classified as it starts to search for insects at the base of a tree trunk before spiralling its way up the tree to the crown and descending to begin its hunting again at the base of the next tree?

The four layer theory shows how food circulates through the ecosystem, each plant and animal having its own unique niche in the woodland ecology. The subject is only touched upon, however, and it is important to visit as many woodlands as possible.

The woodcock is the only wader found regularly in woodlands and therefore has no feeding competitors.

Gazetteer

LIKE every naturalist I have my favourite woodlands and to include them all would be impossible. I have made the selection easier by not listing those reserves requiring a permit and there is therefore free access at all times to the woodlands mentioned. Anyone wishing to discover woodland reserves which do require a permit should contact their local County Naturalist Trust, the address of which will be available from your local library. The woods are grouped into the counties of England in alphabetical order with separate sections for Scotland and Wales. The numbers in brackets after each entry indicate where the woods are to be found on the map on pages 202–203.

AVON AND SOMERSET

Weston Woods (1)
Situated on the coast near Weston-super-Mare the area is best visited in summer when butterflies seem to be everywhere, the main species being peacock, small tortoishell, comma and brimstone. The woodland has been planted in recent years mainly with sycamore, oak and ash, but there are some sweet chestnuts, poplar and hazel. There are not many flowers but toothwort grows well.

Brockley Combe (2)
A nature trail organized by the Avon Wildlife Trust lies just off the A370 between Weston-super-Mare and Bristol. The limestone valley has delicate growths of ash, hawthorn and elder with clematis very much in evidence. Birds include linnet, long tailed tit, yellowhammer and greenfinch with summer visitors including whitethroat, lesser whitethroat and redstart.

Cloutsham and Hornerwood (3)
A magnificent damp oak wood with a rich understorey and flower layer. The trees give way to open moorland studded with gorse and have resident raven and buzzard while red deer wander the open slopes finding shelter in the woods. Along with the nearby Hornerwood, Cloutsham is reached by turning off A39 Lynton to Minehead road at Porlock. Cloutsham has free access but the National Trust ask visitors to Hornerwood, which is more than 1,000 years old, to stick to the marked paths. Ivy leaved bellflower, bitter vetch, scaly male fern and wood spurge all thrive here as do dippers and grey wagtail enjoying the fast tumbling streams.

BEDFORDSHIRE AND HUNTINGDONSHIRE

Aversley Wood (4)
Situated off the A1 to the north of Huntingdon this still extensive stretch of woodland, much of it of ancient origin has thick patches of blackthorn providing ideal habitat for the black hairstreak butterfly. Wild service trees are also a feature but the real glory is seen when bluebells fill every light filled space between the oaks and ashes.

The Lodge, Sandy (5)
Directly on the A1 at Sandy, the Lodge is the headquarters of the RSPB and opens daily. On Sundays entry is restricted to members of the bird society and of the Bedfordshire and Huntingdonshire Naturalists Trust. Some of the paths have been eroded by 1,000s of footsteps. Redstarts, woodpeckers and several titmice breed here and there are occasional sightings of birds of prey, especially sparrowhawks.

BERKSHIRE

Windsor Great Park (6)
A huge area of around 6,000 hectares (15,000 acres) run by the Crown Estate Commissioners. An ancient hunting forest, the park is best reached via the A3022 or A332.

Much of the ancient woodland survives including an 800 years old oak close to the forest gate and the fungi, beetles and flies have been carefully studied over many years. The bird life is also plentiful and in areas of deep quiet, sparrowhawks hunt by day and tawny owls by night despite the close proximity of the park to areas of huge population.

BUCKINGHAMSHIRE

Ashridge Park (7)
This estate in the Chilterns covers 165 sq km (60 sq miles) and pushes into Buckinghamshire, Bedfordshire and Hertfordshire. Most of this area is owned by the National Trust and areas of the woodland date back to Saxon times. These are full of spring bluebells and breeding jays while in the open areas birds foot trefoil grows providing nectar for the chalkhill blue butterfly. The edible dormouse occurs at Ashridge which is only 40km (28 miles) from London.

Chalkdell wood (8)
A tiny beechwood of around 1 hectare ($2\frac{1}{2}$ acres) run by the woodland trust interesting for its rookery and tangled shrub layer, which includes old man's beard, bramble and wild rose. There are varied fungi beneath the beeches

surrounding an old chalk quarry. Chalkdell wood is near the junction of the A4128 from High Wycombe and the A413 from Amersham to Wendover.

Church wood (9)
Lying between the A535 Slough to Beaconsfield road and the M40 this RSPB reserve is a delightful tangle of tree and shrub, ancient and modern, native and alien plants. Pools ensure growths of yellow iris and encourage sedge warblers to breed and butterflies include the white letter hairstreak. The profusion and variety of fruits and seeds means a regular passage of winter migrants such as field fare, redwing, siskin and redpoll.

CHESHIRE

Alderley Edge (10)
A national trust area of woodland standing on a sandstone ridge with commanding views of the Cheshire plain and the valley of the River Bollin. Scots pine, oak and birch provide good habitat for all three British woodpeckers and sparrowhawks also breed. Close to Manchester the area, with its overtones of witchcraft, is reached along the A34 and is well signed.

Dunham Park (11)
A National Trust owned house surrounded by trees, the river Bollin and the Bridgewater canal. Dunham has a deer park, duck pond and some splendid stretches of woodland. An oak wood shows layering while on the opposite side of a large car park is a beechwood with nothing but mosses and fungi on the ground. Dunham is signed off the A56 just south of Altrincham.

Tatton Park (12)
Run by the Cheshire County Council and within walking distance of the centre of Knutsford, Tatton consists of a nineteenth century house and a couple of meres surrounded by woodland. A signed 'Foresters walk' leads through a variety of trees including Scots pine, oak, ash and especially birch. There is a variety of fungi and woodpeckers drum on and nest in the hollow trees. Nuthatches sing their bell-like notes from the mighty beeches and the meres are famous for their winterwildfowl.

Lyme Park Country Park (13)
Lyme Park is a deer park managed by the National Trust and clearly signed off the A6(T) at Disley. Nature trails run through woodlands with good stands of oak, beech, ash and horsechestnut. All three woodpeckers have been recorded and woodcock appear in the summer. Pipistrelle and long eared bats are also common.

CORNWALL

Coombe Valley (14)
Situated just to the north of Bude off the A39 the reserve is owned by the Cornwall County Council, and holds a variety of native deciduous trees. These, and the varied understorey, is good habitat for the silver washed fritillary butterfly as well as commas and peacocks. A stream has a fast area suitable for dippers and slower deeper spots which attract kingfishers. Flowers are plentiful and include the winter heliotrope and autumn crocus.

Peter's Wood (15)
10 hectares (25 acres) of trees overhanging steep valleys provide many secret places for a variety of nesting birds including buzzard, blackcap, whinchat, yellowhammer and a number of warblers. Pipistrelle, daubenton's, long eared and noctule bats are also common. The splashing streams provide ideal wetland habitat in which many ferns grow, including the Tunbridge filmy fern and the Royal fern. Peter's Wood is signposted from Boscastle.

CUMBRIA

Arnside Knot Nature Trail (16)
A short journey from Carnforth just off the A6, Arnside Knot is under the joint control of the National Trust and the Arnside Parish Council. The knot is a fine example of a limestone woodland. Ash and juniper thrives in the cracks of rock, orchids are plentiful and red squirrels are often seen. Green woodpeckers, pied flycatchers and many species of warbler occur and there is the occasional spotting of a hawfinch.

Bardsea Country Park (17)
The coast road A5087 from Ulverston to Barrow passes the Cumbria County Council woodland overlooking shingle and mudflats. Oak and beech dominate but outcrops of limestone allow growths of lily of the valley, some spectacular orchids and fellwort. Birds include jackdaw, green woodpecker and sparrowhawk. Red fox, badger and brown hare can all be seen occasionally in the clearings.

Friars Crag, Keswick (18)
A National Trust woodland within easy walking distance of the town. The walk skirts the lake and there are lovely views of Derwentwater through the stands of Scots pine, oak and birch.

Glencoyne Wood, Ullswater (19)
A mixed National Trust woodland overlooking Ullswater with carpets of spring daffodils, masses of autumn fungi and echoing to the sound of summer bird song. After rain the crashing Aira force waterfall hurls a mist of spray and ensures a variety of liverworts, mosses and ferns. The wood is easily reached from the M6 motorway turning at exit 40 and following the A592 to Glenridding.

Lake District National Park (20)
The area is as famous for its woodlands as its lakes and mountains. Most are open to the public including the Forestry Commission Grizedale forest as well as smaller, mainly deciduous areas controlled by the National Trust, and the Cumbria Naturalist Trust. The woodlands surrounding Tarn Hows are at their best in winter when the trees overhanging the frozen waterfalls are alive with thrushes, tits and finches.

DERBYSHIRE

Dales (21)
Many footpaths cut through Monk's Dale and Lathkill Dale centred around Bakewell and Buxton, linked by the A6. Permits from the NCC are needed to visit some areas but there is plenty to see in an area dominated by the Peak District's carboniferous limestone. The ash woods are spectacular with guelder rose, hazel and rowan plus the very unusual rock whitebeam and wild privet. Lily of the valley, herb Paris, green hellebore and yellow star-of-Bethlehem are also treasures. Bird watchers will see black grouse, ring ouzel and merlin on the fringes of the woodland and breeding warblers within it.

Elvaston Castle (22)
A lovely walk of almost 2km ($1\frac{1}{2}$ miles) through native trees interspersed with rhododendron runs in a circle from the Derbyshire County Council centre at Elvaston. Wide clearings allow carpets of bluebells, primrose and ramsons to flourish and the streams have kingfishers breeding and feeding in them. The area is just south of Derby on the A6(T).

Hardwick Country Park (23)
Just north of Mansfield and reached via junction 28 or 29 from the M1, Hardwick has a nature trail weaving in and out of ponds and the damp areas include bulrush, common spike rush, horsetail, marestail and a number of ferns. Common woodland birds include titmice, thrushes, jay, little owl, treecreeper and nuthatch.

DEVON

Lady's Wood(24)
On the edge of Dartmoor on the A38 before the turn off for Totnes (A385). The Devon Trust for Nature Conservation administer the area dominated by oak and ash but coppicing goes on among the hazel area – a breeding area for the common dormouse. Coppicing always encourages spring flowers and Lady's wood is a real joy in spring and early summer.

Wistman's Wood (25)
Situated within the Dartmoor National Park, Wistman's Wood is reached by footpath from Two Bridges near the junction of the A384 and B3212. The beauty of this wood is not in its rich wildlife because there is little to see, but in the thrill of seeing gnarled oaks fighting the harsh climate in the valley gouged by the torrential West Dart draining the gaunt slopes of Dartmoor. You would expect to find sessile oak here but it is the lowland species – the pedunculate oak – which grows here. The moss flora is very rich.

Yarner Wood (26)
This lovely wood is part of Dartmoor reached by taking the B3344 off the A38 Plymouth to Exeter road. Dominated by oak with a lot of birch marked trails run by the Nature Conservancy Council reserve. A permit is required if visitors wish to leave the trails. White admiral, holly blue and meadow brown butterflies flutter in the rich undergrowth and both wood warblers and pied flycatchers breed here in the summer.

DORSET

Brownsea Island (27)
Run jointly by the Dorset Naturalists' Trust and the National Trust this reserve can only be reached by boat either from Poole Quay or Sandbanks Ferry. No dogs are allowed on the island which has a great variety of habitats, including a fine woodland with sika deer, red squirrel and the second largest heronry in Britain. There are many exotic trees as well as areas dominated by native species.

DURHAM, CLEVELAND, TYNE AND WEAR

Collier Wood (28)
A tiny but fascinating reserve organized by Durham County Council, Collier wood is at the junction of A68 and A689 roads near Tow Law. A short trail of less than 0.4km ($\frac{1}{2}$ mile) leads through oak, ash, beech and some conifers, with open areas in which cowslips, primroses and bluebells grow. Butterflies, including small copper, orange tip and small tortoishell, are common and the bird life includes jay and the occasional influx of crossbills.

Hamsterley Forest (29)
A forestry commission woodland but enough of the native woodland remains to ensure variety. Sloping banks of trees drain into Bedburn Beck on which dippers and grey wagtails have established territories. Pennington beechwood is part of the forest and at almost 300m (1,000ft) is one of the highest such woods in Britain and very popular with wintering bramblings. Lady's mantle and foxglove reflect the acid nature of some areas whilst the richer parts support growths of bluebell, golden saxifrage, wood sorrel and ramsons are so common that the whole wood smells strongly of garlic. Pied flycatchers, redstarts, and wood warbler nest here and crossbills and siskins are common winter visitors. Hamsterley is reached via a toll road from Bedburn signed off the A68 north-west of Bishop Auckland.

Hardwick Hall (30)
This Durham County Council reserve is located off the A689 just beyond its junction with the A1(M). A boarded walk allows the damp alder woodland to be seen at its best. Marsh marigolds and lady's smock light up the spring and the lovely colours of the long tailed tits do the same on cold mornings of winter. At one time the area was a lake which has long since silted up.

ESSEX

Belfairs Wood (31)
Southend-on-Sea Borough Council has made the most of this mixed woodland which occupies 36 hectares (90 acres) opposite Canvey Island. The hornbeams are particularly impressive but there are also plenty of fine oaks and birches. Heath fritillary butterflies are the delight of visiting entomologists.

Epping Forest (32)
Until the late thirteenth century almost the whole of Essex was beneath the canopy of the mighty forest of Epping. Only a tiny fraction now remains and even some of this is threatened. It is still possible, however, within 20km (12 miles) of London to stand beneath ancient oaks, smell the sweet summer nectar of small leaved limes, watch the Essex skipper butterfly and the gold tail moth and see the rare crested newt swim with common toads in one of the many ponds. This is one of the most vulnerable woodlands in Britain and every effort must be made to preserve it.

Hatfield Forest Country Park (33)
A National Trust property consisting of 420 hectares (1,100 acres) of what was once the Forest of Essex. There is evidence of the coppicing when oaks were needed for houses and ships between which there are open spaces. This is ideal for common woodland birds. Orange tip butterflies feed on Jack-by-the-hedge, and among the rich collection of flowers are lesser celandine, ground ivy, bugle and germander speedwell. There are wet areas in which yellow flag and marsh cinquefoil grow and provide cover for nesting reed buntings and even the occasional snipe. The park is close to the A111. The old forest is now part of Hertfordshire.

The woodlands of Britain

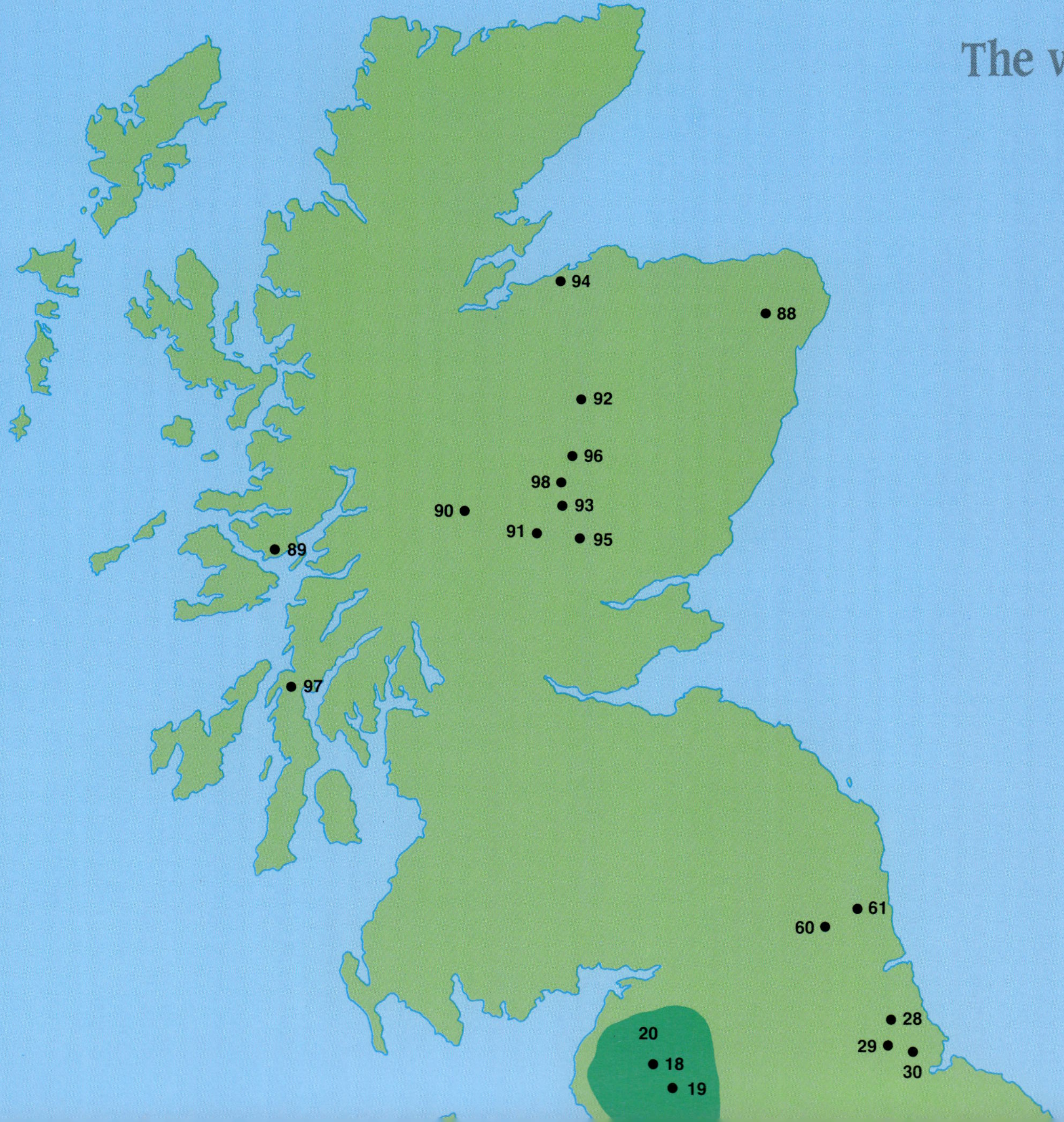

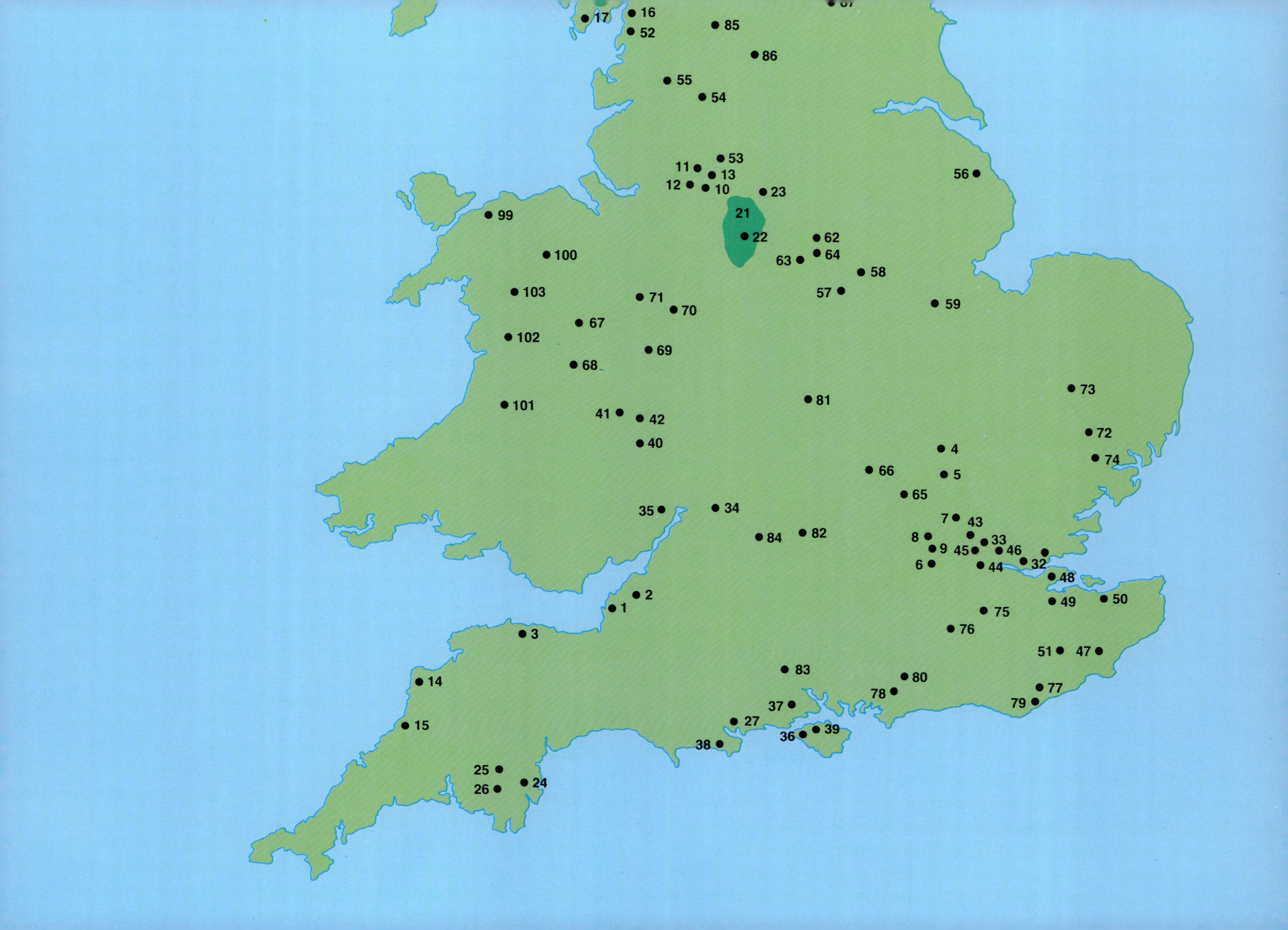
17
16
52
85
86
55
54
53
11
13
12
10
23
56
99
21
22
62
64
63
58
100
57
59
103
71
70
67
102
69
68
73
81
101
41
42
72
40
4
74
66
5
65
35
34
7
43
84
82
8
33
9
45
46
6
44
32
48
2
50
49
1
75
3
76
51
47
83
80
14
77
78
79
37
27
15
36
39
38
25
24
26

GLOUCESTERSHIRE

Buckholt Wood (34)
A lovely beechwood in the care of the Nature Conservancy Council and situated to the south of Gloucester just off the A46 connecting Stroud to Cheltenham. Coltswood limestone ensures a rich tapestry of plants in the clearings including travellers joy, ploughman's-spikenard and green hellebore. Damper areas are dominated by alder beneath which are strands of pendulous sedge – ideal habitat for wintering finches and tits and breeding warblers. Bird nest orchid is also found beneath the beeches.

Forest of Dean (35)
Almost 11,000 hectares (27,000 acres) sounds a lot of woodland but the Dean squeezed between the Rivers Wye and Severn has also been squeezed by man's demand for timber. Its future seems more secure and within it are areas under the control of the RSPB, the Gloucestershire Trust for Nature Conservation, the Forestry Commission and the Nature Conservancy Council. The Dean has provided charcoal for smelting, oaks for mighty ships and timber for building. The presence of sheep since the middle ages has prevented the development of a substantial understorey but the lichens are spectacular and the limestone outcrops have colonies of herb Paris, autumn crocus and birds nest orchid. Noctule, daubentons and a number of other bats have been recorded as well as several other mammals' including badger. The bird life is also rich. The B4226 runs through the centre of the forest.

HAMPSHIRE AND THE ISLE OF WIGHT

Fort Victoria Country Park, Isle of Wight (36)
Close to Yarmouth and just off the A3054 are a series of wooded limestone cliffs which periodically collapse during heavy rain. The nature trail follows a safe path through tangles of ideal butterfly habitat and there are spectacular sproutings of old man's beard.

New Forest (37)
A huge area of 37,555 hectares (92,800 acres) between Southampton and Bournemouth the New Forest is the last of the Royal hunting forests designated by William the Conqueror to survive almost intact. The wild gladiolus (*Gladiolus illyricus*) is found growing among the bracken, buzzards scream over the trees and the wild ponies graze in the glades. The New Forest guide map is published by the Forestry Commission and lists the history of the area and marks car parks.

Selborne (38)
Made famous by Gilbert White the hanging beeches are the special feature of this wooded hill. Oak is also present and the understorey includes blackthorn, holly, hazel, buckthorn, ash and dogwood. Dog's mercury, nettle leaved bellflower, woodruff and ivy dominate the field layer and harts-tongue fern is also common.

Windmill Wood, Pyle, Chale, Isle of Wight (39)
An ancient woodland on steep west facing sandstone which has a rich ground flora and in spring is densely carpeted with bluebells. Wet areas have stands of reed mace and soft rush. Nightjar breed here and the wood must be preserved from any form of disturbance if they are to survive here.

HEREFORD AND WORCESTER

Broadway Tower Country Park and Fish Hill (40)
A mixed woodland with two trails winding through it to a high point from which there are magnificent views into Wales. The bird life is rich and badgers and foxes are present. Nearby is Fish Hill Woodland Trail which has a splendid lime-loving flora and good views over sweeping countryside into Wales. Broadway is situated south of Evesham at the junction of A44 and A46.

Croft Caste Woodlands (41)
Reached via the B4361 and B4362 and between Leominster and Ludlow this National Trust property offers magnificent views and varied wildlife. Pied flycatchers, redstarts and warblers call from the summer trees, goldcrests are resident in the conifers and buzzards hover in the currents of warm air rising from the limestone rocks.

Wyre Forest (42)
Massive stands of oak, graceful birches, damp areas sprinkled with meadowsweet, hemp agrimony and water mint, stretches of river with resident dipper and kingfisher, many species of butterfly are just a few of the glories of the Wyre which is one of our few remaining native woodlands. Footpaths run through the forest but a permit may be needed to go into some protected and ecologically sensitive areas. Bewdley is the best starting point and the B4194 to Buttonoak runs through the forest.

HERTFORDSHIRE

Ashridge Nature Trails (43)
Trails running through broadleaved woodlands containing muntjac, fallow deer and red fox. Woodcocks can be seen roding in the breeding season and there is a resident population of redpoll and nuthatch. Ashridge is between Tring and Hemel Hempstead on the B4056. It is National Trust property but the Hertfordshire Natural History Society and Field Club are involved in the management.

Northan Great Wood Country Park (44)
Just north of Potters Bar on the B157. This area is noted for its nightingales and stands of beech interspersed with hornbeam, birch and oak. Coppicing is still part of the management strategy which is under the control of the Welwyn and Hatfield District Council. The M25 motorway runs close by and the park can be reached from exit 24.

Oughton Head Common (45)
This Hertfordshire County Council reserve is more famous for its river which sports heron and kingfisher, but its wet woodlands dominated by willows are rich in wildlife. Plants include hemp agrimony, meadowsweet, purple loostrife, tussock sedge and marsh marigold. Sedge warblers breed and in winter siskin and redpoll are common. Muntjac deer are also resident. The site is just off the A505 road from Hitchin to London. Visitors can go without permit providing they stick to the marked paths on the 16 hectare (40 acre) site.

Wormley Wood (46)
Just off the A10 between Cheshunt and Hoddesdon is Wormley Wood, a magnificent mixture of native broadleaves. Wood anemones and bluebells dominate the parts of the woodland which are ancient, but there is a dense bird-rich scrub covering the sites of abandoned fields. There is a good car park and it is marvellous to find such an unspoiled wood so close to London.

KENT

Ham Street Woods (47)
A Nature Conservancy Council woodland showing the classic management technique of coppice with standards. Nightingales and hawfinches breed and an array of moths including lime hawk and buff tip. Ham Street is south of Ashford at the junction of the A2080 and the B2067.

Northward Hill (48)
Reached along the A228 out of Rochester as far as High Halstow. The RSPB reserve is signed off Northwood Avenue. Although Northward suffered badly from Dutch elm disease there is now some recovery. The largest heronry in Britain (over 200 pairs) and rooks, nightingales, little owls, long eared owls and all three woodpeckers are to be found. The white letter hairstreak butterfly also breeds among the tangle of brambles.

Queendown Warren (49)
Between the M2 and the A249 Queendown Warren is an important refuge for wildlife on the North Downs. The Kent Trust for Nature Conservation administers this 7 hectares (16 acres) site which dates back to the time of Henry III when it was a commercially operated rabbit warren. Beech and elder are common but there are also oak, birch, wayfaring tree, wild cherry and hornbeam. Birds foot trefoil, rock rose and wild thyme all grow well as do many species of orchid including fly, spider and bee. Adders and common lizard occur as do red fox, stoat and weasel.

Westfield Wood (50)
On the A299 just off the M20 is Westfield Wood which lies on the old Pilgrims road from Winchester to Canterbury. The Kent Trust for Nature Conservation look after the 5 hectares (12.5 acres) of steep chalk dominated by gnarled old yews. Butchers broom and green hellebore both grow and the wild cherry is a delight in the spring.

Yockletts Bank (51)
To the north of Wye and sandwiched between the A28 and the B2068 is the rich chalk woodland at Yockletts Bank a Kent Trust for Nature Conservation. Crammed into just under 25 hectares (62.5 acres) cowslip, salad burnet, woodruff and the rare lady orchid all occur here. A badger sett has been in use for many years and foxes may be seen. Birds include nightingale, green woodpecker, blackcap and willow warbler.

LANCASHIRE AND GREATER MANCHESTER

Eaves Wood, Silverdale (52)
Eaves Wood, Waterslack Wood and Castlebarrow make up an area of 44 hectares (113 acres) administered by the National Trust and the Lancashire Naturalists Trust. The whole area is a site of special scientific interest (SSSI) and overlooks Morecambe Bay. Yew is very common on the sloping limestone hillside on which the wood is sited and from which it gets its name. 'Efes' is medieval English for a sloping wood. Green woodpeckers feed on wood ants which abound here.

Etherow Country Park (53)
The River Etherow is one of the tributaries of the River Mersey and the river runs through a wooded gorge with oak, ash and sycamore. Pheasants, finches, thrushes are common and siskins and long tailed tits are often seen in the alders. Swifts, swallows and house martins swoop around Compstall Mill once powered by the river. A reservoir also associated with the mill is a haven for wildfowl. Administered by Stockport Council and reached on the A626.

Healey Dell, Rochdale (54)
A disused railway line, the twisting River Spodden and a variety of trees make this Rochdale Borough Council reserve one of Lancashire's most treasured cloughs. A clough means a wooded valley. The acid nature of the surrounding moors ensure a growth of heather, bilberry, bog asphodel, tormentil and wavy hair grass, whilst the tons of limestone used as ballast when the railway was built has allowed plants such as harts tongue fern, birds foot trefoil and harebell to thrive. Both northern and southern orchids and their confusing hybrids also grow here. The area is signed off the A6066 from Bacup to Rochdale.

Hodder Woods (55)
Lower Hodder Bridge is between Whalley and Longridge on the B6246. A footpath follows the river to the Higher Hodder Bridge with magnificent broadleaved woodlands sloping down to the water. Bluebells, primrose, toothwort, wood anemone, lords and ladies and the pungent smelling ramsons, grow in profusion. Birds include nuthatch, treecreeper and woodcock, while kingfisher, dipper and grey wagtails are found by the waterside. Sika and roe deer have been recorded as have mink, stoat, weasel and both grey and red squirrels.

LINCOLNSHIRE AND SOUTH HUMBERSIDE

Bradley Woods (56)
On a minor road off the A18 south west of Grimsby is Bradley Wood, under the control of the local council. There is an occupied badger's sett among the tangle of wild cherry, blackthorn, bramble and dogwood. Oak and ash with some elm and conifers are the dominant trees but there are plenty of open spaces filled with spotted orchids and bluebell while butterflies flit about in the sunlit glades.

LEICESTERSHIRE AND RUTLAND

Beacon Hill (57)
Leicestershire County Council are custodians of this high spot at the junction of the B591 and B5330 to the south west of Loughborough. Many native trees including oak, beech and hawthorn with a rich understorey ensure a wide variety of insects and birds.

Swithland Wood (58)
Fringed by the B5330 to the north of Leicester this wood has some very uncommon plants including saw-wort, adders tongue and betony. The bulk of the wood is of ancient origin dominated by oak but with the damp areas dominated by alders and sedges. Dragonflies, butterflies and moths are all common in this 58 hectare (150 acre) site.

NORTHAMPTONSHIRE

Castor Hanglands (59)
To the west of Peterborough off the A47(T) are 45 hectares (115 acres) of castor hanglands, a mere remnant of the old Forest of Narborough run by the Nature Conservancy Council. Wild service trees occur and this species is typical of old woodlands. Standard oaks tower over coppices of ash, hazel, and more oaks. Fallow deer wander among the scrub of crab apple, guelder rose, buckthorn and privet. There is some grassland and a number of ponds frequented by dragonflies, moorhens, wildfowl and herons.

NORTHUMBERLAND

Holystone Forest Walks (60)
The village of Holystone can be reached just off the B6341 between Alnwick and Otterburn. There is a Forestry Commission spruce plantation but also magnificent old oak and beechwoods – a rare sight in Northumberland. These are rich in ferns and are a haunt of red squirrels. For the historians there are hill forts and signs of charcoal burning among the once coppiced oaks.

Thrunton Wood (61)
A Forestry Commission wood reached along the A697. Roe deer are common here and do some damage to seedling spruce, larch and western hemlock. Grouse from nearby moors used the area for shelter during the winter and pheasants also graze among the rides colourful in late summer by purple clumps of heather which are very popular with butterflies.

NOTTINGHAMSHIRE

Clumber Park (62)
Signed from the B6005 south of Worksop, Clumber Park's 1,275 hectares (3,200 acres) are owned by the National Trust. Many years ago part of the old Sherwood Forest, a few fine trees remain providing a rich variety of understorey plants. The great lake cutting through the park adds wildfowl to the wide variety of woodland birds.

Oldmoor Wood (63)
Leaving the M1 at junction 26 and following the Ilkeston road leads to the Woodland Trust's reserve to the north east of the town. There are tall beeches, gnarled oaks and larches which look marvellous in their spring greenery. Each of the 15 hectares (38 acres) abounds with spring bird song and summer flowers.

Sherwood Forest Country Park (64)
The Country Park is signed from the M1 north of Nottingham and fringed by the A614(T) to the east of Mansfield – it is but a fragment of Robin Hood's ancient forest. The beetles of the area have been studied in detail and there are still some mighty oaks and groves of birch.

OXFORDSHIRE

Aston Rowant (65)
Situated very close to exit 6 of the M40 is the Nature Conservancy Council reserve which is part of the Chilterns. There is a nature trail but no public right of way or access to areas other than the trail itself. This is wise since the habitat must be protected from any further erosion. Among the beeches grow white and violet helleborine while the clearings have patches of hawthorn, holly, guelder rose, bluebell, enchanter's nightshade and woodruff. Green hairstreak, dingy skipper, chalkhill blue, and the Duke of Bergundy are among the butterflies found here and among the birds, hawfinch and sparrowhawk both breed.

Blenheim Park (66)
The park surrounding the house built in the 18th century for the Duke of Marlborough has some splendid oaks overlooking a lake. Entrance to the estate is off the A4095 south west of Woodstock. Treecreepers, nuthatch and all three woodpecker may be seen and jays are also common.

SHROPSHIRE

Colemere Country Park (67)
Signed clearly from the A528 from Shrewsbury to Wrexham the County Council run reserve occupies 50 hectares (125 acres) of mixed habitats including a lake and grassland as well as woodland. The woodland overlooks the Shropshire union canal and alder, oak, ash, yew, sycamore and rowan with a very rich understorey ensure a variety of birds. Some areas are covered by rhododendron in which nest thrushes, blackbirds and dunnock.

Hope Valley, Woodland (68)
A narrow woodland of only 13 hectares (33 acres) actively managed by the Shropshire Trust for Nature Conservancy. Existing conifers are gradually being replaced by oak and other native hardwoods and will increase the number of bird species. Pied and spotted flycatchers both breed along with redstarts and several species of warblers. A lovely stream attracts kingfisher, grey wagtail and dipper. The reserve is on the A488 south of Shrewsbury.

STAFFORDSHIRE

Cannock Chase (69)
A lovely mixture of bog, heath and woodland the 870 hectares (2,200 acres) of Cannock Chase is managed by the Forestry Commission. Situated to the north of Cannock there are many access points off the A460, A34(T) and A51. Ancient oaks, wood anemones, bluebells, climbing corydalis, lesser celandine plus a variety of fungi including fly agaric under birches please the botanists. Fallow deer trot around the clearings and the list of woodland birds is impressive. There is a fine information centre and museum.

Coombes Valley (70)
The RSPB reserve is reached via the A523 Leek to Ashbourne road and following the signs along a minor road to Apesford. A very steep woodland hanging over a brook with both kingfisher and dipper. There is a badgers' sett, but the reserve is beautifully managed for birds and long eared, tawny and little owls are all present and woodcocks weave in and out of oaks and wood warblers sing from the foliage. Nuthatches, treecreepers and all three woodpeckers are present.

Greenway Bank Country Park (71)
Signed off the A527 road from Stoke-on-Trent to Congleton this country park is of special interest because of its arboretum planted to celebrate the Silver Jubilee of Queen Elizabeth II in 1977. The collection concentrates on British species. There is also an established mixed woodland in which redstart, spotted flycatcher, jackdaw, jay and warblers breed. A reservoir built to feed the nearby canal attracts wildfowl and there are resident kingfishers.

SUFFOLK

Bradfield Woods (72)
The Suffolk Trust for Nature Conservation's reserve is

south of Bury St Edmunds off the A134. Bradfield woods are ancient coppices with rights of way through them. Visitors are asked to keep to the paths. Oxslip, herb Paris, water avens, primrose, dog's mercury grow under holly, alder and hazel. Adder and grass snake both occur and butterflies include white admiral, brimstone, orange tip, wall and common blue.

Brandon Country Park (73)
The B1107 north west from Thetford leads directly to Brandon Park. Paths lead through Thetford Forest and Warren which are mainly coniferous but there are often rides with some scrub suitable for warblers and butterflies including red admiral and common blue. Mammals include stoat, weasel, red fox and grey squirrel.

Wolves Wood (74)
A woodland of 38 hectares (92 acres) belonging to the RSPB, Wolves Wood holds a wide variety of woodland birds because of the many species of tree including oak, ash, field maple, aspen, willow and, especially, hornbeam. There are flowers and butterflies in profusion and breeding birds include nightingale, garden warbler, great spotted and lesser spotted woodpecker. The reserve is close to Hadleigh at the junction of the A1071 and A1141.

SURREY

Box Hill Country Hill Park (75)
Between Leatherhead and Dorking off the A24, Box Hill overlooks the River Mole and is in the care of the National Trust. The 250 hectares (650 acres) of chalkland is strewn with yew, ash, birch, elder, wayfaring tree and, of course, the box from which it gets its name. Deadly nightshade, sainfoin, autumn ladies tresses, marjoram, salad burnet, horseshoe and kidney vetch.

Butterflies find copious nectar and the edible snail, thought to have been introduced by Roman gourmets, easily finds the essential calcium from which to build its shell.

Frensham Country Park (76)
A lovely area directly on the A287 from Farnham to Haslemere and an excellent example of a heathland grading into woodland dominated by birch and Scots pine over a carpet of purple moorgrass. The more acidic areas have round leaved sundew and bog asphodel and the marshes have breeding reed buntings and reed warblers among the bullrushes and both yellow and sweet flag.

SUSSEX

Fore Wood (77)
An RSPB reserve close to the historic town of Battle, the area has been coppiced for sweet chestnut. Birds include hawfinch, sparrowhawk, all three British woodpeckers, tawny owl, nuthatch and treecreepers. There is also some coppiced oak which allows enough light onto the woodland floor to encourage primrose, wood sorrel, violet and moschatel to grow.

Kingley Vale (78)
A Nature Conservancy woodland dominated by ancient gnarled yews which means a very limited ground layer because of the dense shade which the tree casts. Situated just off the A286 Chichester to Midhurst road the wood has such a unique atmosphere that it should not be missed. There are also surrounding patches of scrub which are a riot of summer colour with wild rose, bramble, wayfaring tree and the climbing white bryony fight for position.

Mallydams Wood (79)
Close to Hastings just off the A259 this 24 hectare (60 acre) wood is managed as an educational reserve by the RSPCA. The habitats vary from wet sphagnum dominated areas to drier rides full of gorse and broom with orchids close to tinkling streams. Birch dominated areas have waves of bluebells in the clearings. Birds include linnet, yellowhammer and tree pipit.

The Mens (80)
A Sussex Trust for Nature Conservation consisting of 155 hectares (390 acres) of mixed woodland reached via the A272 from Petworth to Billingshurst. The effect of coppicing can be seen but there is plenty of splendid beech and oak with an understorey of hazel, midland hawthorn, crab apple and spindle. The rich field layer includes wood anemone, bugle, bluebell and, in damp areas, pendulous sedge. In early spring white drafts of blackthorn blossom grace the area.

WARWICKSHIRE AND WEST MIDLANDS

Edge Hill Nature Trail (81)
A 3.2km (2 mile) nature trail found by following the A422 from Stratford-upon-Avon to Banbury. Primroses, bluebells, wood sorrel and violets grow on the slopes under oak, ash and hazel and through which there are spectacular views of Cotswold country.

WILTSHIRE

Colerne Park and Monk's Wood (82)
South west of Chippenham in the angle between the A4 and the A420 are the limestone woodlands of Colerne Park and Monk's Wood. Both angular and common Solomon's seal occur here and in May, especially after rain, the heavy scent of lily of the valley permeates the area. Butterflies including the small copper, wall brown and comma are found. Great spotted woodpeckers, green woodpecker and tree pipits are among the varied bird life.

Pepperbox Hill (83)
A magnificent viewpoint in its own right, the National Trust area of Pepperbox Hill is one of the few sites where juniper still thrives. Together with good specimens of yew, dogwood, wild rose, hawthorn, wayfaring tree and wild privet the area is a wonderful spot for butterflies and small birds such as linnet, yellowhammer and winchat with the occasional stonechat. The lovely black and red burnet moths are a feature of the site which lies at the junction of the A36 and A27 to the south of Salisbury.

Severnake (84)
Situated just south of Marlborough the forest occupies 930 hectares (2,300 acres) although it was once much more extensive and used as a royal hunt. The dominant trees are oak and beech, the latter also having been planted by Capability Brown. There is also birch and conifers have been planted by the Forestry Commission. The lichen flora is rich, and the fungi are prolific. Four species of deer – red, roe, fallow and muntjac may be seen wandering the

glades and the dormouse is also a resident. Leave the M4 motorway at exit 15 and eight miles south the forest lies between the A4 and A346 to Andover.

YORKSHIRE AND NORTH HUMBERSIDE

Grass Wood, Grassington, Yorkshire Dales (85)
A lovely ash woodland on limestone with a rich flora including lily of the valley, bloody cranesbill, wild thyme and rock rose. Bird life includes nuthatch, pied and spotted flycatcher and occasionally a hobby has been spotted. The area is reached from Skipton on the B6265 and also supports both common and birds eye primrose.

Hardcastle Crags, Hebden Bridge (86)
A National Trust woodland with a lovely stream tinkling down through the valley. Oak, beech and Scots pine provide perfect habitat for red squirrels. Green woodpeckers, crossbills, and chaffinches occur whilst in winter bramblings are a feature. The Crags are signed from the centre of Hebden Bridge where there is a splendid Information Centre.

Pickering District Forests (87)
Situated at the junction of the A169 and A170 Pickering is an ideal spot from which to explore the five forests of Dalby, Wykeham, Langdale, Falling Foss and Cropton. Pine, larch and spruce dominate the Forestry Commission plantations but the wildlife is rich and includes jay, red fox, roe deer and badger. Parking is easy and there are a few roads pushing deep into the forest and a small toll is payable on some of them.

SCOTLAND

Aden, Mintlaw (88)
Follow the A92 from Aberdeen to Fraserborough to the junction with the A950 Peterhead/Banf. At Mintlaw, Aden Park is well signed. Once an extensive estate the area is now a well wooded country park with a stretch of the River Ugie ideal for brown trout. Roe deer come to the river to drink and wood mice, red deer, fox, stoat and weasel all occur. There is a good variety of birds, flowers and fungi. A camp site and facilities for children make this an ideal woodland for the naturalist with a young family.

Ardtornish Ash Wood (89)
A magnificent ash wood growing on slopes overlooking loch Aline opposite the Island of Mull. Although remote and reached via the Corran ferry off the A82 Oban to Fort William, Ardtornish is well worth the effort. Buzzards are common and eagles are often seen as well as smaller birds of prey such as sparrowhawk, kestrel and merlin. The mosses and lichens are prolific and varied and Scots argus butterlies flit among the heather, bracken and tormentil thriving in the open clearings.

Black Wood of Rannoch, Tayside (90)
A fine remnant of the ancient forests of Scotland the Black Wood fringes loch Rannoch and there are fine views through ancient pine and graceful birches. Wild cats, pine martens, red squirrels and both red and roe deer roam free. Birds include capercaillie, black grouse, great spotted woodpecker and a pleasing assortment of summer warblers and resident tits. Plants include chickweed, wintergreen, common wintergreen and tawyblade. Access is off a minor road between Kinlochrannoch and the Bridge of Gaur.

Birks of Aberfeldy (91)
Signed from the lovely town of Aberfeldy on the River Tay the birches fringe tumbling waterfalls so loved by Robert Burns. The damp climate encourages ferns, liverworts and mosses while bilberry and cow wheat grow under the shade of old birches. Buzzards and long tailed tits are resident and spotted flycatchers and black redstarts are summer visitors.

Carrbridge, Invernesshire (92)
Off the A9 between Aviemore and Inverness. Carrbridge visitors' centre not only has a theatre and shop, but also a short and excellent walk through an old pine wood with red squirrel, sparrowhawk and crested tit. To preserve the wood a board walk is provided but this does not detract from its beauty.

Graigower Hill, Pitlochry, Perthshire (93)
The 450m (1,300ft) Craigower once used as a beacon hill is in the care of the National Trust for Scotland. Lodgepole pine, spruce and larch fringe the summit but there are splendid views over the Perthshire countryside. Sundew, heather, butterwort and lovely tufts of yellow mountain saxifrage and bog asphodel all grow in profusion. Goldcrests and sparrowhawks are among the varied bird species. The slots (footprints) of roe deer can be found in the soft streamside mud.

Culbin State Forest (94)
Once known as the Culbin sands this magnificently varied area is on the southern shore of the Moray Firth and is almost 9.7km (6 miles) long and 2.2km ($1\frac{1}{2}$ miles) north of Forres. The Forestry Commission and the Nature Conservancy Council have both ensured the retention of the native pines growing in sand hills as well as native plants including the wintergreens, but the fungi, lichens, liverworts, mosses and ferns are also worth travelling many miles to see. Capercaillie, crossbills, buzzards, tits and hooded crows are all found in the forest.

Dunkeld, The Hermitage Woodland Walk (95)
Under the control of the National Trust for Scotland, the Hermitage walk leads directly off the A9 at Dunkeld. The Dunkeld larches grow here fed upon by red squirrels while dipper (*Cinclus cinclus*) and grey wagtail (*Motacilla cinerea*) are common on the river Braan flushing through the woodlands on its way to meet the Tay. The Hermitage is an 18th century folly overlooking magnificent trees and spectacular waterfalls.

Glenmore Forest Park (96)
Some 7 miles from Aviemore on the A9 the extensive woodland walks are overlooked by the lowering mountains of the Cairngorm range. Crested tits and capercaillies delight the ornithologists while red squirrels are common and there is also a tame herd of reindeer. Goosanders (*Mergus merganser*) swim in the lochs and nest in the tall conifers. Although dominated by spruce and other cash crop conifers, there are many areas of Scots pine and birch.

Knapdale Forest Walks (97)
An extensive area around Crinan reached on the B814 from Lochgilphead this forest is an interesting mix of native birch, alder, oak, ash, hazel and willow. Surrounded by savage and yet haunting scenery looking through the trees and across the water to Jura, the Knapdale forest's 3,500 hectares (8,750 acres) should be explored slowly. Hooded crows, red squirrels and brown hares are often seen with

the occasional golden eagle soaring on the thermals and otters playing in the chuckling burns.

Linn of Tummel Woodland Walk, Killiecrankie, Perthshire (98)
Run by the National Trust for Scotland since 1944 and well signed from the A9, this woodland has areas which are clearly divided into the four layers. Otters frequent the damp areas near the Rivers Tummel and Garry running through the woodland. Hazel is common and enjoyed by the acrobatic red squirrel and ferns are prolific.

WALES

Coedydd Aber Trail (99)
Between Conway and Bangor on the A55 lies the village of Aber and this is a good point from which to explore the woodlands administered by the Nature Conservancy Council and the Forestry Commission. Bat boxes have been set up to attract the pipistrelle and long eared bat. In addition to the conifers there are good stands of oak, alder, sycamore and beech. Primroses, wood sorrel and bluebells grow well and great spotted woodpeckers can be heard drumming in spring.

Gwydyr Forest, Llanrwst, Gwynedd (100)
A Forestry Commission area reached on the B5106 and 4.8km (3 miles) from Betwys-y-Coed. The whole area is 8,182 hectares (20,218 acres) and includes plantations, farms and bare hilltops thus ensuring varied wildlife. Trees include Scots pine, lodgepole pine, spruces, Douglas fir and larches. Buzzards, green woodpecker, jay and goldcrest are resident birds and mammals include hare, rabbit, badger, pine marten, polecat and the occasional otter.

Rheidol Forest (Bwlch Nant yr arian) (101)
Reached along the A44 from Aberystwyth the visitors' centre (small charge) is well signed as are the paths into the forest. Very much a working forest, but magnificent views from picnic sites across to Aberystwyth on Cardigan Bay. Sparrowhawk, buzzard, coal tit and goldcrests are among the surprisingly rich bird life.

Tan y Coed Forest Trails, Dyfi (102)
A Forestry Commission trail leads from a picnic area off the A487 Dolgellau to Machynlleth road. There are fine examples of Douglas fir, western hemlock and silver fir but native trees such as sessile oak, birch, beech and rowan all thrive. Woodwarblers, woodcock, chiff-chaffs and willow warblers breed and screaming groups of jays are resident.

Ty'n-y-Groes (103)
To reach the Forestry Commission woodlands leave the A494 Barmouth to Bala road via the A470. Ty'n-y-Groes is signed after 4km (3 miles). A 3km (2 mile) trail leads off from a pretty picnic site, and is a walk for all seasons. In winter fieldfares, redwing and woodpeckers feed and in summer flycatchers and redstarts search for nest sites. Hard fern and beard lichens are a botanical feature and the occasional fallow deer and badger may sometimes be spotted or more likely signs of their presence be found.

Kingfishers are found in many woodlands through which a gentle river flows.

Acknowledgements

During the writing of this book I have been given help by many friends. Firstly I would like to thank my wife Marlene whose knowledge of natural history as well as my handwriting was helpful in converting an idea into a manuscript. At Bell and Hyman continual encouragement was given and I am particularly grateful to Connie Austen Smith and Emma Jones for their understanding and sympathetic editing. Paul J. Freethy and Brian H. Lee kindly read the proofs. Illustrations are a vital part of any book of this type and I have been well served by a number of photographers whose work is separately acknowledged. The line drawings were done by Carole Pugh who combines the talents of naturalist and artist to perfection.

The author and publishers would like to thank the following for the use of their photographs on the pages listed:
Richard Abernethy: page 107; Heather Angel: pages 118–19; Will Bown: pages 139, 155, 190; Mick Chesworth: pages 13, 24, 26, 40, 47, 60, 89, 173, 176, 180, 147, 182, 192; Michael Clark: pages 166, 171, 179; John Clegg: pages 36, 42, 54, 63, 64, 69, 74, 82, 115, 148, 157, 196, 197; Michael Edwards: pages 46, 48, 51, 52, 77, 78, 79, 80, 90 (top), 91 (bottom), 92, 102, 106, 135, 137, 141, 150, 153, 164, 177, 191; Mary Fuller: page 107; John Glover: pages 2–3; Lorraine Harrison: pages 202–3; John Heap: pages 62, 75, 110; Alan Heath: page 34; Margaret Hodge: pages 45, 89, 93; Robert Howe: pages 22, 126, 142, 146, 162 (top), 163, 173 (top), 178; Michael Hunter: 131; Institute of Agricultural History and Museum of English Rural Life, University of Reading: pages 16, 18; Dick Jones: pages 134, 186, 187; Bernard Lee: page 14; Brian H Lee: pages 6, 10, 39, 49, 59, 122; Charles Linford: page 184; Barry Ogden: pages 90–91; Brian Oldfield: pages 154, 162 (bottom); R Smithies: end-papers and pages: 50, 83, 194–5 and Ian Spellerberg: page 35.

Bibliography

Alvin, K L, *The Observers Book of Lichens.* Warne, 1977.
Anderson, M L, *History of Scottish Forestry Vol. 1.* Nelson, 1963.
Anderson, M L, *History of Scottish Forestry Vol. 2.* Nelson, 1967.
Beckett, K and G, *Planting Native Trees and Shrubs.* Botanical Society of the British Isles, 1974.
Beirne, B P, *The Origin and History of British Fauna.* Methuen, 1952.
Bennett, D P and Humphries, D A, *Introduction to Field Biology.* Arnold, 1974.
Bishop, O N, *Natural Communities.* John Murray, 1973.
Blatchford, N, *Your Book of Forestry.* Faber, 1980.
Bristowe, W S, *The World of Spiders.* Collins, 1958.
Brook, M and Knight, C, *A Complete Guide to British Butterflies.* Cape, 1982.
Brown, L, *British Birds of Prey.* Collins, 1976.
Bunce, R G H and Jeffers, J N R (Eds), *Native Pinewoods of Scotland.* Environmental Research Council, 1975.
Burrows, R, *Wild Fox.* David & Charles, 1968.
Burton, John, *Conservation of Wildlife.* Blackie, 1974.
Burton, R, *Animal Senses.* David & Charles, 1973.
Chinery, M, *A Field Guide to the Insects of Britain and Northern Europe.* Collins, 1973.
Clapham, A R et al, *Excursion Flora of the British Isles.* CUP, 1968.
Clapham, A R and Nicholson, B E, *The Oxford Book of Trees.* OUP, 1975.
Cloudsley-Thompson, J L, *Microecology Institute of Biology Studies in Biology No. 6.* Arnold, 1967.
Cloudsley-Thompson, J L, *The British Naturalists' Guide to Woodlands.* Crowood Press, 1985.
Condry, W, *Woodlands.* Collins, 1974.
Corbet, G B and Southern, H N (Eds), *Handbook of British Mammals.* Blackwell, 1977.
Cousens, J, *Woodland Ecology.* Oliver & Boyd, 1974.
Cousens, J, *Introduction to Woodland Ecology.* Oliver & Boyd, 1974.
Darlington, A, *Pocket Encyclopaedia of Plant Galls.* Blandford, 1968.
Darlington, A, *The World of a Tree.* Faber and Faber, 1972.
Davis, Paul and Jenne and Huxley, A, *Wild Orchids in Britain.* Chatto & Windus, 1983.
Deal, W, *A Guide to Forest Holidays in Great Britain and Ireland.* David & Charles, 1976.
Dowdeswell, W, *Ecology – Principles and Practice.* Heinemann, 1984.
Edington, J M and M A, *Ecology and Environmental Planning.* Chapman & Hall, 1977.
Edlin, H L, *Forestry and Woodland Life.* Batsford, 1947.
Edlin, H L, *Trees, Woods and Men.* Collins, 1956.
Edlin, H L, *The Living Forest.* Thames & Hudson, 1958.
Edlin, H L, *The Tree Key.* Frederick Warne, 1978.
Edwards, C A and Lofty, J R, *Biology of Earthworms.* Chapman & Hall, 1977.
Elton, C E, *The pattern of Animal Communities.* Methuen, 1966.
Fitter, M and R, *The Penguin Dictionary of Natural History.* Penguin, 1978.
Ford, E B, *Butterflies.* Collins, 1945.
Ford, E B, *Moths.* Collins, 1955.
Freethy, Ron, *The Making of the British Countryside.* David & Charles, 1981.
Freethy, Ron, *How Birds Work.* Blandford, 1982.
Freethy, Ron, *Man and Beast. The Natural and Unnatural History of British Mammals.* Blandford, 1983.
Freethy, Ron, *British Birds in their Habitats.* Crowood Press, 1985.
Godden, R, *British Butterflies – a Field Guide.* David & Charles, 1978.
Godwin, H, *The History of British Flora.* CUP, 1975.
Griffin, D R, *Listening in the Dark.* Yale University Press, 1958.
Hart, C and Raymon, C, *British Trees in Colour.* Michael Joseph, 1973.
Hickin, N, *Natural History of an English Forest.* Hutchinson, 1971.
Hill, Jack, *The Complete Practical Book of Country Crafts.* David & Charles, 1979.
Hinde, Thomas, *Forests of Britain.* Gollancz, 1985.
Hollom, P A D, *Popular Handbook of British Birds.* Witherby, 1968.
Howarth, T G, *Butterflies of the British Isles.* Viking, 1984.
Hubbard, C, *Grasses.* Pelican, 1983.
Imms, A D, *Insect Natural History.* Collins, 1947.
Jackson, R M and Ran, F, *Life in the Soil, Institute of Biology Studies in Biology No. 2.* Arnold, 1968.
Jones, Dick, *The Country Life Guide to Spiders of Britain and Northern Europe.* Country Life, 1953.
Kosch, *The Young Specialist Looks at Trees.* Burke, 1972.
Lewis, J G E, *The Biology of Centipedes.* CUP, 1951.
Linssen, E F, *The Observers Book of Common Insects and Spiders.* Warne, 1973.
Malcolm, M D C, Evans, J, Edwards, P N (Eds), *Broadleaves in Britain.* Institute of Chartered Foresters, 1982.
Matthews, L Harrison, *Mammals in the British Isles.* Collins, 1982.
Mellanby, K, *The Mole.* Collins, 1971.
Mitchell, A, *Trees of Britain and Northern Europe.* Collins, 1974.
Neal, E G, *Woodland Ecology.* Heinemann, 1969.
Ovington, J D, *Woodlands.* English Universities Press, 1965.
Packham, J R and Hording, D J L, *Ecology of Woodland Processes.* Arnold, 1982.
Pennington, W, *The History of British Vegetation.* English Universities Press, 1974.
Perring, F and Morris, B, *The British Oak.* Classey, 1974.
Perrins, C, *British Tits.* Collins, 1979.
Peterken, George, *Woodland Conservation and Management.* Chapman and Hall, 1981.
Phillipson, J, *Ecological Energetics Institute of Biology Studies Biology No. 1.* Arnold, 1966.
Pollunin, O, *Trees and Bushes of Europe.* University Press, 1976.
Rackham, O, *Trees and Woodlands in the British Landscape.* Dent, 1976.
Rackham, O, *Ancient Woodland.* Arnold, 1980.
Russel, Sir John, *The World of the Soil.* Collins, 1957.
Ryle, G, *The Forest Service.* David and Charles, 1969.
Sankey, J, *A Guide to Field Biology.* Longman, 1958.
Savory, T H, *Biology of the Cryptozoa.* Merrow, 1971.
Sharrock, J T R (Ed), *Atlas of Breeding Birds in Britain and Ireland.* B T O Poyser, 1976.
Sheail, J, *Nature in Trust.* Blackie, 1976.
Simms, E, *Woodland Birds.* Collins, 1971.
Simms, E, *British Thrushes.* Collins, 1978.
Skinner, Bernard, *Moths of the British Isles.* Viking, 1984.
South, R, *The Moths of the British Isles.* Warne, 1973.
Steven, H M and Carlisle, A, *The Native Pinewoods of Scotland.* Oliver & Boyd, 1959.
Storey, Edward, *A Right to Song – The Life of John Clare.* Methuen, 1982.
Sutton, S L, *Woodlice.* Ginn, 1972.
Tubbs, C, *The New Forest.* David & Charles, 1968.
Turrill, W B, *British Plant Life.* Collins, 1948.
Unwin, D M, *Microclimate Measurement for Ecologists.* Academic Press, 1980.
Wallwork, J A, *Ecology of Soil Animals.* McGraw Hill, 1970.
Warren-Wren, S C, *Willows.* David & Charles, 1972.
Watling, R, *Identification of the Larger Fungi.* Hulton, 1973.
Watson, H, *The Scots Pine.* Oliver & Boyd, 1947.
Wilkes, J H, *Trees of the British Isles in History and Legend.* Muller, 1972.
Willis, A J, *Introduction to Plant Ecology.* Allen & Unwin, 1973.

Index

Page numbers in **bold** type indicate illustrations